The
RESIGNATION
REVOLUTION

How to negotiate your exit package like a pro

Alex Monaco with Will Burrows

Edited by Jenny Monaco

The Resignation Revolution:
How to negotiate your exit package like a pro

Published by:
Monaco Digital
Peckham Levels Unit 601
Floor 6, 95a Rye Lane
London
SE15 4ST
United Kingdom

Edited by Jenny Monaco
Cover and chapter illustrations by Lydia Baker/Baker On Sunday Street
Cover design by Sian Tomlinson
Cover photography by Sarah Cresswell
Interior book design by Susana Cardona

ISBN 978-1-9164590-0-7

Love this book? Visit the website www.resignationrevolution.co.uk

This book is dedicated to Isabella

Contents

PART ONE

Leaving employment: negotiating tactics

PART TWO

Leaving employment: specific scenarios and claims

Case studies and examples of documents used in negotiations and employment tribunals

Appendices

Foreword

It is daunting to be in a dispute with your employer. Views can be polarised and working relationships become very difficult. Part of you may want to claim, or even resign and do so, but part of you may just want to put it behind you, and your employer may want that too. Family and friends may have opinions ranging from the helpful to the downright misleading which can do more harm than good: 'man in the pub legal advice' some people call it.

As lawyers I suppose we would say that you need to see a lawyer (although I believe I can be a bit more objective now I am a Judge – I do see people representing themselves in Court and it is really not easy to do). As Alex and Will rightly stress, even this (truly excellent) book cannot be a substitute for a lawyer. But what is refreshing about this book is that it gives you the tools to negotiate a deal yourself even if you need a lawyer later on – including to formalise the agreement you have negotiated and make it legally binding as they explain.

A lot of experience and wisdom has been poured into this book, which is laid out in a user-friendly way in straightforward language with none of the jargon we lawyers use ! It cannot train you to be a lawyer but it explains your rights clearly and gives you the tools and confidence to use your own skills to negotiate a deal effectively. I would commend it to you. I wish it had been around when I was a barrister negotiating agreements!

HHJ Jim Tindal
Circuit Judge, former Employment Judge and Barrister
July 2018

Preface

Finally, the Resignation Revolution is here! Until now, the mainstream media have portrayed employee rights as 'red tape' and damaging to the economy. They would have you believe that people who 'claim compensation' are simply out to make a swift buck at the expense of the rest of us who are diligent, hardworking and pay our taxes.

In countries such as Germany and Sweden, employees have more rights than we do, and their economies are more efficient. Perhaps knowing that your employer is not entitled to fire you unfairly can give you the sort of confidence which allows you to relax into your role and work hard, without your health being affected by worries of losing your job.

You probably had no real opinion on such matters, until, that is, you were directly affected by an issue at work....

What generally happens when you are treated unfairly or illegally at work is that you just resign from your job and try to get another one. In the meantime you might become ill with stress or anxiety. Or you might be more stoic about it. Either way, the whole affair can be messy and, understandably, not really something you want to talk about.

We have decided to bring the conversation out into the open, starting right here with this book. From now on, wouldn't it be great if our culture encouraged employees to get a fair deal and to negotiate an exit package – known also as a 'settlement agreement' – for themselves? That way, if you had to leave your job, you could leave with your head held high, not to mention with the money you would need to tide you over until you got another job.

Sure, no employer is going to admit that they have treated you unfairly, but by agreeing to pay you a decent settlement agreement then, symbolically at least, they have apologised. You can then go into your next job interview with confidence, knowing that you weren't bad at your job, but that in fact you were subjected to unfair, and possibly also illegal, treatment.

But this book isn't a self help book which just aims to make you feel better about the whole thing. It's a detailed practical guide with step by step instructions on how to negotiate a decent exit deal for yourself. It is the first and only book of its kind in the UK.

And why are we the best people to write it?

Well, we are lawyers who for many years have focused solely on negotiating settlement agreements for employees who have been, or are being, badly treated at work. It's all we do and there are very few firms who can say that.

Lawyers, contrary to popular belief, can be benign individuals concerned with actually helping people rather than simply cashing in on their misfortune. Some shining examples include Nelson Mandela, Mahatma Gandhi and Abraham Lincoln to name but a few.

We're not saying we're quite like those people (!) but we do care passionately about helping employees to even up the odds. Since the Magna Carta was drawn up in 1215, justice has supposedly been available to all. But in practice those with deeper pockets, such as companies and corporations, get to do what they want because the 'little guy' hasn't the knowledge or power to stand up to them.

For a number of years at my firm, Monaco Solicitors, we have found new clients by publishing advice about employment law online and appearing at the top of the Google results page when people search for related information. One day when we were auditing our website we realised something – we had enough material there to form the basis of a book.

Wouldn't it be easy, we thought, to develop the website into a book and publish it? Turns out we were wrong about the 'easy' part, but certainly we have had so much positive feedback from employees about our website that we wanted also to offer something like it in book form.

One of the best things about employment law is that generally you, as a claimant, don't get hit with a bill for the other side's legal costs if you lose a trial at the employment tribunal. Although tribunals are a long way down the line from negotiating exit packages, this does help because employers know that you could take them there risk free. It also means that you, as a lone individual, could start a tribunal claim and so long as you play fair then the worst that could happen is that you lose. However, it's quite a complicated process, and it's much easier just to settle out of court.

We seek to demystify the process of negotiating a fair exit package, so that at least you have the information to assess what is involved. This book is obviously not as good as having an actual lawyer working alongside you, but it certainly helps. If you do decide to 'go it alone', then keep a copy with you and we wish you the very best of luck!

Acknowledgements

I'd like to thank my mother Jenny for editing this book, which took a huge amount of time and skill. Jenny turned it from a collection of individual articles into a coherent and readable volume, often researching points of law and deciphering 'legalese'. She also encouraged me throughout my career to stick with it, especially as a junior lawyer when times could get really tough.

During those early days, Steve Fairburn and Piers Marquis were amongst some of the lawyers who inspired me to succeed in establishing my own law firm and later to take on the challenge of writing this book.

I'd also like to thank Will Burrows for his outstanding contribution in writing sections of this book with me, and for his ongoing insights into running my law firm. Will's technical employment law knowledge, combined with his strategic mind, really helped to craft my friendly advice into hard-hitting negotiating tactics.

My team of lawyers at Monaco Solicitors have contributed to some of the specialist content, especially Nicola Welchman (sections on discrimination) and Chris Hogg (sections on tax and employers' tactics), with support also from Dippalli Naik and Lorna Valcin.

The team at Monaco Digital has been very helpful in publishing the book as well, especially Katharine Horsman with her energetic drive for us to get it finished within the deadline, also proofreading by Sian Tomlinson, technical help from Mel Macaluso, Ben Mills, Joe Reed, Tim Mortimer and Steve Peacock, and fantastic illustrations by Lydia Baker.

Alex Monaco
Senior Partner
MONACO SOLICITORS

Introduction

About the book content and structure

This book is a guide to negotiating a 'settlement agreement' with your employer when you leave your job. In essence, a settlement agreement is a legally binding document in which you settle a dispute with your employer. The deal is that you receive a financial payment, and sometimes other benefits, when you leave your employment. In return, you agree to give up any rights to sue your employer in a tribunal or court. We sometimes also use the term 'exit package' to mean essentially the same thing as settlement agreement.

The contents of the book are presented in three parts:

Part One

This section gives you tactical negotiating advice related to gathering evidence and raising grievances at work. It explains how to handle negotiation meetings and correspondence, with guidance on when and how to use 'without prejudice' rules. This advice is applicable across all the different employment exit scenarios. Part One also covers the end of the negotiating process, such as how much money you should get, the contents of settlement agreements (your preferred solution) and the process of employment tribunals (your last resort). Everyone should read Part One.

Part Two

The next section addresses the most common case scenarios, such as unfair and constructive dismissal, redundancy and discrimination. It includes specific advice on how you can negotiate an exit package and settlement agreement in those scenarios. You are of course welcome to read all of Part Two if you would like to, but you will probably be most interested in those chapters which apply directly to your particular case.

Part Three

The final section contains a small collection of example letters and documents which will give you an idea of exactly how to set out your case to the other side (your employer). It's rounded off with two case studies which track the progress of two end-of-employment cases, from start to finish, together with commentary from the lawyer working on each case and all relevant correspondence. Part Three is handy if you want some concrete examples of successful negotiations and how they have been conducted.

How to use the book

All the advice we offer in this book is tactical, and because your own circumstances are unique, you should not take it as 'legal advice' per se. It is practical guidance for you to use, with advice and tactics for you to adjust to your own individual case as appropriate. It has been written to help you to negotiate the best deal possible when leaving employment.

The book is aimed at regular employees from all industries so we don't expect you to be familiar with employment law or legal jargon. If we have to use any legal language, then we will do our best to explain what it means in plain English. In Appendix One we also provide you with a glossary of some of the acronyms, words and phrases commonly used in employment law, so you can double check definitions there if you need to.

There are various legal individuals and organisations which help sort out problems arising between employers and employees. Below we just mention a few, so that you will already be aware of them when you come across references to them later in the book. We also touch on the definition of being an employee.

Lawyers

This book isn't intended to be a substitute for the sound legal advice that only an experienced employment lawyer can offer once they understand your situation. We can't tailor the guidance in this book to you, or tell you exactly when to make the right moves in your particular case, whereas a good lawyer who understands your case can.

It follows that a good lawyer is also very likely to be able to win a higher settlement amount for you, even after deducting their fees. We wouldn't discourage you from going it alone if you think you can, but be aware of your limitations in what can be a complicated and complex legal arena, and beware of the strengths of the lawyers who will be acting on your employer's behalf.

If you decide that you do want to instruct a lawyer, there are different kinds of law firms out there. Most employment lawyers handle employment dispute cases for both employers and employees, plus other types of cases such as conveyancing and divorce. Some specialise only in employment law and some only in representing employees and not employers.

There are also different types of fee structure available. Most lawyers charge by the hour, some charge a fixed fee, and others charge on some kind of 'no win no fee' basis. If you just want a defined task doing, such as writing a specific letter to your employer, then a fixed fee is usually possible.

If you want your lawyer to take over the entire case and do all the negotiating for you, then look for a deal where your fee is an agreed percentage of any increase the lawyer can get for you – over and above any amount already offered to you by your employer. This can encourage great teamwork between you and your lawyer because your incentives are aligned.

Employment tribunals

Employment tribunals were established to enforce the rights of employees. Before tribunals, employees would just go on strike en masse, and that wasn't good for either side. Now, the threat of employment tribunal proceedings underpins most settlement agreement negotiations, because that is what employers are trying to avoid. Employers are more likely to respond more positively to you in negotiations if they think you would have a fair chance of winning an employment tribunal. That is why it's important to gather strong evidence for your negotiation.

In theory the employment tribunal system is straightforward and free to use. However, in reality, employees face a fierce uphill battle to ensure justice is done; in terms of complexity, cost, resources, controlling the evidence and the amount of stress involved. This is why we would always advise you to negotiate and settle cases before you resort to taking claims before an employment tribunal.

Just be aware of how the tribunal system works so that you can use it in what we refer to as 'the carrot and stick' approach in your negotiations. In actual practice, the stick you would use is to negotiate and behave in such a way that your employer believes that you would be prepared to take your claim to an employment tribunal – without you in any direct way threatening such action. It's a ploy which you can use to encourage your employer into a good settlement. The 'carrot' is the relatively easy bit. It's what you offer your employer in return for a good settlement; namely, agreeing to leave your job (assuming you haven't left already) and giving up rights to any future claim.

It's important to note that nearly all tribunal claims have a three month 'limitation period'. This means that, unless you start the claims process within three months of the date of the incident which you complain about, you will not be able to bring a claim to tribunal. If you cannot bring a claim, then you cannot use that claim as a negotiation tactic in settlement discussions with your employer.

More information about employment tribunals and details of how to make an employment tribunal claim can be found in chapter 6.

ACAS

Before you are allowed to start an employment tribunal claim, you have to obtain a certificate from ACAS (the Advisory, Conciliation and Arbitration Service). ACAS is a UK government body which supports the employment tribunal system and provides a 'pre-claim conciliation service'.

This means that when you submit your claim summary to ACAS, they will call you and ask you how much money you want in order to settle your claim. They will then call the other side (the employer) and see whether they will accept your offer, or whether they have a counter offer. In this way ACAS is able to settle some claims quickly. The most common claims for ACAS to settle are ones where the two sides aren't talking at all and there has never been any proper negotiation.

Don't expect ACAS to be able to settle your claim for you if you have already tried to do this yourself. Because ACAS conciliators are neutral, they are not there to put forward your strongest case, or advise you how much you should be asking for in a settlement. They are more like a messenger service, simply carrying messages between the two sides. And they aren't lawyers....

Civil courts

Civil courts (e.g. county courts and the High Court) are separate from employment tribunals. The types of employment-related claims which can be heard in the civil courts tend to be claims based around the contract of employment between you and your employer. These are separate from types of 'statutory' claim such as unfair dismissal or discrimination, which are derived from laws made in Parliament, rather than from the contract of employment itself.

The benefit of using the civil courts for breach of contract matters is that there is no cap to the amount you can claim there, whereas in employment tribunals, there is a cap of £25,000 for each individual breach. On the down side, civil courts are a 'cost-shifting jurisdiction' which means that the loser pays the winner's legal costs, or in other words, the bill of the lawyer on the winning side. Unfortunately, legal costs in civil claims regularly exceed the principal amount being fought over. So you can imagine the stress involved when the stakes don't just involve the prospect of winning or losing, but also of having to pay the fees of your employer's lawyer.

Are you an employee or not?

The chances are that, if you are reading this, you are an employee. Employees make up the bulk of the UK workforce and enjoy the most rights and protections of any other kind of worker. Most settlement agreements are between employer and employee.

If you have a contract of employment, work for a business on premises owned by the business, use the equipment of the business and are paid by the business on PAYE (Pay As You Earn), then you are almost certainly an employee. The legal definition of an employee is as follows:

a) There must be an obligation for the employer to provide the work and for the employees to undertake it.

b) Employees allow the employer to direct their actions on a day-to-day basis.

c) The other provisions of a contract between an employee and an employer are consistent with its being a contract of employment. This may mean, for example, that the employer:

   i) provides the employees with tools and equipment to undertake their duties,

   ii) pays the employees via Pay As You Earn taxation,

   iii) pays the employees' tax and national insurance contributions,

   iv) insures the employees against risk,

   v) provides a workplace or office for them.

The list of examples of these 'other provisions' is potentially endless, but in determining whether someone is an employee or not, a judge will look at the totality of the evidence presented and then, on balance, make a ruling. If you are an employee then you have some rights and protections including the following:

- Protection from unfair dismissal after two years' service.
- Periods of notice dependant on your length of service, from one week up to 12 weeks.
- A statutory redundancy payment if made redundant.
- Protection from discrimination.

Self-employed people

If you perform your job during hours you choose and in a manner which you decide, then the chances are you are self-employed and not an employee. A modern example of this would be an electrician hired by a building contractor to undertake the wiring of a new house. If you are permitted to send another person in your place to perform the duties under your contract, then this too would most likely mean that you are not an employee.

If you are self-employed then you do not have any unfair dismissal rights, so you will probably not be able to negotiate yourself an exit package or settlement agreement. However, self-employed people do have protection from discrimination and from making protected disclosures (commonly known as whistleblowing).

Partners

It gets a little trickier when dealing with people who are, for example, partners of legal firms, accountancy firms and the like. However, the general test for those scenarios is the definition of an employee above, plus the ability to make genuine profits or losses from the performance of the business.

For example, if you are labelled as a partner in a business, but you're paid a fixed salary which makes up the majority of your remuneration, with a bonus based on performance, then it is arguable that you could be classified as an employee.

If, on the other hand, your remuneration depends entirely upon performance, so if the business had a bad year then your remuneration would be much lower, then the chances are that you are not an employee.

Other information

You can find a wealth of other information for employees about employment issues on our website. One of the most popular tools available there is our settlement agreement calculator, which gives you an estimate of how much you should get in a negotiated exit package. You just input your case details, press calculate, and a figure pops up.

Another useful resource is our wide-ranging collection of letter templates and examples which you can download and adapt for use in your case. These supplement the ones to be found in Part Three of this book.

PART ONE

Leaving employment: negotiating tactics

Introduction

In Part One we offer a range of practical advice and tips on how to negotiate with your employer and in particular on how to:

- Negotiate using 'protected conversations' and 'without prejudice' rules together with a range of other negotiating tactics.
- Understand your employer's approach to negotiating.
- Put together evidence to support your case.
- Make formal grievances (or complaints).
- Estimate how much you should get in your settlement agreement.
- Assess whether all relevant payments are included in your agreement.
- Understand how tax is calculated on settlement payments.

Finally, we look briefly at employment tribunals and how they work in practice. We offer advice on how to use the prospect of a tribunal claim to enhance your negotiating position with your employer and – as a last resort – on how to go about making a tribunal claim.

Chapter 1

Negotiating a settlement agreement

Introduction

There are many tactics which skilled negotiators use across a variety of employment leaving circumstances and in this chapter we give you an insight into some of them.

We'll help you understand how to negotiate with your employer in ways that will stand up to legal scrutiny – both in writing and in meetings – and how to respond to settlement offers made by your employer. There are lots of valuable practical tips and advice in this chapter, while examples of letters that you could use during the course of your negotiations are provided in chapter 12.

In particular we'll introduce you to two important technical terms, and the practices associated with them, that you will have to learn about if you're negotiating a settlement agreement. These are 'protected conversations' and 'without prejudice' communications.

In practice, these two conventions both offer the two parties using them (i.e. employer and employee) protection from the contents of the exchanges being disclosed, should the dispute ever need to be settled in court. The main difference between the two is that protected conversations are used when there is not a dispute between the parties, whereas without prejudice exchanges are used between the two sides when there is a dispute.

1.1. Protected conversations

A protected conversation is a legal construct that enables your employer to have an 'off the record' chat with you, and make you an offer to leave the business, without you being able to refer to that conversation later in a tribunal claim.

Under the rules, an employer can just take you aside, ask you for a protected conversation and tell you, for example, that your work is substandard, that they want you to leave and that they'll offer you a payment in return. So long as there are no allegations of whistleblowing, breach of contract, or discrimination (see below), then a protected conversation is off the record. For your employer to use a protected conversation with you, there doesn't need to be an existing dispute between you.

Your employer must act 'properly' when conducting a protected conversation. If they act improperly, for example by threatening that unless you take what is being offered, then you will be dismissed; or by applying excessive pressure to ensure you accept their terms, then the conversation is no longer protected. In that case it can be referred to by a judge and used as a reason for you to resign or to sue for unfair dismissal.

There are however a couple of important limitations to the scope of protected conversations which you can use to your advantage, namely:

- Your employer cannot dismiss you, or tell you that you will be dismissed, under the guise of a protected conversation. They can say that if you do not accept the offer then they will start a disciplinary or performance management process, but they cannot tell you that this process will lead to you being dismissed.

- Your employer cannot discriminate against you in a protected conversation. If you think you have been selected for the protected conversation due to your gender, race, age, because you are pregnant etc., or because you have raised concerns about discrimination, then the conversation will not be protected. For example, it's not uncommon for employers to attempt to have protected conversations with women returning from maternity leave, but this will almost always give rise to a claim of maternity discrimination.

Employees can use protected conversations too. You're better off making sure your employer knows you have an issue first though, otherwise there is no reason for them to agree to pay you an 'ex gratia' settlement amount (see chapter 5). As such, it would be better for you to have a without prejudice conversation (see below) at the appropriate time, rather than seeking to have a protected conversation before you've raised a dispute.

What to do if you're asked to have a protected conversation

If you're invited to have a protected conversation with your employer, agree to have one. There is no harm in hearing what your employer has to say and it may be of benefit to you – especially if you're already unhappy in your job. When you're in the meeting:

- Listen to what your employer has to say but don't respond to any offer made or to any criticisms of your performance or conduct. Say you'll consider what your employer has said and that you will come back to them at a later time.

- You should, however, clarify any points about the offer that you are not sure about e.g. are you going to be required to work your notice period, and what tax treatment is the employer going to apply to the payments? You should also clarify what will happen if you don't accept the offer. With any luck your employer will slip up and say that you will be dismissed, meaning that the conversation is no longer protected – allowing you to negotiate a better deal.

- Ensure you take good notes of what your employer says in case there is any later dispute. After the conversation you should carefully consider the offer that has been made and any ways you may be able to improve it.

TOP 3 TIPS

- Do agree to have a protected conversation – it never hurts to listen
- Don't respond to any offer made or engage with your employer – take time to reflect
- Do ask what will happen if you don't accept any offer made – it's important to know

---

By the time you start negotiating for a settlement agreement, your exchanges with your employer will usually follow the without prejudice rules explained below.

1.2. Without prejudice communications

What does without prejudice mean?

'Without prejudice' is a legal term short for 'without prejudice to any right or claim'. This means that whatever is said or done on a without prejudice basis cannot later be used in a tribunal or mentioned at work in any context other than negotiations.

This gives an element of protection for the parties in a dispute if they have discussions on a without prejudice basis. Any discussions undertaken under the cloak of this protection are confidential between the parties, irrespective of whether those discussions are in person, in a letter, email, text, on the phone or other format.

For example, let's say you set out a lot of complaints in a without prejudice letter, along with a suggested resolution of a settlement agreement. Your employer won't then be able to refer to those complaints in a grievance meeting with you, because you raised those complaints on a without prejudice basis. Similarly, if the case goes to tribunal, then the without prejudice item cannot be brought to the attention of the tribunal.

In order for this protection to apply, there must be a genuine dispute between the parties, the correspondence or conversation must be expressly declared to be on a without prejudice basis, and the discussions must be a genuine attempt to resolve the dispute.

Why does the rule of without prejudice exist?

Without prejudice was introduced into English law to make it easier to achieve out of court settlement agreements, and therefore to save taxpayers' money by cutting down on the amount of cases which end up in court. Because everyone knows that you can't use without prejudice offers as evidence of guilt in court, people feel safe in making such offers. If the without prejudice protection was removed, then no one would make any offers. You wouldn't offer to accept a £7,500 settlement if you thought that the judge would find out about it, because you'd be telling the judge that your claim was worth £10,000.

Without prejudice and open communications

If a document/correspondence is not marked as being without prejudice then it's regarded as 'open'. Open correspondence is any email, letter, phone call or meeting which doesn't have without prejudice protection. So, you might write an open letter to your employer resigning from your job, or raising a grievance; or during a tribunal case you might request disclosure of vital evidence or contact details for a witness.

All open correspondence can be referred to in front of a judge. For example, you can point out to the judge that you wrote an open letter to your former employer requesting copies of your HR file, but no response was ever forthcoming, therefore they must be hiding something. Judges don't want to see draft settlement agreements or any other written material that's marked as without prejudice.

Use of without prejudice communications in legal proceedings

You can't generally use without prejudice communications in legal proceedings. You can't use anything which is discussed in without prejudice discussions, to build your case or as a reason for your resignation, except in specific circumstances (see below). So, if your employer raises an issue with you in a without prejudice discussion which could breach trust and confidence, you cannot use this against your employer.

But without prejudice exchanges can be used in legal proceedings in a couple of specific circumstances:

- If without prejudice exchanges uncover evidence of unambiguous wrongdoing or criminal behaviour, for example fraud, 'undue influence', perjury, blackmail, or discrimination.
- To help a judge make a ruling about any outstanding costs issued after the conclusion of a case.

How is without prejudice implemented in practice?

Firstly there has to be a dispute between the parties in order to qualify for without prejudice protection. So, if you have a grievance against your employer (no matter what it may be about), or if your employer has what they think is a genuine issue with, for example, your performance, then you can usually assume that it will qualify as being a dispute between the parties.

This should be contrasted with the scenario where there is absolutely nothing on record as being a problem between you and your employer. In that scenario, any letter which your employer marks 'without prejudice' is arguably not without prejudice at all, and could be referred to in court.

We have caught out many employers in this way. Imagine their horror when they realise that the settlement agreement which they offered you in return for you leaving your job could be shown to a judge in tribunal. 'Why such horror?', we hear you ask. Well, because you could legitimately point out to the judge that your employer constructively dismissed you when they did that. Their action in trying to get rid of you breached your trust and confidence in them, to the extent that you had no choice but to resign and then claim compensation for loss of income. (See chapter 7 for more on constructive dismissal.)

So, to sum up so far, there are three elements required to making a communication or settlement agreement document without prejudice:

1. It needs to be clearly marked with the words 'without prejudice', or 'without prejudice and subject to contract', or if it is a verbal conversation then you or your employer need clearly to say, 'do you mind if we speak without prejudice?'.

2. There needs to be some kind of issue or dispute in existence between the parties.

3. There needs to be a genuine attempt to settle the issue out of court, for example an offer of an amount of money. It is not enough to just talk about the merits of the case and say the words 'without prejudice' as it is likely in that scenario that the protection would not apply.

Without prejudice negotiations opened by the employer

Generally, if your employer wishes to open negotiations about the termination of your contract, on a without prejudice basis, they will either call you to a without prejudice meeting, or ask in a regular meeting if you can speak on a without prejudice basis. Your employer will then set out the reasons for the discussion and their proposal for a financial settlement in return for the termination of your employment. They will often then hand you a letter marked 'without prejudice' which will set out the details of that offer and, sometimes, the reasons for the offer and the consequences of not accepting (for example, they will commence a performance management procedure, or there will be a redundancy exercise).

Your employer may seek to remove you from the office during negotiations. If your employer wants to put you on leave while you consider their offer, this is actually good news for you, especially if you want to leave and negotiate a settlement. So always accept. The longer you are out of the office, the harder it will be for your employer if you decide to go back. Most people will know you are going to leave, your employer may even have let it slip; so if you come to an impasse in your negotiations, you can threaten to return to work – which you know your employer doesn't want you to do. Your employer cannot prevent this without breaching your contract, neither can they allow it without looking ridiculous to your colleagues: check-mate. Your employer will have to give you what you want.

Without prejudice negotiations opened by the employee

If you, the employee, wish to initiate negotiations with your employer, a good approach would be for you to send a without prejudice letter or email to your employer setting out the reasons for wishing to negotiate, and the terms on which you are willing to settle.

1.3. Without prejudice meetings and phone calls

It's usually your employer who will ask you to a without prejudice meeting or who will phone your lawyer (if you have one) during a negotiation and before a claim is issued, and ask to speak on a without prejudice basis. This would become a without prejudice phone call. Then the employer will explain how much they are willing to offer as an exit package for you.

It is less common for you, as an employee, to ask for a without prejudice meeting or phone call, although there are occasions when it would be appropriate to do so (see more on this below). It's usually easier for you to set out the issues in written form rather than to initiate verbal discussions, mainly because you're probably not used to this kind of formal conversation.

On the other hand, if you have a lawyer, they will often just pick up the phone to discuss your case with your employer. A lawyer will be confident in knowing what to say and how to say it on a without prejudice basis.

Below are a few basic pointers to be aware of when it comes to meeting your employer on a without prejudice basis. The required approach is slightly different depending on whether it was your employer, or you, that suggested the meeting.

TOP 3 TIPS

- Let your employer be the one to suggest the without prejudice meeting
- Listen, don't speak (apart from seeking any factual clarification)
- Take detailed notes of what is said and by whom

Without prejudice meetings usually take place when you are still employed. For example, meetings may occur after you have submitted a written grievance but before the grievance is investigated, or when your employer believes there are serious performance concerns and wants you to leave the business. Your employer would then ask to speak without prejudice, and suggest an exit package for you.

Without prejudice meetings are less common after tribunal proceedings are issued. This is simply because by that point you've probably left employment and therefore it is more effort to get people together. However, in some high-value cases it can be beneficial to have a without prejudice meeting even at this late stage.

Be careful if there is only a verbal agreement to speak without prejudice. Where there's only a verbal agreement to speak without prejudice, then obviously there is an element of trust involved and you need to be careful what you say and who you say it to.

Deciding whether or not to attend a without prejudice meeting is not always easy. There is no legal requirement for you to attend a without prejudice meeting that your employer has asked you to go to, and it cannot later be held against you at work or in tribunal if you do not attend. Often when the employment relationship has broken down, and your employer has caused you a lot of stress and anxiety, you may not feel physically or mentally able to attend a meeting with them.

If this is the case, then you could just ask your employer to put their points across to you in writing. It is actually quite a good idea to say something along the lines of: 'As I'm currently signed off sick with stress and anxiety I'd like this process to be conducted in writing.' If you have legal representation, then you can ask your lawyers to write everything for you, to be sent under your name, or to communicate directly with your employer on a without prejudice basis.

Be aware of how to act in a without prejudice meeting. If you do decide to attend a without prejudice meeting requested by your employer, then normally our advice would be to say as little as possible, apart, perhaps, from seeking clarification on any point they make which is unclear. Don't be tempted to pour your heart out to HR or complain about how badly treated you've been – they probably won't be on your side. Plus, you might reveal something which they could use against you somehow. Just turn up, keep quiet, listen to what they have to say and try to take detailed notes.

How to respond to an offer made in a without prejudice meeting

If HR or management make you a without prejudice offer, the best advice would be to say that you'll consider what they have to say and get back to them. It's often worth asking them for a breakdown of how they calculated the figure – for example, does it include your notice pay or not? Better still, ask them for a written draft that you can study further in your own time.

Try to avoid appearing to be pleased by the level of the offer, or desperate to conclude negotiations as soon as possible – keep a straight face, even if the offer is higher than you expected. When you have had a chance to think about it you can get back to them. (See below on responding to an offer in writing.)

As with any negotiation, it is unlikely that your employer will put forward their best offer first. Also, the people who attend without prejudice meetings on behalf of your employer often do so with specific instructions about how high an offer they are allowed to make. If you reject their offer, then they may need to go back to senior management for approval to raise the ceiling before they can offer you more. So be patient.

If you do reach some common ground and the offer seems acceptable to you, then bear in mind that most exit packages are put in writing in the form of a settlement agreement. When you receive the settlement agreement from your employer's HR or legal department, it will probably be at least ten pages long. (See chapter 12 for an example of a settlement agreement document.)

There will inevitably be some points included in the agreement which you haven't agreed in your without prejudice meeting. For this reason, it would be best for you to agree terms 'subject to the wording of the settlement agreement'. This gives you more room to manoeuvre once you actually receive the document. This means that in principle you are happy with the offer itself, but in practice you want to check the wording of the settlement agreement document to see exactly what it is they want you to sign.

In summary of the above:
- Don't say too much.
- Don't agree to anything on the spot.
- Ask for a written breakdown of any offer made.
- Be patient during negotiations.
- Agree terms 'subject to the wording of the settlement agreement'.

Whether to request a without prejudice meeting yourself

If you decide to request a without prejudice meeting yourself, then you would be well advised to do so from a position of strength. That means after you have put your legal case forward and fought for your rights, either through the grievance process, the initial stages of the tribunal process or through written without prejudice correspondence.

Generally, we would advise against you requesting a without prejudice meeting too early because it can be seen as a sign of weakness. It can indicate that you are going to crack under pressure and may not have what it takes to pursue a just and fair result. But each case is different, and if you are confident that you could achieve a good settlement quickly, then requesting a meeting could work.

If you have a lawyer you could ask them to attend the meeting with you or to be part of a conference call when it comes to without prejudice discussions. Such discussions are not like formal grievance/disciplinary meetings where you are only permitted to bring a trade union representative or a colleague.

1.4. How to write without prejudice letters and emails

When writing a without prejudice letter it is often helpful to set out the strongest points of the case. This means listing, in bullet points or numbered paragraphs: dates, times, places, and details of who said or did what.

Then you need to set out your proposal for a resolution, normally being an amount of money which you would accept in settlement. It's also worth reminding your employer about the additional costs which they will incur if they don't settle. These would include legal fees which they would have to spend fighting the case, and an estimate of the amount of compensation which they would have to pay you if they lose (preferably with a realistic breakdown of that estimate).

Then you can set out the discounted amount which you would accept to settle by way of a settlement agreement, and state a deadline for their acceptance of, say, seven days. Deadlines are a good idea as they put the cat amongst the pigeons and will have HR and/or management sitting up and paying attention, rather than being tempted to put your case to the side and assign it a low priority.

Likewise, if you are responding to an initial offer from your employer, then you may wish to put down your thoughts in a letter rather than by verbally speaking with them. This puts things on a formal platform and allows you to set out your case professionally.

Examples of without prejudice letters and emails are given in chapter 12.

Making allegations or accusations

In your first correspondence, be selective and keep some issues in reserve for the final negotiating stages. Try not to over-emphasise all the ways you think they've mistreated you. Instead, stop and think if there is a way you can more subtly mention their behaviour.

That's not to say you shouldn't set out the facts that you are relying upon to negotiate. You should, but you can do this without making damaging allegations against named individuals, especially individuals who have the power to offer you a settlement agreement.

The more you make allegations and accusations in a without prejudice letter, the more your employer will defend those allegations: it's a natural thing to defend yourself when you're accused. They are likely to investigate further and and this will generate still more letters. The parties may become entrenched, with the likelihood of a settlement disappearing over the horizon. All this, when what you really need is a quick, painless deal which leaves you financially better off, and able to look for another job free from immediate financial pressures.

Simply set out the facts

It is best to set out the facts in a neutral and objective way. Those facts, if they form the basis of a claim, will speak for themselves. Remember, you are dealing with an employer, not a colleague, and your employer will have an HR department as well as lawyers or advisers who specialise in employment law on their side.

Therefore, once your letter gets passed to these individuals for their views, they will understand that you may have a claim against the company or that you present a risk to the business. They will know what claims you may have and what they are worth. There is usually no need to say that Mr X has it in for you and that's why he failed to score your performance procedure correctly, or that Mrs Y has maliciously breached your contract and that you have an unfair dismissal claim.

This is, in our view, the way to set out most without prejudice letters for ordinary unfair or constructive dismissal cases (e.g. redundancy, performance, conduct etc.), breaches of contract and other contractual claims such as unpaid bonuses or holiday pay. By setting the facts out in a neutral way, you will appear professional and easy to deal with rather than overly emotional and irrational. The company will appreciate this and is much more likely to want to deal with you.

Without prejudice letters in cases such as discrimination or whistleblowing

In such instances as these, and contrary to the general advice given above, it's often best to set out the allegations themselves. Try to do this in a neutral and objective manner that does not antagonise your employer too much. Set out the allegations, the dates on which they occurred, the witnesses to them, reference any evidence that you may have to support your case (see chapter 2) and then explain – again, as objectively as possible – why you consider the allegations to be, for example, discrimination.

Make it look professional

It may sound obvious, but if you're not used to writing legal letters, then it's important to make sure that your letter is typed on a computer and in the correct letter format. If you're not sure of the correct format for a formal letter, use one of the examples in Part Three.

If you intend to send the letter electronically, print off a copy, sign it, scan it and then send it to your employer. Alternatively, use an electronic signature and convert the document to a PDF file if you can. Avoid sending your letter in an editable format.

If you want to be taken seriously, use the correct terms, write in complete sentences, use paragraphs, bullet points and headings, and above all make sure your use of language is correct in terms of grammar and meaning. Use a spell checker and don't ignore those red and blue lines under words on your screen – they usually mean that something needs correcting!

Use a three step formula when drafting your letter

When drafting a letter there are three steps: the introduction, the facts of the dispute, and the resolution. This is the anatomy of any good without prejudice letter which has a decent chance of leading to a successful negotiation. Each step is detailed further below:

Step 1: Writing the introduction

This should be the opening of the letter in which you introduce yourself, your role, what you do for the company, how hard you have worked and for how long. You should mention any commendations or accolades you have received from the company and any successes you have personally had, or contributed to, in the last year or two.

Say how much you have enjoyed working for the company and that you value its work. Every employer wants to know how much you enjoyed working for them. They are much more likely to deal with you if you are respectful and come to negotiations out of a sense of genuine regret, rather than showing malicious intent.

This sets the scene for you to tell your employer what they have done wrong. Explain how important this is to you and how hard it has been for you to decide to take the step of writing the letter. This creates an element of guilt for the company, and possibly of shock that one of its employees can be so unhappy.

Step 2: Presenting the facts of the dispute

Now is the time to tell your employer exactly why you are unhappy. Set out the key facts that you think could lead to a claim, but don't actually mention a claim, merely that these things have happened to you and that you feel very unhappy and hurt by them. Stick to the most important facts, leave out the trivial matters and don't be tempted to exaggerate. Concentrate on recent events and ignore events from years ago unless they are directly connected to more recent happenings.

Set out the events in date order and make references to evidence that you have collected. If you feel it appropriate at this stage, you can send a copy of the key items of evidence with your without prejudice letter. If you are going to do this, then you should use the format discussed in chapter 2 on how to build your case using evidence, and reference the evidence by the tabs in your evidence file.

Don't make this section too long: remember, you are trying to capture and hold your employer's attention and you are unlikely to do this by writing a lengthy letter making dozens of allegations. Ideally, your entire letter should fit on no more than three sides of A4 paper, and that includes the headings and your signature.

It is a real art and a science to try to write a concise without prejudice letter while still maintaining the full impact of all the contents. If you can master it, your employer will probably think you have been helped by a lawyer, and be more inclined to offer you a settlement deal.

Step 3: Setting out your proposed dispute resolution

You have presented your employer with a problem (the facts of the dispute), now you need to present them with a solution: a settlement agreement, termination of your employment and a payment. In this part of your letter, if you want to leave your job then you need to say so and also detail when you want to leave. Be humble about it, say you regret this decision very much, but you see no other option. Again, don't mention an employment tribunal as this can often kill any existing goodwill stone dead and prevent an agreement being reached.

The best way to set out your offer is as follows:

1. Proposed termination date.
2. That you want payment in lieu of notice.
3. That you want your outstanding holiday pay paid.
4. That you want an agreed reference.
5. Any other non-financial terms you require.
6. Your proposal for an ex gratia payment (see chapter 5), set out in gross months' salary, for example six months' gross salary. Of course, the first £30,000 of this will be tax free.

Points 1-4 above are easily negotiable and most employers will agree to these if the first parts of your letter are well drafted. Therefore, for the purposes of presentation, you should set out the easy points first. This gets your employer, or the reader of the letter, used to saying 'yes, that seems reasonable' in their head, so by the time they get to point 5 they are more receptive to your additional proposals.

In terms of how much to ask for, that depends on the case you have, but remember, you are asking for a quick deal, so you should accept less than you could hope to achieve at an employment tribunal. Remember also that by settling, you won't have to pay for legal representation or incur the very real risk of losing your case. You'll also get the tax advantages of settling under a settlement agreement. 'A bird in the hand is worth two in the bush', as the saying goes.

We deal with the question of how much you should settle for in greater detail in chapter 4, but in general terms most negotiations settle for between 'notice pay plus one month's gross salary' and 'notice pay plus four months' gross salary'. If you have an excellent case, or represent a risk to the business in terms of clients, then you should be aiming higher, maybe notice pay plus six months' gross salary.

So, if you have an idea of the amount you can realistically settle for, you need to pitch a little higher when making an opening offer: a little higher, but not ridiculously so. If you can realistically aim for three months' salary plus notice, and you offer twelve months' salary, then your employer is not going to take you seriously. Ironically, if you plan to use a lawyer, it can be a good tactic to offer a ridiculously high amount straight away, then instruct a lawyer to negotiate on a sensible basis.

Normally though, you should be asking for up to double what you can realistically achieve, depending on the strength of your case. So, if you can expect three months' gross salary plus notice then you could try pitching for six months' gross salary plus notice in your initial offer.

The last line of your letter before the signature should always be, 'I look forward to hearing from you'.

1.5. Responding to an offer in writing

We considered earlier (in section 1.3.) how to respond to a verbal settlement offer made in a without prejudice meeting, but if you've already been made an offer in writing, you need to respond – also in writing.

By this time, you are in an excellent position to secure a settlement agreement on favourable terms as it's evident from your employer making the offer that this is what they want to achieve. Therefore, the structure of the letter needs to be slightly different. You can still set out the introduction in a similar way to that outlined above, only start by saying that you are surprised and a little hurt that your employer wishes to terminate your employment. Then state how hard you have worked and how much your job means to you. This should elicit sympathy and create goodwill.

In the second part of the letter, you should respond to the points your employer has made. They are hoping you will agree with those points, so that they can use them to form the basis of a settlement agreement with you. However, you should not just accept them passively: fight your corner if you need to, but without being aggressive or making too many accusations.

Correct mistakes if your employer has made them. Let them know that you are not prepared to accept their version of events and then present your own version. Use evidence to highlight the differences in the two accounts. Study the small print in the agreement carefully and seek to clarify anything which is unclear, or ask for changes to any clauses that are unacceptable. Build a case related to your employer's reasons for offering you a settlement agreement, and let them know that getting rid of you isn't going to be as easy, or as cheap, as they think.

The 'resolution' part of the letter should be the same as if you were taking the first steps. You should be able to get an idea of a realistic response to the initial ex gratia offer from your employer by reference to what they have offered you. So, if they have offered two months' gross salary plus notice (a common starting point), then you should be looking to achieve between four and five, and therefore be responding to that offer proposing six months' gross salary plus notice.

1.6. When your employer doesn't play ball: breaking deadlock

It may not surprise you to learn that most of the time employers don't simply agree with you after the first letter, or your initial response to their offer, and give you everything you want straight away. This is where the value of keeping some of your ammunition in reserve comes into play. It is likely that, following a well-crafted letter, your employer will have made an improved offer; but it is also likely that this offer still falls short of what you want and can realistically achieve.

So, you should respond to your employer in writing and use some of those arguments which you have been holding back for just such a time as this. While your language should continue to be professional, now is the time to explain that you consider your employer's actions to be unlawful. Moreover, you can explain that you have a potential claim in the employment tribunal, and while you do not wish these issues to end up in the tribunal, unless they are settled now then that's where things may conclude.

Your letter should also say that, while you welcome the fact that your employer has increased their offer, it is not enough for you to accept. Set out how the facts relate to the claim you have: mention witnesses, introduce any evidence you have, so that at this stage your employer should have all the evidence they need to determine the risk you present to them. Make it clear that you are prepared to stand your ground and are not going to be a pushover.

Now may also be the right time to instruct a lawyer if you haven't already done so. You have an offer on the table and a settlement agreement is likely, so you just need the final push to get you exactly what you want.

A lawyer entering the fray at this stage is sometimes enough for your employer to recognise that this is going to get serious unless they offer an acceptable deal. It also shows that you have at least some of the same resources available to you that they have, and that often breaks the deadlock. A quick letter or call from your lawyer often gets you what you want, and it's not going to cost you very much, given that you have already carried out a lot of the legwork. Bear in mind that you will need a lawyer anyway to review and sign your settlement (this is a legal requirement that is normally paid for by the employer), so if you can instruct one now then you will get the most value from their time.

1.7. Accepting an offer

It's sometimes difficult to know when to accept an offer, but the general rule is that when both parties are not happy with the deal, then this is a good time to accept. What do we mean by this? The explanation below should give you a better idea:

The art of a compromise is exactly that: a compromise. This means that both parties think that they are giving something away that they are not necessarily entirely happy with. Sometimes you'll be entirely happy with the deal, which is fantastic, and you'll know when this is because you'll be celebrating. However, in the majority of cases, both your employer and you will leave the negotiation not entirely happy with everything, but with a deal you can work with.

Sometimes it's OK not to be immediately happy with the final offer. What we often find is that, although you may not have been entirely happy with the final offer (i.e. you wonder if you could have received more), it is an amount that you planned to accept had the offer been made. So in the next day or so after some initial disappointment, you become satisfied with the deal and relieved to be moving on with a fair sum of money.

So how do you know when this situation arises? Well, it's not necessarily when your employer says that this is a 'final offer' as that can just be a negotiating tactic. If this happens, you will have to work out whether you believe them to be bluffing or not. In our experience, if an employer says, 'final offer' then you can probably get them to move a bit more – and sometimes a lot more.

Another tactic is to propose a compromise on your employer's latest offer. Suggest that if you meet in the middle then that would be acceptable, but with the intention of taking slightly less than that. You would say something like: 'If you would be willing to move to X amount, then I will accept your offer', or, 'then we will have a deal'. For example, your employer is offering an ex gratia payment of £16,000, and you are offering £24,000. Then you suggest that, 'if you move to £20,000 then we have a deal'. This is sometimes enough to generate an offer of £19,000, as the employer will think that they are winning because they are offering less than you suggested. They don't know that this is what you wanted them to do all along. This is a good time to accept.

Know what to do if your employer won't move further. If your employer is unwilling to move further on the ex gratia element of the package and you have tried everything to get them to move, either instruct a lawyer, or try to come to agreement on another element of the package that will give you higher remuneration. For example, ask for your car allowance to be paid for the same duration as your notice pay, or for the benefits that would have accrued during your notice period (such as pension, healthcare etc.) to be paid as damages. If they offer this, then it's probably time to accept. Of course you can still submit a formal grievance or an employment tribunal claim in the right circumstances. If you're still employed, and you wish to claim for constructive unfair dismissal (see chapter 7), then you would have to resign in order to issue an employment tribunal claim, and resigning is a risky business in a settlement agreement negotiation.

Know what to do when you're ready to accept an offer. If you feel you have reached the stage where you wish to accept an offer, then you need to write to your employer telling them that you will accept the offer 'subject to contract' (ie your settlement agreement). This means that while you are willing to do the deal, the deal isn't done until you've signed the contract. This is important, as it allows you or your lawyer to alter elements of the deal as and when they arise.

1.8. Additional negotiating tactics

To round off this chapter we introduce a few additional negotiating tactics for you to consider:

● **Your manner when negotiating**

Be polite, but not too nice. Not surprisingly, simply asking your employer for a large lump sum of cash for your settlement agreement just doesn't work. Remember, it's not so much what you ought to receive because you've been such a loyal employee and generally nice person; it's more what they owe you for mistreatment and for forcing you out of your job in one way or another. You're going to need to be tough. Negotiating a settlement agreement is not for the faint hearted and even if you do have lawyers on your side you'll still need to be prepared to dig in for a fight. Hopefully, it'll be worth it.

Be resolute but not nasty. It's no good ranting and raving about how badly you've been mistreated and how you're going to take revenge on your employer if they refuse to agree to your demands. This is not a hostage situation! No matter how badly you've been treated, try to maintain a sense of decorum. There's nothing wrong with stating matter-of-factly, in a without prejudice letter, that unless the settlement agreement negotiation is successful, you will take further action, but try to take some of the emotion out of the situation, or at least use no more emotion than strictly necessary. We're not asking you to hide your feelings, just don't come across as too angry.

Consider the 'unpredictable employee' approach. We don't recommend this approach in the majority of cases, but there is something to be said for using this tactic in some scenarios. It involves you being totally unpredictable and liable to do or say anything at any point, including things to your own (and the employer's) detriment.

Your employer is unsure how to deal with this approach and HR is afraid because this scenario is outside of their training. This is a rarely used, but actually fairly effective tactic in international diplomacy (think Donald Trump and Kim Jong-un) and does, in certain cases, make employers pay way over the odds just to get rid of an employee. The tactic works especially well with large employers with reputations to protect.

If you are going to adopt this unconventional approach, then make sure you do nothing illegal or in breach of your contract, and that you don't make threats that could be taken to be blackmail. Threatening to 'go to the local or national press', or to sue a director for civil harassment, or something similar, are all last-ditch tactics that could work. Deployed correctly, they can break a deadlock.

Try using 'The flinch'. This is where you express your shock or disappointment at the inadequacy of the other side's offer. It will strike a note with the recipient, no matter how steely-nerved they are trying to be.

● **Use the whisper number**

If you have a lawyer, see if they think it's timely to use what's known as the 'whisper number'. This is where the lawyer will typically say to the other side, 'I don't have my client's instructions on this but theoretically could you go up to this amount?'. By talking about an amount which you haven't authorised, your lawyer can sound out the opposition without committing to anything and still play a get-out card if need be.

● **Use inside information**

If you have any information relating to malpractice by your employer, which would help to motivate them to give you a better deal, then what better time to mention it than when negotiating a settlement agreement? It is especially relevant when such behaviour is the cause of you having to resign in the first place. Indeed, by revealing your employer's bad behaviour, you are probably helping to ensure that they change their ways going forward. Of course, you can't blackmail your employer by asking for money just to keep quiet about certain information; but it can be used to point out the strength of your potential whistleblowing claim, and therefore be a perfectly legitimate bargaining chip.

● **Don't negotiate against yourself**

Sometimes a cheeky employer will reject your first offer and ask you to come back with something more palatable to them. So, rather than making a counter offer, they want you to revise your offer downwards. This would amount to negotiating against yourself. Instead, stand fast, tell them that you've set out your offer and if they want to make a counter offer they should do so by a certain date, failing which you'll take action without further notice.

● **Don't make threats in open correspondence**

Don't mention employment tribunals in open correspondence such as a grievance letter or a normal email to your employer. If you 'openly' threaten to sue your employer this can be construed as breaching the relationship of trust and confidence which is supposed to exist, and technically it could be a firing offence. Don't openly say that the trust and confidence has broken down either.

● **Keep strictly to deadlines**

Deadlines in negotiations: set a deadline in your without prejudice letter and say that your offer will be withdrawn if it is not accepted by that deadline. And then stick to it. It's no good running a settlement agreement negotiation using deadlines and then giving the other side one more chance – they'll think you're soft – so only brandish deadlines if you're prepared to use them. The kind of thing you could do to threaten your employer (apart from withdrawing the offer) might include submitting a formal grievance or issuing a tribunal claim. Also remember you can use the words 'final offer' when you've really reached your bottom line.

Conversely, when your employer gives you a deadline to negotiate a settlement agreement, don't think that you have to stick to it. Often employers put arbitrary deadlines on their offers which give you little or no time to consider matters properly and/or seek legal advice. There is often no reason for doing this other than to put pressure on you. And once these deadlines slide, 95% of the time their offer will still be available to you. They've done the maths and calculated what they'd be prepared to pay you, and that won't change just because some arbitrary tactical deadline has passed. This can be a bit of a 'white knuckle' ride for you, but it does show them that you are not prepared to dance to their tune any more – you're in charge of the negotiation now.

Deadlines in tribunal claims: whatever happens, remember to issue an ACAS certificate for employment tribunals within three months. Don't let your settlement agreement negotiation side-track you into overlooking the time limit for tribunal claims. Your employer may try to stall you or string out the negotiations in the hope that you do miss this deadline, and if you do, then you might as well forget it, because tribunals are very strict about this. For more about employment tribunal time limits see chapter 6.

● Submitting grievances during negotiations

Submitting a grievance can be a good way to further a settlement agreement negotiation when without prejudice correspondence has reached a deadlock. By requiring a written response, formal grievances force your employer to address the matter head-on rather than turning the other cheek and hoping you'll go away. It is also a handy way to see what defence your employer has up their sleeve before you issue your tribunal claim. You can flush out any crafty moves which they are planning to make in their defence, so that you can fine tune your claim and anticipate their response. Always appeal your grievance response, as explained below.

● Use your appeals

At all stages in the 'open' process, whether that process be redundancy, dismissal, performance review, or grievance etc., you should take full advantage of all the appeals which your employer offers you. If they offer you the right to appeal, use it. If there are two levels of appeal available, use them both. Don't be tempted to take the easy exit and not use your appeal rights. If it's harder work for you, then it's also harder work for your employer, so it's more likely that you'll succeed in negotiating a settlement agreement.

1.9. Employers' approaches to settlement negotiations

If you want to get the best outcomes from negotiating with your employer, it's useful to have an idea of what they're thinking about during negotiations and what sort of tactics they use. Employers usually approach settlement negotiations with a number of questions in mind, including the following:

- **Precedent:** what has been done in other similar situations? Will settling your case make other people come forward? Are you being treated fairly in light of other cases?

- **Disruption to business:** what is the business cost of not settling; including management time and disruption to the normal operations of the business?

- **Direct costs of not settling:** is there paid sick leave or a prolonged period of agreed paid leave? How long will they have to pay you for if they do not settle the case?

- **The risks of not settling:** how likely are you to bring a claim and what is the likely cost of this claim in terms of damages? Larger employers in particular are likely to settle, just so they can avoid legal fees.

- **Reputational risk:** what's the risk of losing clients from bad publicity if your case is not settled?

Precedent

This can sometimes work to your advantage. Some employers have a history of making generous termination payments; particularly in cases of performance and redundancy. If you know that such payments have been made in the past you can use this to argue that you should be paid a similar amount.

Precedent can also work against you. For example, in a large redundancy exercise it is very difficult to convince your employer to increase any settlement offer as they will be worried that others will seek the same increase. Also, employers may be reluctant to settle a claim that they don't think is worthwhile in case it creates a precedent which encourages others to seek a settlement.

Disruption to business

Dealing with such matters as grievances and performance plans is time consuming and costly for an employer, so they may well prefer to settle with you instead.

Direct costs of not settling

If your employer has to pay you money to do nothing, this gives them a powerful incentive to reach a settlement. For example if you are on paid sick leave your employer will be motivated to settle as they will be paying you in any event. The same applies if you are suspended and there is likely to be a prolonged investigation.

The risks of not settling

If you have a strong claim against your employer and they think that you are likely to bring the claim to tribunal, this will also encourage them to settle. They may test your motivation by not settling until you actually issue a claim, particularly if you have already resigned or been dismissed.

Reputational risk

Your employer is more likely to settle if their failure to do so is likely to result in bad publicity or have a detrimental impact on customer service.

Employers use a variety of tactics to try to minimise settlement amounts. These include setting short deadlines, making low final offers, and requiring you to reduce your offer, as discussed earlier in this chapter.

Chapter 2

Evidence:
how to build your case

Introduction

All legal cases stand or fall on the quality or quantity of the evidence that is presented either to the court or to the other side. The same is true in a negotiation between employee and employer. This is because your employer might not know exactly what happened to you at work. It might be HR who is dealing with your negotiation, whereas it may have been your line manager who mistreated you – and if it's just one word against the other with no evidence, HR might believe the line manager over you. In other cases, HR may well believe that you were mistreated, but they don't believe that you could prove it in court, so they see no litigation risk and therefore no reason to negotiate with you.

So, if you want to negotiate with your employer, then you must first gather, and then present, evidence to the other side. You need to select this evidence carefully and try to be rational and critical about what you include, just as a lawyer would be. Remember, large companies employ lawyers 'in-house' or they instruct outside law firms to handle their legal work. The chances are that your without prejudice letter will be passed to a lawyer, so you have to be able to argue your case in a manner which a lawyer understands. If a lawyer cannot understand the points you are making, or cannot see how the evidence ties together to support those points, then you probably won't get a good deal.

This chapter discusses the methods used both to gather evidence and to present that evidence to your employer in the most effective and concise way. We look at the common forms of evidence; how to gather evidence; why sometimes gathering evidence can lead to unintended consequences; how to get witness evidence and how to present evidence to your employer.

2.1. Evidence: a practical overview

Deciding what evidence will support your case

Before gathering evidence to support your case, it helps to determine what your potential claims are and where the evidence is likely to be found to support these claims. Some of the possible claims you may have are discussed in detail in Part Two of this book, but here we give you some broad tactical advice on how to decide which areas of employment law are relevant to your particular case.

Try to undertake this evaluation before starting to gather evidence, as the type of claim you may have against your employer will affect the sort of evidence that you need to gather. For example, if you believe you are being harassed by a colleague at work, there is no point in asking for a copy of your contract, or searching through emails if the harassment is taking place verbally.

Likewise, if you believe that you are being unfairly dismissed for an incident on the factory floor witnessed by two colleagues then a trawl of your emails from years ago is not going to support your case. Or, if you believe that you are not being paid equally when compared to a colleague of the opposite sex, you need to be asking your employer directly for information about your colleague's pay.

Critically and carefully select your evidence

It is tempting for some employees to trawl through as much evidence as possible in an attempt to make some of it support a potential claim: this is not generally recommended, as undertaking this sort of exercise can often lead to weak and unsubstantiated allegations which will not help you to achieve what you want. Lots of unrelated incidents over several years are unlikely to be sufficient to establish a case of constructive dismissal; nor is the fact that your manager made a pass at you at the Christmas party two years ago going to help you establish a case of unfair dismissal if you are accused of negligence in performing your duties.

If you simply amass as much evidence as you can and then accuse your employer of anything you can think of in a 'throw as much mud as possible and see what sticks' approach, this is not only going to fail to get you what you want, it may actually be counterproductive and even lead to your employer taking action against you.

Evidence should support your strongest arguments

By far the better approach is to focus your evidence on the main argument you have. For example, if you believe that you have been constructively dismissed because of a breach of trust and confidence (see chapter 7), search for evidence over the last six months that will support the three or four incidences that you believe are the strongest. A tight and focused approach will always be more effective in a negotiation than wide ranging allegations.

Remember, although this book is written to enable you, as an employee, to negotiate a settlement agreement, you are actually gathering evidence that could be used in an employment tribunal or civil court. Your employers are much more likely to take your negotiation seriously if you can provide them with evidence that a) supports your case, and b) could be used against them in an employment tribunal, as it presents a risk to your employers in terms of compensation, legal costs and their reputation.

2.2. Taking confidential documents

Before looking at the main types of evidence that can be used, it is worth exploring whether you can or cannot take any document you want. (For the purposes of this section, the term 'document' is used to include emails and other forms of text-based communication.) These issues are particularly relevant to documents which your employers would argue are confidential.

Be careful: you can be sacked for taking confidential documents

The case of Brandeaux vs Chadwick (2010) looked at when an employee can take confidential documents from an employer and use them in an employment tribunal case. In this case Ms Chadwick, the employee, had forwarded a vast volume of confidential material to her personal email account. When she did this there was no whistleblowing dispute – she was just trying to gather evidence to show unfair dismissal. The upshot? If you do this is and your employer finds out, you can be lawfully sacked for gross misconduct, which is exactly what happened to Ms Chadwick.

If, on the other hand, there is a serious regulatory matter, such as fraud or other misconduct by your employer, then you may be entitled to take documents from your employer and use them in an employment tribunal case or negotiation. But you shouldn't take hundreds of documents like Ms Chadwick did – only consider the most relevant ones – and you should be careful how you copy the information.

If you have a genuine regulatory or whistleblowing concern, you can use your employer's confidential information to make a report to the regulator, but it would be best to avoid sending your employer's confidential data to your personal computer. You could, for example, compile a report using the information on the system at work, without actually removing it.

TOP 3 TIPS

- Don't email confidential documents to yourself
- Make sure there is a regulatory breach before you copy anything
- Only copy the minimum number of documents

Remember, anything done on a computer or smartphone, even if deleted, can in theory be detected by your boss, and furthermore they can sometimes 'track' what you print. At the start of any litigation, some employers may order a forensic examination of a computer and/or smartphone to see if they can catch you out. If you are determined to take documents, photocopying hard copies might be an option, or taking screen prints or photos.

What about after dismissal?

After you have been dismissed you have more room for manoeuvre. For example, if you still have access to the server or to emails on a smartphone, then using or forwarding data would not destroy a future case, because your employer can't argue that it was a reason to sack you (because they've sacked you already). Confidentially sensitive information however shouldn't be taken. For example, information about products or other employees.

Case study

How you come by evidence is important. Some months ago one of our lawyers advised a woman who, soon after telling her employer that she was pregnant, was sacked. After her dismissal she was anonymously forwarded a copy of an email sent from her boss to another member of staff. This email made clear that the firm intended to sack her because she was pregnant. She was entitled to keep this copy because it was sent to her, but if she had instead hacked into her boss's email account before she had been dismissed to 'steal' the email, the situation would have been trickier. Needless to say, we achieved a large payout on this case!

2.3. Gathering different kinds of evidence

Once you have established what type of claims you may have to base your arguments on, and have a general understanding of what areas of evidence are likely to be able to support your case, the time has come to search for and secure that evidence. Here, we will look at the main types of evidence that are used to substantiate allegations in negotiations and employment tribunals.

2.3.1. Emails

The world is run on emails; countless millions pass between colleagues and companies each day. Decisions are communicated in emails, adverse comments are made in emails, and so the majority of the documents in most trial bundles in employment tribunals these days are emails. This, therefore, is logically where you should start your search for evidence.

Emails that have been sent to you from within your company are the emails most likely to hold evidence you can use. You can search for these emails in your inbox or deleted items folder in the usual manner and save the useful ones, either in a separate email folder or in an electronic document folder. Gathering email evidence is the easy part, preserving them in a safe place is the more complicated part.

Company email policies

Most email communications these days come with a disclaimer at the bottom explaining that the email, its contents and any attachments are the property of the company. Furthermore, as an employee, you are likely to be subject to an email policy, a company property policy and a confidentiality policy. These policies will state that emails are company property, may contain confidential information belonging to the company and therefore must not be removed from the company.

These policies are designed to prevent you from taking all sorts of actions including forwarding company emails to your own private account, electronically downloading or uploading company emails, or printing out emails and removing the print outs from the company premises.

There are many legitimate reasons for a company to have policies such as these; however, there is a direct conflict with such policies and your right as an employee to gather evidence to use for the purposes of litigation. It is a fine balance and – as discussed earlier – many employees have been subject to threats, disciplinary action and even dismissal for moving confidential emails from the company servers to their own personal email accounts.

By and large these policies amount to matters of civil law rather than criminal law. After all, you are not trying to defraud the company. So if you breach them, the worst case scenario would be that you get sued for financial compensation by the company, rather than arrested or anything involving the police.

General rule on removing emails

Although every case is different, the general rule is that it's best not to remove emails from the company server. In a normal case it shouldn't be necessary to take these steps. For example, if you continue to remain in work, and are gathering evidence for a normal case of unfair dismissal or constructive dismissal, and you don't suspect your employer of attempting to destroy evidence, you should gather together the emails that support your case in your company inbox or store them on the company server.

If you feel you have to remove emails (if, for example, you suspect you will suspended and not granted access to systems or that your employer is deleting evidence), then it is risky to remove confidential commercial information contained in emails or as attachments, from the company servers, even if this supports your case. Examples here include price lists and client lists. This can lead to legitimate allegations that you have breached company policies and your duties of confidentiality, which will not only undermine your negotiation but could lead to disciplinary action in and of itself – as exemplified in the Brandeaux case mentioned earlier.

Exceptions to the general rule on removing emails

There are nearly always exceptions to rules, however, and here is an example of a case we handled which demonstrates this: our client had retained the whole of her email inbox on her phone. She had been entitled to have this because the email system was synchronised to her phone. The employer tried to use against us the Brandeaux case mentioned above, but because our client hadn't done anything against company policy, she won that particular battle and went on to achieve a decent settlement figure. Perhaps she should have returned the emails once she'd been dismissed, but by then the employer couldn't argue that it was a reason for dismissing her.

The other feature of this case which distinguishes it from the Brandeaux court case is that there was a whistleblowing issue – the employer had been 'cooking the books' or committing corporate fraud. Therefore our client was much more likely to be treated leniently by the tribunal, and allowed to use the emails which she had in her possession.

The same strict rules don't apply to standard day-to-day communications even if those communications are vital to your case. For example, if your boss has used aggressive language or threats in an email, the company is going to be hard-pressed to claim that the communication contained confidential information. So, if you do forward it to your own email address you will most likely be on stronger ground than if you have forwarded a list of clients or financial information.

2.3.2. Letters

Letters addressed to you from your employer are usually important evidence, so you should preserve them. Taking copies is sometimes a good idea so that you have spares as back up should something happen to the originals. Letters addressed to you are your property, therefore you are able to remove them from the office and store them at home without any issues. You should be able to locate these letters easily. If you have lost the original you received then ask HR for a copy and they should provide you with one.

If you believe that letters exist that support your case, and that you can search for these letters in a lawful manner (i.e. without breaking into colleagues' offices or filing cabinets, which is likely to lead to disciplinary allegations), then you should commence this search. Bear in mind that letters that you come into contact with as part of your job are generally the property of the company and taking the original letters could lead to allegations of theft of company property or misuse of confidential information. If, during your search for letters that support your case, you do find evidence that you believe will help your case, the best thing to do is to take scans or copies and then replace the originals where you found them.

2.3.3. Documents

Documents relating directly to you such as performance reviews, sales records etc., are almost always legitimate documents to use in a negotiation. Documents you have obtained that relate to you, but were not sent to you in the normal manner, are likewise fine to use as long as you haven't obtained them in an unlawful manner or in breach of your employee obligations.

The same caveats regarding company property and confidential information apply to company documents: they are not your property and so removing them from the office risks disciplinary action. If you require documents for litigation and cannot preserve them in any other manner, then there is no guarantee that you will be protected by the law if you take them. Just bear in mind the risks discussed above.

2.4. Formally requesting documents and information

2.4.1. Requests for disclosure

If you have conducted a search for emails, letters and documents, but cannot find what you are looking for, you may wish to consider writing to the company (usually the HR department) and making a formal request for the company to hand over specific documents. The advantage of this approach is that the request for evidence will be made on a formal basis and you have acted properly in making this request. It will, however, put your employer on notice that you intend to do something that may cause them trouble.

What to ask for

If you are going to make such a request then you need to make a list and description of the documents you wish to have disclosed to you, ideally including dates (approximate is fine) when the documents were created or circulated.

What not to ask for

A reasonable employer should disclose the documents to you, especially if they relate to you directly. They will almost always resist disclosing documents that do not relate to you or which they consider are nothing to do with you, or none of your business. For example, if you ask for the minutes of partnership meetings for a private partnership then you'll be facing an uphill struggle.

What to do if your employer doesn't disclose the documents you want

If the company refuses to provide you with the documents you want to see, then you should consider either a 'questions procedure' (formerly known as a discrimination questionnaire) under the Equality Act 2010, or a 'subject access request' under the General Data Protection Regulation (GDPR) 2018. See below for further details of both.

2.4.2. Questions procedure in discrimination cases

If you believe you have been discriminated against at work then you have the right to engage the formal questions procedure. This procedure gives you the right to ask your employer, and expect responses from them to, a range of questions about possible discrimination against you. We discuss these below and also in chapter 9 on discrimination.

The most important advice we can give you here is to ask direct and pertinent questions and ask for disclosure of clearly identified documents. Much like the approach to gathering evidence generally, if you are too wide-ranging in your questions, or in your request for disclosure, then it is likely that your questions will be rebuffed or your request for disclosure not completed adequately.

If you focus on the specific areas where you think you have been treated less favourably, under just a few main headings, and then ask direct questions under those headings, your employer must either answer the questions, or risk drawing an adverse inference at an employment tribunal. In other words, if your employer doesn't answer your questions in a straightforward manner, the tribunal will probably think they are being evasive because they have a weak case.

The same goes for requests for documents under the questions procedure: the more focused the request, the more reasonable it will seem, and if the employer doesn't comply, then that's likely to be held against them at an employment tribunal. Also try to ask factual questions about things like numbers or dates. If you ask subjective questions about why people did things, for example, this actually helps the other side because not only will they deny any wrongdoing but also they get a chance to refine their arguments while at the same time understanding your plan of attack.

For further advice on what questions to ask, ACAS has produced a helpful booklet called *'Asking and responding to questions of discrimination in the workplace'*, with a section in it which offers employees (or questioners as they are called) guidance in six steps. You can download this booklet from their website: www.acas.org.uk

When to submit your discrimination questions

Because of the need for focus in your questions, the time for submitting them is usually once you have a good idea of the nature of your discrimination case. It will be after you have exhausted your search for documents in the usual manner, and when you are able to make your points clearly and concisely.

2.4.3. Subject access requests

You may have heard about your right to make a 'subject access request' and that this can be a good way of encouraging your employer to enter into a settlement agreement with you. So here we look at what a subject access request is, and how best you should use your right to make one. We have provided a couple of examples of subject access requests in chapter 12 for you to use and adapt to your case.

What is a subject access request?

A subject access request is a right under the General Data Protection Regulation (GDPR) 2018 (formerly the Data Protection Act 1998), to request all information that your employer (as a data controller) holds, which relates to you. Importantly it includes the right to ask for information contained on your employer's computer system. For example, if your manager has been emailing people about you, you are entitled to see this information.

The courts have recently confirmed that you are entitled to this information even if you are just seeking evidence to use in a claim against your employer. Don't let your employer tell you that you are not allowed to issue a subject access request to gather evidence for your claim.

Be aware though, that although your employer has 30 days to respond to a subject access request, if they argue that the request is 'manifestly excessive' they can ask for up to three months to provide the information. So be careful, because if you ask for too much information then your employer may play the 'manifestly excessive' card and drag the whole thing out for months.

Furthermore, although in the majority of cases there is no charge, your employer is permitted to 'charge a reasonable fee'. No one actually knows what this means yet and it will take some time for case law to develop and for that to become clear.

Does an employer need to provide every document that mentions you?

There are some limitations to what your employer needs to provide you in response to a subject access request. Exceptions include:

- **Documents containing information about others.** If any document contains information about someone else, your employer may be able to exclude this document or to delete the information about the other person. This can make what is left in the document hard to follow.
- **Documents subject to legal privilege.** Your employer does not need to disclose details of any legal advice that they may have requested about you, although this only applies to legal advice from lawyers and barristers, not from HR professionals.
- **Disproportionate requests.** Your employer does not need to respond to a request if it would be 'disproportionate'

to do so. There is not much guidance on what would be disproportionate but it is important to ensure your request is targeted toward the information that you actually need to assist with your claim/grievance.

How can a subject access request assist in negotiating a settlement agreement?

Making a subject access request can be a great way of obtaining a satisfactory settlement agreement or improving an offer which is already on the table. Sometimes your employer may be aware of incriminating emails about you and may want to settle to avoid these emails surfacing. You may also obtain documents in response to your request which help your case, strengthening your negotiating position.

We have seen numerous cases whereby management have exchanged internal emails about the employee, discussing how to engineer their departure from the business. Even internal communications from HR have to be included in the documents disclosed in response to a subject access request. We have experience of smaller companies whose board members or bosses have disparaged employees in emails and WhatsApp groups and so, because of this, a subject access request has really brought them speedily to the negotiation table.

Even if your employer has nothing to hide, searching for and reviewing the information you have requested can cost them a lot of money in time and resources. Sometimes an employer will agree to settle just to avoid the costs associated with complying with a subject access request.

Sometimes however, making a subject access request can be counterproductive. If your settlement discussions are already progressing well, it can annoy your employer and make settlement harder. Also, large employers are used to dealing with such requests. This means the fact you have made a subject access request is unlikely to faze them as much, although you can still obtain useful information as a result.

How do I make a subject access request?

Making a subject access request is easy. All you need to do is write to your employer requesting the personal information that they hold about you. Your employer should have a designated data protection officer. If you know who it is then your request should be sent directly to them.

Knowing exactly what you should be asking for is a bit harder. You should think about the following before making a request:

- What information would be of the most use to you to assist with your claim/grievance?
- What information is your employer least willing to disclose?
- Who is likely to be the author of the information you need?
- What types of communication are used in your organisation e.g. email, Slack, WhatsApp, text message, chat rooms etc.?
- What time periods are likely to include relevant information?

Once you have considered these details you should ensure your subject access request is targeted towards them to avoid your request being disproportionate. Say which types of communications you want searched, involving which people, and between which dates. It is also helpful to provide suggested search terms e.g. your first and last name or initials. Some people are surprised that even SMS text messages, Facebook messages and WhatsApp communications can be used as evidence in a tribunal claim.

The subject access request must be done on an 'open' basis, so you shouldn't refer to any communications you have had with your employer on a without prejudice basis. You can, however, refer to the subject access request in without prejudice communications.

─────────────── **TOP 3 TIPS** ───────────────

- Consider carefully whether a subject access request will help you or whether you will only annoy your employer and make a settlement agreement less likely

- Ensure your request is carefully targeted at the information that is likely to help your claim/grievance
- Include reference to named individuals who may have discussed you and the specific messaging services they may have used within identified date ranges

2.5. Making/using audio and video recordings

One of the questions that we are asked regularly is: 'Should I record the conversation?' This is entirely up to you, but you may not be able to rely on it in the future if no one knows you are making a recording. Some employment tribunals will allow secretly recorded evidence to be heard in a hearing, others will not. It rather depends on the circumstances of the recording and the relevance of the evidence on the recording to the proceedings.

The same applies to negotiations as in tribunals: your employer may not wish to hear a recording of a disciplinary hearing or grievance meeting you have made covertly, when they already had an HR representative taking notes. This is because the notes protect the employer and also because the employer will feel undermined if you have made a recording without their knowledge. Often recordings made in meetings don't uncover much, as people are on their best behaviour on such occasions and may expect a recording device to be present.

On the other hand, sometimes recordings of meetings show bad behaviour, for example an aggressive approach by your line manager, especially when there is no HR representative present, and the top brass might be very interested to hear one of their managers shouting at a member of their staff.

Where recordings are of serious value is when they uncover evidence of heinous wrongdoing such as discriminatory harassment. In such cases an employer will almost be duty bound to hear/watch it and an employment tribunal would most likely allow the recording to be admitted as evidence to the hearing if the claim is disputed. Importantly, if you have audio or video recordings of you being discriminated against or treated unfairly, you can, subject to compliance with RIPA (Regulation of Investigatory Powers Act 2000), disclose them to your employer as evidence to support your case in negotiation.

Having said that, covert recordings undermine trust, so deploy them only when you have to.

2.6. Witnesses

The incidents which you plan to bring to your employer's attention in the course of a negotiation may well have been witnessed by one or more colleagues. You may want to consider asking a colleague to be a witness to support you in your negotiation. However, you may be surprised to learn that this is not always helpful during a negotiation for a couple of reasons:

- An employer will usually want any settlement agreement to be confidential. This includes the facts of the allegations you intend to make being kept confidential from other employees. If you ask other employees to be witnesses then you will necessarily disclose facts of your case to them, making the employer less likely to agree to a settlement agreement.
- Witnesses are only useful to support disputed allegations. Often in employment negotiations, if allegations are disputed then they usually remain disputed, but the parties agree to disagree and settle. If witness evidence, such as a witness statement, is produced, the employer is likely to instruct lawyers and start to defend the allegations, which is not what you want to happen if you are looking for a settlement.

If, however, you have been subject to discrimination or harassment and the only way you can make your case to your employer is by using witness evidence, then you may want to ask your colleagues to provide evidence to support your claims. Be aware though that your colleagues won't necessarily want to get involved. They may not be willing to expose themselves to the same problems you have suffered, or they may simply disagree with you.

It's very common at employment tribunals for the claimant to be the only witness because no one in the company will come forward to support them. So don't be surprised if you approach a colleague to be a witness and he or she is reticent or simply refuses.

If you are going to approach witnesses, the best ploy is to ask them to make a written witness statement and then to sign and date it there and then, while they still feel inclined to do so. Alternatively, if you raise a grievance, you could ask the company to interview witnesses for you, although this may well let the employer persuade the witnesses into giving evidence favourable to them and not you.

2.7. Keeping an events diary

One classic way of keeping a record of ongoing events is by keeping an events diary. To do this, simply record the events that you wish to complain about in work whenever they occur, then sign and date the record, either electronically or physically.

Employers at employment tribunals used to dispute the truth or dates of events diaries, but as modern software can date-stamp, employees can now prove that they recorded certain events on a certain day.

2.8. Presenting evidence to your employer

You should try to build your case selectively, rationally and critically when you start the process of negotiation. This also extends to how you would present the evidence that you have gathered. There's no point in spending days or weeks gathering evidence only to present it to your employer (accompanied by a without prejudice letter), when it's set out in a chaotic and disorganised way.

You will need to refer to any evidence you have gathered in your without prejudice letter. So you must figure out a method of identifying the evidence that you have disclosed in your letter so that your employer can easily refer to that evidence when they're reading it. The best way of doing this is to put your hard copy evidence into a file, such as a lever arch one, and then use tabs and an index, as outlined below.

Firstly, arrange your documents in order – usually in date order, oldest to most recent – then between each separate document place a file tab. Tabs can be bought from any stationery retailer and each tab will have a number or letter on it. Make sure you place the tabs in order from A-Z or 1-20.

It's best not to duplicate email chains, so try to include one email chain as one document and then don't add any part of that email chain again.

Once you have placed the tabs between each document, you can then create an index for the documents by using the following template example:

Tab no.	Document description	Date
A	Email from Mr Bloggs to Mrs Brown Re: Bonus payment	01.05.18
B	Letter from Bloggs Ltd to Mrs Brown Re: Withheld bonus	07.05.18

In your accompanying without prejudice letter, you can refer to the documents by using the tab numbers. This will make it easy for your employer to understand not only your case, but also the evidence supporting it.

2.9. Can employers investigate your private communications?

So far in this chapter, we have focused on what evidence you can collect in building a case against your employer, and the forms of evidence that can legally be used to substantiate your claim. To conclude the chapter, we look briefly at what means employers can use to collect evidence about you, in order to substantiate their own case, or to defend themselves against your claims. To help with this, we use a case study drawn from an actual employment tribunal case.

Case study

The key question that the Garamukanwa v Solent NHS case below gives rise to is this: can your employer check your emails? As the case study exemplifies, the short answer is 'yes' – if they are sent from your work email address and/or impact on work-related matters.

In this case, the claimant was a manager for the NHS trust. He got into a relationship with a nurse. However, things started to go wrong when he became suspicious that the nurse had formed a relationship with a female colleague. He was upset about this and anonymous malicious emails about the nurse were sent from various fake email addresses to management. The nurse also began to think that the claimant was harassing and stalking her.

As a result, the Trust carried out an investigation. They concluded that there were items on the claimant's iPhone that linked him to the anonymous emails. He was therefore dismissed for gross misconduct.

The claimant brought a claim for unfair dismissal in the employment tribunal. During the proceedings he unsuccessfully argued that his employer had breached Article 8 of the Human Rights Act by looking into matters purely related to his private life.

Article 8 of the European Convention on Human Rights enshrines the right to privacy. It states that: 'Everyone has the right to respect for his private and family life, his home and his correspondence.'

The Employment Appeals Tribunal decided that Article 8 was not breached (on the facts of this case) by the employer investigating emails, on the basis that the emails had a potential impact on work, and dealt, at least in part, with work-related matters.

It is important to note that Article 8 does extend to protect private correspondence and communications and, potentially, emails sent at work where there is reasonable expectation of privacy. However, in this case the emails had impacted on work related matters and the emails were sent to work email addresses of the recipients. The emails greatly upset colleagues, potentially affecting their work.

This meant that the employment tribunal was entitled to conclude that Article 8 was not breached and the claimant had no reasonable expectation of privacy in respect of such communications.

The lesson to be learned from this case is that you shouldn't send emails to other colleagues which insult another colleague, or which you would not want your employer to see, even if they're sent outside of working hours and from your private email address.

Can employers monitor your communications?

Your employer may also attempt to monitor your electronic communications if they believe that you are setting up business in competition with them or perhaps acting in a way contrary to any restrictive covenants (see chapter 11). In general, corporate espionage is more common than you may think.

TOP 3 TIPS

- Don't use your work emails for your legal advice
- All company computers and phones leave data trails, even if you delete files
- Your employer may have the right to monitor your communications

---

It is illegal under RIPA to monitor live communications unless you have been made aware that calls are monitored. What is legal however, is for your employer to look into your previous communications, including your work emails, by examining the hard drive on your machine or data stored on the server.

Skype instant messenger, for example, stores written 'chat' conversations on Excel files on the hard drive of your actual computer. This is not held on the cloud or on Skype servers, unlike with personal email accounts.

The legal situation is less clear so far as personal email accounts are concerned, but it is worth bearing in mind that everything you ever write using a computer can be reconstructed from examining that computer's hard drive. The only way to be sure that no information can be reconstructed is to put a screwdriver through the hard drive, or to dispose of it in some other way (not that we are suggesting that you do that; we're just trying to paint a clear picture for you). Better still, don't write it in the first place!

Conclusion

In conclusion, be methodical about collecting and presenting evidence, and be clear about exactly what it is that you are trying to prove – 'less is more'. Armed with the above knowledge you should be ready to navigate the stormy waters that evidence collection can entail.

Chapter 3

Grievances
and how to raise them

Introduction

If you have a problem or complaint at work, you might want to take this up formally with your employer. This is called raising a grievance. Raising a grievance is a difficult step to take: it means putting your head above the parapet and making your employer aware of serious issues. It will nearly always make you fear the repercussions, whether directly in terms of an immediate backlash, or indirectly in terms of future impact on your career.

In practice, employers very rarely react negatively to a grievance in the first instance, at least on paper. They will usually follow their grievance procedure, or the ACAS Code of Practice on grievances (see below) and attempt to deal with your complaints. They will rarely admit that any of your complaints are justified however.

Before raising a grievance, you should ask yourself: 'What am I hoping to achieve by doing this?' Below we consider circumstances where raising a grievance is a good idea, and indeed where it's a bad one.

3.1. When to raise a grievance and when not to

Our general rule is that if you want to leave your employment and negotiate a settlement agreement, then write a without prejudice letter first, and only if that doesn't result in a decent settlement, should you raise a grievance.

Raising issues with your employer formally and openly by way of a grievance forces them to investigate the allegations, possibly to instruct lawyers, and then to spend time and money in managing the process. That is time and money which could have been spent by them in negotiating a fair deal for you.

Raising a grievance places a legal obligation on your employer to act fairly and to not do anything in reaction to the grievance that may be seen as victimisation. For example, if you raise a formal grievance regarding discrimination or whistleblowing, an employer will almost never propose a settlement agreement with termination of employment for fear of being held liable for victimisation. Whereas if you raise the same issues on a without prejudice basis and suggest termination and a settlement agreement, they are free to negotiate as you have made the first move regarding settlement.

This rule isn't always to be followed as there are circumstances in which raising a grievance and then starting settlement negotiations can apply pressure on HR to consider settlement rather than having to conduct a potentially disruptive grievance investigation.

However, if a settlement is what you actually want, then don't sit and wait for your employer to make an offer of settlement, as it is unlikely that it will be forthcoming. Instead, be proactive and initiate without prejudice discussions for a settlement while keeping the formal grievance procedure in reserve.

When raising a grievance is the right thing to do

If you want to make your employer aware that you have been subject to breaches of contract, including breaches of trust and confidence, and wish to start negotiating an exit package, you should write a without prejudice letter. But if you have raised a grievance already, don't worry, you can still start a without prejudice negotiation as well.

If you have been subject to unlawful deductions of wages, your contract has been breached or changed and you wish to work under protest, then you should consider raising a grievance if informal efforts, such as raising the issue with your line manager, have failed.

If you have been the victim of harassment or discrimination, it can be best to raise a formal grievance as these are serious issues which your employer needs to be aware of, especially if you wish to remain in employment and fight through the trouble. This not only makes your employer aware of the issue, but can also afford you protection from victimisation and, in some circumstances, from unfair dismissal.

When raising a grievance is the wrong thing to do

It's not a great idea to raise a grievance about trivial matters, especially when those matters could have been resolved through informal channels via your line manager or HR.

If, for example, you believe that your manager is not affording you proper opportunities to progress, or is not crediting you properly for your achievements, then this is not the sort of matter which should be the subject of a grievance. Likewise, if you have had a disagreement with a colleague, you may be seen as disruptive if you raise a formal grievance rather than attempting to resolve the matter informally with them or via your line manager or HR department.

To sum up on raising a grievance

You should see raising a grievance as a tool to get you what you want, namely leaving your employment and negotiating a settlement agreement. A grievance is a means to an end, and not an end in itself. By raising a grievance you may think this will be the end to all your problems, but this is unlikely. Indeed it may just be the start of them, so be smart and know what you want to gain from this process before even sitting down at your computer and starting to type. If you can't think of a resolution, then perhaps you should consider not raising a grievance in the first place.

3.2. Grievance procedures

Understanding the grievance process is crucial if you wish to successfully raise a grievance with your employer. If you have tried raising a matter verbally or informally in writing, and there is still no resolution, then, subject to the points mentioned above, it's time to consider instigating a formal written grievance process. Often, taking this serious step may mean that you have already decided to leave your job. Or perhaps you just want to record the fact that you have been mistreated and wish to seek a resolution in the workplace.

3.2.1. The ACAS Code of Practice on grievances

The difference between submitting a formal grievance and an informal email detailing an issue at work may seem quite small. On paper, they would both set out your complaint – but there is a big difference in practice. This is because the ACAS Code of Practice sets out a procedure which employers should follow upon receipt of a grievance letter. The Code specifies:

- That you must submit your grievance in writing.
- That your employer will respond by inviting you to a grievance meeting and will then investigate your complaints and provide you with a written outcome, which you have the opportunity to appeal.
- That if you decide to appeal, your appeal must also be in writing.
- That your employer will then hold an appeal meeting, decide whether to investigate further based on your grounds of appeal, and then provide you with a final written decision.

Your grievance must be investigated and resolved within a reasonable time frame and your employer must investigate your complaints to the extent that they are able to do so reasonably.

3.2.2. Writing a grievance letter

The grievance letter is the most important part of the entire grievance procedure. It must be written carefully, in neutral language and should set out the complaints you are making as clearly as possible. It should also be as concise as you are able to make it. Don't submit a 30-page letter setting out everything that's happened to you in the last two years, instead, focus on the issues that you are raising which support your main legal arguments.

─────────────────── **TOP 3 TIPS** ───────────────────

- Remember to specify the details – who, when, how and what
- Don't mention compensation
- Don't mention tribunals

──

Locate your employer's grievance procedure

The first thing you need to do is find your employer's grievance procedure. It should be readily available on the internal intranet or sometimes in hard copy. The procedure should tell you to whom your letter should be addressed, which is in itself an important piece of information to have.

Include the words 'Formal Grievance' in the letter heading

Once you know to whom the letter is to be written, you should format it like any other formal letter you would send, except you should include the words 'Formal Grievance' as the heading.

Introductory paragraph(s)

In your introduction, you should be conciliatory. Explain that you regret having to raise a formal grievance, but you felt like you had no other option. Set out the attempts you have made to resolve the issues you will refer to informally, and explain that this letter is a last resort. This will put you in a good light with your employer.

Employers don't like it when employees raise grievances for no reason as it causes disruption and takes up management time. However, if you explain how you have been left no option, then your employer's frustration will often be directed at management, or HR, rather than at you. This is important as you are seeking to persuade your employer that you have been treated badly, which is a crucial step in attempting to negotiate a settlement.

Summarise the issues you are raising

You should next set out the events that relate to your grievance. Try and do this using as few words as possible, but also enough words to convey the facts of the situation.

Use numbers for each incident, as this forces your employer to investigate and then respond using your numbering, rather than just omitting to answer certain points (which will happen if you don't number your points).

Try to keep a professional tone and do not make inflammatory allegations unsupported by the facts – in extreme cases doing so can leave you vulnerable to disciplinary action. Try and refer to specific evidence if possible (see chapter 2 for how to do this) and also give your employer the information they need to investigate incidents: this could be times, dates, details of emails etc.

Set out exactly the behaviour of any employee that you wish to complain about, in chronological order, giving as many facts as possible. In employment law, the key facts would be:

- **Who** – who was present?
- **When** – state the time and date.
- **How** – was this in a meeting, an email or a phone call?
- **What** – what was said or done? Describe the event.

Only suggest a resolution if you want to remain in employment

To conclude, if your intention is to remain in employment you should then suggest a resolution. If your intention, by raising a grievance, is to commence without prejudice negotiations simultaneously, then do not suggest a resolution as you will do that in your without prejudice correspondence. Instead, explain to your employer that you feel badly treated, let down and will have to consider your options.

The importance of a good grievance letter

How to write an effective grievance letter to your employer is an important skill. It is not only important for getting things off your chest, but also for giving you the maximum chance of entering into a settlement agreement and receiving sufficient payment to last until you find a new job. Writing a good grievance letter can also form the basis for drafting your 'ET1' form (that's your employment tribunal claim form, as explained in chapter 6). An employer will know this and it should give you more negotiating power in settlement discussions.

3.2.3. Attending a grievance meeting

After you have sent your grievance letter, you should be invited to a meeting and given the chance to bring a colleague or a union representative. This is supposed to happen within a reasonable length of time after the grievance letter is submitted. If your employer is delaying the meeting, then send them an email or letter reminding them of their duty under the ACAS Code.

This meeting will probably be attended by a manager and an HR person who will take notes. You should make sure that you take your own notes, in as much detail as possible, or your colleague could take notes if they are willing, and good at note-taking. As soon as possible after the meeting, type up your notes, adding any other details which you remember. Then send a copy of your notes to your employer's HR representative inviting them to comment.

Anything which is not written down will inevitably become lost and forgotten, and by the time you reach a tribunal hearing both sides will have completely different recollections of what was said at any given meeting. This advice applies to any type of meeting. Note-taking is a serious skill which lawyers are trained in for years. It sounds silly but in the heat of a grievance meeting notes may become a distraction and you may forget to keep on writing everything down or your handwriting may become illegible. Before the meeting, have a go at writing really quickly and see if, for example, capital letters are easier for you to read back afterwards.

We recommend writing people's initials in the margin to indicate who is speaking as there will inevitably be more than one person present. Include times in the margin every now and then, especially if it is going to be a long meeting. One particularly helpful tip is to refer to the numbered paragraphs which you used in your grievance letter. That way it saves you writing down the subject of each part of the discussion. You can just write '1' for example, if what is being discussed at that moment refers to the first point raised in your grievance letter.

3.2.4. Outcome letter

Shortly after your meeting your employer will send you an outcome letter (99% of the time a grievance is dismissed). This letter should outline your right to appeal. It should set out why your grievance was not upheld. This commits your employer to state in writing their reasons for dismissing your grievance, which is an advantage for you as it means that they are unable to change their story later on.

A clever employer will sometimes uphold part of your grievance, but you will find that overall the more serious allegations are not upheld. This will enable your employer to claim that they acted fairly overall and gave it due consideration. If you believe that your employer has failed to uphold the serious parts of your grievance despite there being evidence to do so, then you must appeal.

3.2.5. Grievance appeal

You can normally appeal to higher management or a different boss (so long as your company is big enough). This grievance appeal letter is similar to the initial grievance letter, but is your chance to comment on the outcome letter.

Focus on why you believe the decision to reject your grievance, or part of it, was incorrect and focus on the evidence supporting your points. Your appeal should refer to the outcome letter and focus on the decision, rather than attempting to have the case heard again. However, if your employer has failed to respond to any part of your grievance in the outcome letter, then you should raise this in your appeal letter.

A meeting will then be held to discuss the points of your appeal and identify if any further investigation is warranted.

Your employer will write to you giving you a final outcome to your appeal. This is normally the final decision and there is no further right of appeal. If you believe that the decision is unfair or unjustified then you can either commence without prejudice discussions, or you can look into making a claim at an employment tribunal if you have grounds for such a claim.

TOP 3 TIPS

- Always put your grievance in writing using numbered paragraphs
- Take detailed notes at the following meeting
- Be prepared to appeal – 99% of grievances are dismissed by the employer

3.3. Advantages of engaging in the grievance process and not just resigning

● **It's a chance for your employer to suggest a settlement agreement**

During the grievance procedure is the perfect opportunity for your employer to offer you a settlement agreement. They will be forced to think about your case at the time and will not want to spend unnecessary hours doing unproductive grievance hearings. In addition, they probably don't really want employees who submit grievances to remain in the workplace as it could affect the rest of the workforce. What better timing for them to offer you a settlement agreement?

● **It helps to set the record straight**

When the letters go back and forth, it makes both sides think about exactly what has happened and to set out their explanation for it. So your employer will have to nail their colours to the mast. This could prove very useful later on in a tribunal. It also gives you the formal opportunity to have your questions answered in writing rather than being fobbed off in endless meetings.

● It may result in additional compensation

If you do go to tribunal and win, the tribunal can award you additional compensation if your employer has failed to follow the grievance process correctly. Similarly, if you have failed to follow it then your compensation can be reduced. The range of possible adjustment is 0-25%.

● It helps prove procedural unfair dismissal

If you are dismissed, it will help you to prove a claim for unfair dismissal if you can show that the proper grievance procedure was not followed. So by doing this now you are helping yourself later on. If your employer sees that you have a good chance of succeeding at tribunal, the more likely they are to offer you a decent settlement agreement, whether or not you actually have any intention of going to tribunal.

Examples of grievance letters are given in chapter 12.

Chapter 4

How much should I get in my settlement agreement?

Introduction

How much you should get in your settlement agreement can depend quite significantly on the strength of your evidence, as discussed in chapter 2. Apart from evidence, there are various other factors influencing how much you should and could get. In this chapter, we have divided these factors into 'internal' and 'external' factors, as well as 'redundancy' or 'dispute'. You can also try the settlement agreement calculator on our website.

4.1. Key factors affecting how much you should get

Internal factors

- **Witnesses**

  Do you have any colleagues who would be prepared to back you up?

- **Evidence**

  What is strength of your evidence – maybe some emails, or even recordings of meetings?

- **Income**

  The more you earn, the more they need to pay you.

- **Length of service**

  The longer you've been there, the more goodwill you've built up.

- **Mistreatment**

  How bad was/is the treatment you have received?

External factors

- **Representation**

  Do you have professional legal representation?

- **Psychology**

  Can you keep calm under pressure and make the right moves?

- **Employer cash flow**

  Do they have lots of money, or, conversely, cash-flow problems?

- **Your determination**

  Does your employer believe you might take them to tribunal?

- **Tax status**

  Can you structure the deal to save both sides tax? (See chapter 5.)

——————————————— **TOP 3 TIPS** ———————————————
- Be prepared to fight if you want more
- Get legal representation
- Assess the strength of your evidence

How much should you get in a redundancy situation?

If your redundancy is genuine and the selection process is fair, then all you're technically entitled to is the statutory minimum payment. If the redundancy is unfair, or the selection process incorrect, then how much you should get will be similar to a dispute situation, as explained below.

Factors affecting how much you should get in a dispute

In a dispute, there are many factors which combine to determine how much you should get, but here is a checklist of some of the most common ones and how they could affect your settlement agreement amount. (Your possible financial awards at tribunal are explained later in this chapter.)

● Annual income

Everything is based around your annual income, since the more you earn, the more you get. This correlates with employment tribunal awards, because in constructive/unfair dismissal cases, tribunals only award successful claimants with an amount of money equivalent to the income they lost while hunting for a new job. This figure would be limited to a reasonable length of time for finding a new job, say six months' salary maximum.

● Bonuses and commission

Often bonuses are discretionary and it's difficult to argue that you were contractually entitled to one, so we would normally try to negotiate a portion of your bonus which you can actually show would have been due to you. Commission is a different matter though, because normally commission is contractual. The other side will probably find some way to dispute the commission figure, in which case we wouldn't normally insist on them paying all your commission, but to get most of it would be a good result.

● Age

If you are nearing retirement age then any claim could be of a much higher value because it could be harder for you to get another job, therefore your economic loss could be greater. This is especially true if your job is quite specialised and hard to come by. If you're over retirement age, however, then you would potentially get awarded less because you were due to retire anyway.

● Number of years worked for current employer

You would tend to get more where you'd worked for your employer for a long time because you probably would have forged more loyalty there. Your level of knowledge about the company might be greater too, so tasks like handovers are more valuable. Also you might know where all the metaphorical 'bodies' are buried in terms of any questionable practices which they want to stay confidential.

● Notice period

Normally we would recommend negotiating for your notice period to be paid as a lump sum, and then asking for a few months' money on top as a starting point, depending on the case. Of course if your notice period is very long, such as six months, then you're less likely to get anything on top of this, because an employment tribunal would normally only award a successful claimant enough money to last them until they found new employment.

● Number of employees

The bigger the company is, the more money they have to spend. Furthermore, bigger companies often prefer not to have legal battles going on with ex-employees and they don't like bad publicity either. (However, employees often think that their dispute would attract media attention when in fact it wouldn't: believe it or not, our media don't like to portray big business in a bad light.)

But, although bigger companies tend to want to settle cases more, they have more red tape and approvals to get past, and they also have more options should they wish to fight – like long drawn out investigations for example. Small companies on the other hand sometimes can't afford to settle a case because they just don't have the money in the bank. So the middle ground here is the sweet spot – the medium sized company.

● Performance improvement plan (PIP)

If you've been put on a performance improvement plan this can actually be a bit of a godsend in terms of a settlement payment – as discussed further in chapter 7.

● Grievance

If you have submitted a grievance then your employer will often want to pay you off rather than spend time and money investigating your complaint. See chapter 3 for in-depth discussion on grievances. However, remember to see if you can short circuit this process by submitting a without prejudice letter first.

● Disciplinary

If you are currently facing a disciplinary then generally you can expect less. This is because, regardless of the strength of your defence, your employer will undoubtedly try to blame you for the situation.

● Whistleblowing

If you are party to information such as fraud or malpractice within the company then they will often want to pay you a lump sum in exchange for signing a confidentiality clause in a settlement agreement. See chapter 10 for further discussion of whistleblowing claims and also below for how much you might get at tribunal.

● Disabled

You could expect to receive more if you are disabled, because your employers may have failed to make reasonable adjustments, as they are required to do to accommodate your disability. It can also be harder for you to get another job. See chapter 9 for further discussion.

● Sick leave

Being on sick leave can help to increase how much you could get, especially where you have lots of paid sick leave remaining. If there's a dispute, it makes sense for your employer to pay you this money as a lump sum rather than keep you on the payroll but off sick – as discussed in further detail in chapter 9 about long-term sickness absence from work.

● Already left/new job

If you've already left, then this is a serious blow to your chances of getting a decent settlement. There's no need for them to pay you off to get rid of you. If you've already got another job this is pretty much the final nail in the settlement coffin because you can't even claim that you have suffered any loss of income.

● Already issued a tribunal claim

If you've issued a tribunal claim then it does make you look more serious. On the other hand you may have burnt some bridges, including any rapport with HR: your case has now gone up to the legal department, and sometimes the legal department think that they have to win every fight rather than settle out of court.

● Tax savings

If you negotiate a deal rather than go to tribunal, then any ex-gratia amount up to £30,000 will be tax free (see chapter 5). Whereas after a successful tribunal claim, both you and your employer would have to pay tax on any tribunal award. So, it makes sense for both sides to settle out of court.

● Public sector

In our experience, many public sector organisations have a policy that they won't negotiate with employees. This means that you have to sue them in the employment tribunal, which is manageable, but it does make life more difficult.

● **Legal representation**

If you approach your company with specialist lawyers on board, then you are likely to receive more money because your employer will realise that you might take them to tribunal and that they should take you seriously. Furthermore they will also need to get 'lawyered up' themselves, and they may instead prefer to pay you the money which they would have spent on legal fees, so long as your opening offer is within a reasonable range. Not to mention the value your lawyers can add by simply doing their job and saying the right things at the right time.

4.2. Financial awards made by employment tribunals

The following exemplify how financial awards made by tribunals are calculated in cases of unfair dismissal, breach of contract, whistleblowing, and discrimination. This should give you an idea of the level of award you might expect to get in related tribunal claims.

Unfair dismissal (including constructive dismissal) claims

There are two main elements in a tribunal award, which are the 'basic award' and the 'compensatory award'.

The basic award is calculated like statutory redundancy pay – a week's pay or £508 (as from April 2018), whichever is lower, for every year of service with an adjustment for an age factor if you are over 41.

The compensatory award is calculated with reference to how much you have lost. There is a statutory cap on the compensatory award which is the lower of £83,682 or 12 months' gross pay (as from April 2018). So, if your gross yearly pay is higher than this amount you can't get any more for this at tribunal. If your gross yearly pay is less than this, the maximum award for unfair or constructive unfair dismissal is one year's pay.

All claimants have a duty to 'mitigate their loss': you must try to find alternative work at the same, or higher, salary. The tribunal will factor in your salary from your new job, and your attempts to mitigate your losses, into the compensatory award. If you do get another job but at lower pay then a tribunal would probably award you a few months' worth of the shortfall, on top of your compensatory award.

Breach of contract claims

A breach of contract would be, for example, not being paid your notice period or wages. For these there is a £25,000 limit in tribunals. For this reason, senior executives will need to consider High Court action, where there is no limit, or preferably just issuing the threat of High Court action (because few people want to go to court at all, never mind the High Court).

Whistleblowing

If successful in a whistleblowing tribunal, you would be entitled to claim your financial loss for as long as you were out of work and actively applying for new jobs (or setting up your own business). This could be around three to six months' income, or a year's income at a push. This is exactly the same as for unfair dismissal, set out above.

Further compensation is available for 'injury to feelings' due to any victimisation, and this is normally between £900-£42,900. This element is similar to that in discrimination claims – see below.

If your whistleblowing case has a USA aspect to it then compensation can be a lot higher. This is because in the USA, companies are fined millions of dollars by the government for malpractice, and the whistleblower is given a reward which is a percentage of the fine. Unfortunately in the UK there is often little or no action taken by the government against companies which break the law. Maybe that is because there is no mechanism to fine them for these breaches. In this regard at least, perhaps we should be more like America!

Discrimination tribunal claims

These types of claims have three elements:

(i) **Financial loss.** This element is based on the same principles as for unfair dismissal, although it is theoretically unlimited rather than being capped at £83,682, which is the limit for normal unfair dismissal claims in the tribunals. In practice this is limited to the amount of money you lost while out of work – so if you got another job straight away on the same or more money, then you have suffered no financial loss.

(ii) **Injury to feelings.** This is always payable to claimants in successful discrimination cases. Guidelines on the amounts of compensation were set out by the Court of Appeal in the Vento vs Chief Constable of W. Yorkshire Police case back in 2002. These have since been updated and are as follows:

- Band 1: £900-£8,600 [one off/isolated incident – this is the most common award by far].
- Band 2: £8,600-£25,700 [more serious discrimination].
- Band 3: £25,700-£42,900 [sustained campaign of the most serious discrimination – rare].

(iii) **Personal injury compensation.** This is theoretically unlimited but in practice it's tightly pegged to the type of injury caused, and it's very difficult to prove, so please don't assume that you'll get anything for this. It's based on the same principles as for, say, a car accident, although the kinds of injuries most common in discrimination employment matters are psychological injuries such as depression. Medical evidence is necessary here, and you have to show somehow that the employer's conduct was the only cause of your condition, and that they should have known that their actions could lead to injuring you.

4.3. Calculating how much you should get

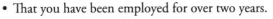

On our website, our settlement agreement calculator is designed to start you off with around two months' gross income plus your notice pay. This can be a good starting point when wondering how much you should get, and then adjust the figure up or down according to your other case circumstances (which you can add on the calculator itself). When recommending that starting point, we make a few assumptions which you need to know about and which are as follows:

- That you have been employed for over two years.
- That you have either been dismissed or forced to resign.
- That you have the evidence to prove that the dismissal (or constructive dismissal if you resigned) was legally unfair.
- That you haven't got another job already. (If you get another job then the amount which you would be eligible to receive from, say, an employment tribunal, would be reduced because the lion's share of your compensation relates to loss of earnings while unemployed.)
- The figure includes a payment in lieu of your notice period, meaning that it assumes that your boss will pay your notice pay but not expect you to work during that time.

Why do we calculate your settlement agreement value like this?

We assume you have been employed for over two years because this means that you will have earned your unfair dismissal rights. In a nutshell, it means that in order to dismiss you for a capability or conduct reason, your employer has to notify you about the problem and give you a chance to improve. The exception to this is dismissal for gross misconduct, whereby no notice has to be given.

Before you've been there for two years you don't have unfair dismissal rights, so they can just simply tell you that you're fired. The situation is different with discrimination and whistleblowing. If you are victimised for these reasons, then you don't need to have two years' service, so in theory you could claim in the employment tribunal after being employed for just one day.

Why do we have a starting point of two months' gross income as an ex gratia payment? Well, we look at what most employees are awarded if they were to win an employment tribunal claim. Judges would tend to award you an amount of money to compensate you for your lost wages while you tried to find another job. But if you were out of work for, say, over six months, then you would need to have a very good reason for not getting a job in that time. (For example you might be a very specific specialist in your field or your type of job might be becoming increasingly rare.) You would need to produce detailed evidence of your job hunt in order to prove that no jobs were available, so on that basis, the maximum which you're likely to receive in a tribunal is six months' wages.

It is worth noting that you would also be taxed on any award received after a tribunal, unlike with a settlement agreement whereby the first £30,000 tends to be tax free, so an employment tribunal award of six months' wages would only look like around four months' wages net to you.

The 'quality of life' value of negotiating a settlement agreement out of court is such that, in our view, you should have no hesitation in accepting half of what you might win at tribunal. For example, for four months' net wages and a long court battle at tribunal which could take more than a year (and which you could quite easily lose), it is surely worth accepting two months' less pay via a settlement agreement, with no risk of losing and no legal costs or the stress of a tribunal.

4.4. Impact of getting another job during your notice period

Bear in mind that if you are fortunate enough to get another job during your notice period, then this would reduce any claim for compensation you might have in an employment tribunal. That is because you have mitigated your loss, as explained in 4.2. above. Say your notice pay was worth £3,000 net, but you earned £2,000 net in the notice period, then you have only lost £1,000 net, so that is the value of your claim.

Of course you don't have to disclose to your ex-employer the fact that you have got a new job prior to issuing tribunal proceedings (but you do need to declare it at that point) so unless they ask you, then they may well assume that you haven't got a new job. At the same time, if it looks like you're about to get another job then it's best to wrap up your negotiation quickly before this thorny issue rears its head, either in the form of reference request from your prospective new employer, or through word of mouth.

Chapter 5

Settlement agreements: legal, practical and tax matters

Introduction

Settlement agreements are individual contracts between you and your employer. As such, their content is not set in stone and there is no single or standard way to do them. There are certain requirements set out by statute, for example that they must be in writing and signed by an independent adviser, but the money element is often open to negotiation. The basic effect of such an agreement is that, in return for a payment, you give up your right to bring claims against your employer at the employment tribunal or in the courts. An example of a settlement agreement is given in chapter 12.4.

5.1. Settlement agreement payments and related benefits

Your agreement should clearly state how and when the payment(s) will be made and exactly when your employment will end. Payment dates are normally around 14 to 28 days after signing the agreement, or after your last day of employment, whichever is the latest.

Some payments are pretty obvious and straightforward, while others are less so. Listed briefly below are some of the more straightforward payments – and possible deductions – that you should check in your agreement. These are followed by additional, and sometimes more complex, payments and other related benefits.

Check your agreement for the following:
- Outstanding salary
- Expenses owed
- Contractual notice pay (or statutory notice pay if that is greater)
- Holiday pay
- Car allowance
- Bonus payments
- Pension payments (see section below on pension payments)

Consider non-cash benefits such as:
- Company car
- Health insurance and life insurance – is there the option for these to continue?

What deductions, if any, will be made? For example:
- Some employers ask for contractual maternity pay to be repaid if you leave before a specified amount of time has passed after your return to work (normally around six months).
- Do you have a 'season ticket loan' or any other loans with your employer?

• Have you taken more holidays than those you will have accrued at the end of your employment?

A note on tax in your settlement agreement

There are tax breaks available for settlement agreements and both sides can benefit from them. This is discussed in detail later in this chapter, but for now it's just worth noting that the most common break is £30,000 tax free when paid as an ex gratia payment.

5.1.1. Ex gratia payments

'Ex gratia' is Latin for 'out of good will'. Ex gratia payments in settlement agreements are great things if you can get them, because they offer a unique tax break only really available to employees who are leaving work after a dispute or redundancy situation.

Ex gratia payments are also known as 'golden handshakes' or 'golden boots'. In essence they refer to a sum of money paid when there is no obligation or liability to pay it under your contract of employment. For example, a lump sum payment over and above the pension benefits of a retiring employee. An ex gratia payment is normally a gesture of goodwill from your employer because they have treated you badly and acknowledge that you deserve some financial compensation. It may also be a way to avoid you trying to sue them in an employment tribunal.

5.1.2. Pay in lieu of notice (PILON)

Pay in lieu of notice means getting paid for the notice period in your contract but not having to work it. For example if your employer has to give you one month's notice to terminate your contract, then, instead of asking you to work for that month, they could just terminate your employment and let you go home but still pay you during that month. This is especially valuable if you have a long notice period.

Pay in lieu of notice is available from many companies if there has been some kind of dispute or disagreement at work, because in such circumstances employers actually prefer to see the back of you rather than risk you staying on and having an adverse effect on your colleagues. So it can just be a case of asking your employer to pay you in lieu of notice – you may not need to negotiate this at all. Of course if your employer offers you pay in lieu of notice then try not to smile too much, and just make out that you expected this as standard; then continue to negotiate the ex gratia element of the deal.

5.1.3. Statutory notice

Statutory notice is the minimum notice period which you should have by law. This is different from your contractual notice period, which is the minimum notice period set out in your contract of employment. Sometimes your statutory notice period is greater than your contractual notice period, in which case the correct notice period to use is the statutory one. This is more common where you have been employed for a long time because statutory notice increases the longer you stay in the same job.

To calculate the statutory minimum notice period that you are entitled to, add up the amount of time worked continuously for your employer. If you have worked for one month or more, your notice period must be at least a week. If it's between one month and two years, you are entitled to one week's notice. For anything above two years' service, you are entitled to one week per year worked, up to a maximum of 12 weeks for 12 years or more of continuous employment.

So, if you have worked for seven and a half years, you are entitled to seven weeks' notice. If you have been employed for 12 years or more, you would legally be entitled to 12 weeks. This minimum amount of notice applies no matter what your contract says.

5.1.4. Sick pay in your notice period

If you are off sick and you have gone down to reduced pay, and then you hand in your notice, should you receive only sick pay during your notice period, or should you receive full pay?

The answer depends on the length of your notice. According to the Employment Rights Act 1996 (ERA) ss.86-89, if your contractual notice period is a week or less above the statutory notice period, then you will be entitled to receive full pay throughout your notice period, despite being absent due to sickness or injury.

If, on the other hand, your contractual notice period is over a week above the statutory minimum notice period, then you cannot benefit from the provisions of the ERA '96 and you will only be entitled to receive your contractual sick pay (or statutory sick pay as the case may be).

So to give a practical example, let's say that you have been employed for four years. Therefore your statutory notice period is four weeks. Now imagine that your contractual notice is one month. In this situation you can benefit from the ERA because your notice period (one month) is not more than a week above statutory notice (four weeks). On the other hand if your contractual notice is two months, then you can't benefit from the ERA because your notice is more than a week over statutory notice.

If this seems complicated to you that's because it is. It's worth asking your settlement agreement lawyer to check this and confirm it for you – that's part of the job as far as we're concerned.

5.1.5. Pensions

Whatever your age it is important to consider your pension, but particular care should be made if you are nearing retirement. The following should be considered:

- Will pension payments continue after your employment has ended?
- Will a lump sum be paid into your pension?
- Do you have all the information, documents and contact details (of your pension provider) from your employer about your existing pension?
- Does the payment in the settlement agreement adequately account for any loss of employer pension contributions and pension rights?

Also see section 5.3. for information about tax payments on pension payments.

5.1.6. Personal injury and pension rights

While the settlement agreement will state that you give up all your claims to sue your employer, there are two exceptions which the law says can't be settled even if you sign a settlement agreement. These are:

- Claims for an unknown personal injury that you are unaware of at the time you sign a settlement agreement, but which later develops into an injury. This might happen, for example, if you were in contact with a substance at work that was believed to be harmless, but many years later caused a disease. In that case you would still be able to bring a personal injury claim when you discovered it, even though you had previously signed a settlement agreement.
- Claims for accrued pension rights. Your pension is always protected and can't be settled, so if it later transpired that your employer failed to pay into your pension when they were supposed to, then you could still sue them for that even if you signed a settlement agreement at the time giving up all claims.

5.1.7. Shareholders/share options

If you are a senior employee of a company, you may have been offered share options as part of a benefits package outlined in your contract, either when you began your employment, or during your work there. If you are exiting the business it is important to ensure these benefits are addressed as part of any settlement.

A share option is the option given by an employer to an employee to purchase shares in the company at a fixed price, or at a discount set by the employer. This is offered as an incentive because it allows you to purchase shares at a tempting price, and to share in the success of the company if the value of the shares increases. But normally these share options only 'vest' after you have been employed for a number of years. Vesting means that you can actually exercise the share options by buying the shares at the agreed price. If the value of the company has increased since you've been employed, then the price at which you can buy them will be lower than their market value. This means that you can sell them and make a tidy profit.

Share options can be the single most financially important aspect of a severance package or ex gratia payment, as they are becoming a more popular incentive for employers to use with their employees than cash-based bonuses. They keep employees in their jobs for years, waiting for their share options to vest, so that they can cash in on the increased value.

Share plans

As is usual with employers, they have various conditions in place to protect themselves, and so as an employee you often have to work hard to actually get your hands on the benefits initially offered as part of your employment contract. Your employer will have a clearly laid out and thorough share plan. This will outline various conditions which you need to meet in order to be eligible to take advantage of any unvested shares, either at the date of termination, or at a future date.

Good leavers and bad leavers

When drafting an agreement and deciding on the inclusion/exclusion of share options, the first thing that will be considered is how your employment ended – and whether you are classified as a 'good leaver' or a 'bad leaver'.

- **Good leavers**

  Examples include those who left due to disability, ill-health, retirement and redundancy (redundancy could also be classified as bad leaver depending on the situation).

- **Bad leavers**

  Examples include circumstances such as capability dismissal, misconduct dismissal and resignation.

Those classified as bad leavers may lose their rights to exercise their share options. This is where you may want to consider using an employment lawyer who could possibly argue with your employer that the reason for the termination of your employment may have been unfair. If you have been unfairly dismissed, then the reason for your termination could be changed to that of good leaver, so that you receive the benefits accruing to a good leaver which are set out in the share plan. This is complicated stuff, which even some lawyers don't fully understand.

Vested and unvested share options

As well as having good leavers and bad leavers, some policies and contracts also make a distinction between vested and unvested share options.

- **Vested share options**

  These are options that you already have the right to exercise (i.e. you could already purchase the shares).

- **Unvested share options**

  These share options are those you have been granted the right to exercise at some future date, or upon fulfilment of a condition, which has not yet been met. Often good leavers are entitled to exercise vested, but not unvested, options.

Can your employer take away your access to the share options?

Most employers cleverly integrate the right to override the provisions of the share scheme under certain circumstances and retract your share options. An example of when an employer could retract your share options is that of post termination restrictive covenants (see chapter 11). If you are categorised as a good leaver and sign a post termination restrictive covenant, which you then breach, you could become a bad leaver and therefore forfeit your rights to unvested shares.

Claiming your share options in the case of unfair dismissal

If you are dismissed unfairly, you may be able to include the value of share options in your claim. This is a possibility even if the criteria and rules within the share plan say that you waive all such rights. This is because the value of the shares is something you have lost as a result of your unfair dismissal. This is a complex area of employment law and you would be advised to consult a specialist if you were to find yourself in these circumstances.

Claiming your share options if you have less than two years' service

If you have less than two years' service when you are dismissed then you can't claim for unfair dismissal – so how could you negotiate any value for your unvested share options? Well, it may be possible to say that you were incorrectly labelled as a bad leaver. You would also need to put forward the argument that there is an implied term in the share contract that you would not be incorrectly labelled as such.

Then you would need to show exactly how your labelling was incorrect. For example if redundancy has classified you as bad leaver, then you would be trying to show that you were not genuinely made redundant, but in fact you were deliberately singled out for dismissal in order for your employer to avoid paying you for the value of your share options. Again, very legally complicated stuff.

TOP 3 TIPS

- When leaving employment ensure you understand the impact on your share options
- Try to ensure that you have good leaver status upon leaving
- If you are a bad leaver then consider whether the reason for your dismissal is genuine

---

5.1.8. Non-disparaging remarks

Employers often ask the employee to agree not to make disparaging remarks or to 'bad mouth' the employer. There should be a reciprocal clause in which they agree, or use their best endeavours to ensure, that they and their staff do not make derogatory comments about you.

5.1.9. Confidentiality clauses

Employers often want the terms and existence of the agreement kept confidential. Be aware of this especially if you have discussed your problems at work. Where possible try to be discreet regarding who knows that you are in negotiations with your employer. In that way, if you are later asked to confirm that you haven't discussed the issues, you won't be in difficulty. Employers usually agree that confidentiality can exclude your immediate family, professional advisers (such as doctors and lawyers) and prospective employers.

5.1.10. Outplacement

Some employers offer outplacement services as part of an exit package in addition to the financial payment. This consists of specialist support in looking for work that can include career counselling, CV writing and interview preparation. It can be excellent and very helpful so it's worth asking your employer to include it, particularly if you are leaving an organisation that has employed you for a long time.

5.1.11. References

An agreed reference commonly forms part of the settlement agreement, but this is one of the things that's often forgotten. Some employers will only confirm dates of employment and duties, whereas others are willing to comment favourably on an employee. What is agreed will depend on the employer's usual practice and the circumstances surrounding your departure.

There is no obligation on any employer to provide a reference and it is one of the advantages of settling a case that a reference can be agreed as part of the agreement. So, if your settlement agreement doesn't have a specific clause dealing with references, then ask for one!

A good reference clause will say something like: 'A reference will be provided upon written request in the form annexed to this agreement at Annex A.' Then there will be an agreed reference attached to the back of the settlement agreement itself, headed 'Annex A'. To make sure that only the agreed reference is provided, you can ask for the clause to say that requests for a telephone reference or a questionnaire will be refused and that any prospective employer will be told that only the written reference will be provided. This guards against an employer giving a bad verbal reference on the phone or in a written questionnaire.

Some settlement agreements will just state that a 'standard reference' will be provided upon request. This implies a very simple reference with just job title and dates of employment. This is great because your employer doesn't have a chance to say something negative in the reference. And if a prospective employer contacts them and ask for more information, they can say that they only provide standard references, and the prospective employer will not think this out of the ordinary.

5.1.12. Welfare benefits

After your employment has ended you may be able to claim Jobseeker's Allowance (JSA). It is worth making a claim for JSA if you meet the eligibility criteria, as for the first six months this benefit is not means tested. Check with the Department for Work and Pensions (DWP) for more information and any recent changes in their criteria.

If you want to claim JSA, the reason for leaving in your settlement agreement should be carefully considered and where appropriate be labelled as redundancy as there is a risk that, if the agreement says you resigned, the DWP will not pay you. Having said that, it is notoriously difficult to convince employers to confirm in writing a reason for dismissal. It is worth asking, but it may not be worth making this a deal breaker.

Depending on your situation you may also be entitled to other benefits and you should check with the DWP to see if you are entitled to any, for example: housing benefit, council tax benefit and tax credits. If you are long term sick or disabled you may be entitled to claim incapacity benefit and/or disability living allowance or its equivalent.

5.1.13. Mortgage/income protection insurance policies

If you have an insurance policy that will pay your mortgage or replace some or all of your income upon redundancy/dismissal, it is essential that you check out the terms of your insurance policy before you sign any settlement agreement. Some policies will only pay out if you have been dismissed or been made redundant. This means that if appropriate the agreement should make clear that the termination was dismissal and/or redundancy. However the same difficulties apply here as mentioned above – employers don't like admitting why they forced you to leave.

5.2. Fees for legal advice on settlement agreements

Individual cases

In almost all cases, your employer will allocate an amount to pay for you to take legal advice. This means that your employer covers your lawyer's fee, not you. The amount allocated will normally be enough to cover the lawyer's time in advising you on the agreement (e.g. identifying any issues lurking in the small print), asking your employer for amendments and signing the agreement.

Occasionally an employer offers a very low fee despite the fact that you may need complex advice on the settlement agreement, or the draft agreement may require significant changes. In such instances your lawyer may wish to ask your employer for an increase.

If you wanted to instruct an employment lawyer to negotiate a better deal for you, there would normally be a separate fee for this. If a lawyer offers to negotiate a better deal for you and only charge you the fee specified in the settlement agreement document itself, then they're unlikely to be able to do the best job for you. Any lawyer worth their salt will add enough value to justify charging you an extra fee!

TOP 3 TIPS

- You are required to obtain legal advice for the agreement to be binding (your employer will provide a set amount of money to pay for this)
- Even if you are happy with the offer the agreement can still be changed to your benefit prior to signing
- Seek an experienced employment lawyer to ensure you get the best out of your agreement

---

Multiple redundancy situations

Unfortunately, changes in business circumstances sometimes dictate that an employer will need to make multiple redundancies in order ensure its survival or competitiveness. This inevitably leads to the employer offering a large group of employees similar settlement agreements.

Specialist employment law firms can often help by sending a lawyer or even a team of lawyers to an employer's workplace or a neutral venue to advise large groups of employees on the effects of their terms of settlement. It can be financially attractive to the employer too, as the law firm may be able to offer them special rates for handling multiple settlement agreements.

5.3. Tax on payments in settlement agreements

Tax on ex gratia payments and other settlement agreement tax queries are often one of the most complicated areas of UK settlement agreement advice. If you are wondering what the tax implications of your settlement agreement are, this section should help. For those who enjoy this kind of thing, it concludes with some guidance on calculating settlement agreement tax. All information and calculations are current for the tax year 2018/2019.

TOP 3 TIPS

- Settlement agreements can save on tax
- Your employer may be concerned about falling foul of HMRC and so not be keen to make tax free payments
- Increase the pressure to get the most tax efficient deal

5.3.1. Tax indemnities

Employers usually ask for one of these and they are a very standard clause in nearly all settlement agreements. The way they read is that if, after the agreement is signed, HMRC deem that tax is due on a payment made to you, they will look to your employer to pay this tax. The indemnity means that you have promised to pay this money back to your employer and, if you don't pay, your employer can sue you for this money. In practice however these clauses are very rarely called upon – hardly ever in fact. So they are not something which you should worry about.

5.3.2. What can usually be paid free of tax (gross)?

The following payments can generally be paid tax free:

- Compensation for loss of employment up to £30,000 (over and above any monies paid in respect of the notice period).
- Payment of legal costs.
- A payment for injury to feelings caused by discrimination or personal injury during your employment.
- Payment for outplacement services.
- Payment made into a pension scheme.

Although it was previously possible to pay notice pay tax free, for terminations after 6th April 2018, all notice pay is taxable. Where you are not employed for some or all of your notice period, the

£30,000 tax free limit only applies to the portion of any settlement payment which exceeds the amount of income you would have received if you had been employed for the entirety of your notice period. The portion equivalent to what you would have received if you had been employed for your notice period is taxed.

5.3.3. What payments are taxable?

The following payments to you will be taxed:
- Salary to the effective date of employment termination.
- Holiday pay – where holiday entitlement has not been taken in full.
- Compensation for loss of employment over £30,000.
- A payment in lieu of notice or other payment equivalent to any period of notice not worked.
- A payment for a restrictive covenant.

Tax on salary and benefits

Salary and benefits payments made until the last day of your employment are subject to tax and national insurance (NI).

Tax on payment in lieu of holiday

If you have unused holidays, your employer is required to pay you in lieu of these and this payment would attract tax and NI as usual.

Tax on ex gratia payments up to £30,000

As mentioned earlier, ex gratia payments are generally exempt from tax for the first £30,000.

Tax on ex gratia payments exceeding £30,000

If your settlement agreement includes compensation in excess of £30,000, the excess is subject to income tax. To work out how much tax would be applicable, see section 5.3.7.

Restrictive covenants

If your employer wants you to enter into new covenants it is important you get specialist advice on the level of compensation offered; there may be tax implications if HMRC later consider the amount paid too low.

5.3.4. Tax on legal fees

If a lawyer represents you in negotiations, then their legal fees can be paid directly by the employer, which means they are effectively tax-free for you. This is great where you are receiving over £30,000. Even if your employer refuses this, any money spent on your legal fees can be set off against your tax bill at the end of the tax year, subject of course to the approval of HMRC.

5.3.5. Tax on pension payments

Normally, the first £30,000 ex gratia payment is tax free, above which the balance will be subjected to income tax. But pension payments in settlement agreements tend to be tax free and therefore worth considering if you are getting over £30,000 from your employer. In this section we explore how to pay a lump sum of money into your pension scheme as part of your settlement agreement deal and the types of practical issues you need to consider.

You may find that you can't pay more than a set limit, for example a £50,000 lump sum, into the pension scheme in total for this tax break to be applicable, so check how much you've paid in already.

Every pension scheme is different, and we would advise that you contact your specific pension provider to ask them what their rules are on paying in tax free lump sums. One common feature across all providers is that if you have a settlement agreement in place, you are normally allowed to pay in a lump sum tax free. You can then draw this money down during your retirement in instalments in the usual way. This is particularly useful if you are nearing retirement age and your settlement agreement settlement amount is over £30,000 in the first place.

TOP 3 TIPS

- Payments into your pension under a settlement agreement are not normally taxable
- Such payments will be locked in to your pension until you're older
- You can only draw the money down in accordance with the pension scheme rules

---

5.3.6. Pension settlement agreement tax case study

One complex case of ours involved negotiating a settlement agreement for a client who was nearing retirement age and was part of a government backed pension scheme. He was receiving over £30,000 from his (soon to be ex) employer, and wanted as much of it to be tax free as possible. Could we help him pay a lump sum of money into his pension scheme tax free?

Firstly we contacted the scheme and it transpired that they had a calculator to tell you exactly how much you could put in and how much you could get out. Our client was able to pay in around £20,000 in return for a monthly payout increase of £1,250. The next highest increment was more than our client was to receive, so he paid in the most he possibly could.

In the end he received around £32,000 ex gratia as well as £21,000 into his pension, and around £1,500 was paid directly to us, his lawyers, based on a small percentage of the deal which we negotiated for him, so that £1,500 was tax free for him. Thus he only paid tax on the £2,000 of the ex gratia payment above the £30,000 tax free limit.

The pension scheme required a letter or a form to be filled out by the employer confirming that our client was still in pensionable employment. This meant that it was crucial to ensure that the EDT, or effective date of termination of employment, was after the date when the lump sum would be paid to the pension scheme. Given that in settlement agreement situations, the EDT is normally prior to the pay out of lump sums, this point required some negotiating and we worked closely with the employer to make it happen.

In the end we agreed to extend the EDT to around 21 days after the last day of being salaried, by changing the employment contract to a zero hours contract.

In other cases the employer organises the payment direct to the pension provider and there is no need to go through complicated application forms or worry about the date of termination of employment.

5.3.7. Calculating settlement agreement tax

Calculating tax on settlement agreements can be a difficult task. In this section we explain how to work out how much tax you will pay on any ex gratia settlement amount in excess of £30,000. This is not for the faint-hearted and it may be of more use to your accountant than to you directly, but we believe you should have the opportunity to consider it.

Employers must use the 0T tax code (rather than BR) in relation to ex gratia payments over £30,000 which are not included in your P45. This could apply if, for example, you are dismissed, issued with a P45, and then your lawyer negotiates a high settlement for you by way of a settlement agreement.

The regulations state that the 0T tax code is to be applied on a 'non-cumulative' basis. For an employee paid on a monthly basis, this means that only 1/12th of the basic rate band (and, if relevant, 1/12th of the higher rate band) is available in the month of payment.

So, if the termination (or other) payment is more than the appropriate proportion of the 20% band, the excess will be taxed under PAYE at 40%, and if the payment is also more than the available 40% band, the excess will be taxed under PAYE at 45%.

TOP 3 TIPS

- If you are receiving no other income in the month it may be preferable be paid before your P45 is issued
- Consider filing a tax return to ensure you don't end up overpaying tax
- Take specialist advice on your position

Firstly, the employer will have to operate PAYE on the basis that none of the personal allowance is available.

Secondly, 'monthly' means tax, rather than calendar, months. Tax months run from the sixth of one calendar month through to the sixth of the next (as each tax year starts on 6th April). This means that payments made on, say, the seventh of one calendar month and the second of the next would fall within the same tax month, with the effect that only one month's bands would be available to share between the two payments.

Finally, there is a risk that the amount of PAYE deducted is more than the actual income tax liability. If you have little other taxable income in the tax year, you could have too much PAYE deducted from the termination payment and have to reclaim some tax through your tax return.

5.3.8. Example of calculating tax

To provide an example, the PAYE that has to be applied to any post-P45 payment in the first month of the 2018/19 tax year (month 1) will be roughly as follows:

- The first £2,875, or the whole payment if it is less than this amount, is taxed at 20%, which means a PAYE deduction of up to £575 (£2,875 is the 20% band for 2018/19 for month 1, found by dividing by 12 the 20% band for the year, £34,500).
- The next £9,625 is taxed at 40%, which means a PAYE deduction of up to £3,850 (£9,625 is the 40% band for month 1, found by dividing by 12 the 40% band for the year which is £150,000 minus £34,500).
- Any amount above £12,500 is taxed at 45% (£12,500 is the combined 20% and 40% bands for month 1, found by dividing £150,000 by 12).

This would mean that if, after the issue of the P45, an ex-employee receives a termination payment:

Of £10,000, £3,425 would be withheld as PAYE. The PAYE is calculated as follows:

- £2,875 @ 20% = £575
- £7,125 @ 40% = £2,850

Of £20,000, £7,800 would be withheld as PAYE. The PAYE is calculated as follows:

- £2,875 @ 20% = £575
- £9,625 @ 40% = £3,850
- £7,500 @ 45% = £3,375

The relative merits (from a cash-flow perspective) of pre- or post-P45 payment will need to be assessed individually in each case. However, if an employer makes more than one post-P45 payment to an employee in a tax year, each separate payment will be subject to PAYE independently, and it will not take account of the earlier payments when working out PAYE on the later payments, paid in a different month.

The key date is when the employee becomes entitled to the amount: simply delaying payment of portions of an amount to which the employee is already absolutely entitled will probably make matters worse as the employer will have to account for PAYE on the full amount on the date of entitlement.

This appears to mean that if a termination payment is paid in a series of monthly instalments then each instalment would be treated in the way described above, and so could be brought (at least in part) within the monthly non-cumulative 20% band (or 20% and 40% bands).

In addition, there may be a cash-flow advantage for an additional rate taxpayer, who does not get a personal allowance in any event and who is likely to suffer tax on a pre-P45 termination payment entirely at the additional rate (assuming that in the tax month of payment, the employee has already received salary payments that have used up the basic and higher rate allowance).

If the payment is made in a subsequent tax month, and following the P45, an additional rate taxpayer will get another chunk of basic rate and higher rate allowance because of the 0T calculation, and this won't be reversed until the taxpayer completes a self-assessment tax return for the relevant tax year.

Chapter 6

Employment tribunals

Introduction

Employment tribunal claims are a wide topic about which several books have been written. What hasn't been written, however, is guidance on how to negotiate your way to an exit package using an employment tribunal claim as a negotiating tool. So that's what we try to explain in this chapter.

Unfortunately, by the time you are in a tribunal, the prospect of negotiating an exit package is fading fast. Both sides have tried to thrash out a deal and failed. Sometimes however, an employer just won't budge and going to tribunal is the only way to get a fair outcome.

If you are looking for an in-depth guide on how to run your case at tribunal, a good one is *Employment Tribunal Claims: Tactics and Precedents* by Naomi Cunningham.

Development of employment tribunals

The forerunners to employment tribunals were 'industrial tribunals'. These were established in 1964 and replaced in 1998 with the present-day system. Nowadays, if you have a claim against your employer for any breach of your working rights (aside from personal injury arising from an accident at work), then the chances are that any claim to enforce those rights would be in an employment tribunal.

The modern system has moved on a great deal since 1964 and has been through good times and bad, usually depending upon the government at the time. For example, the introduction in 2013 of fees (of up to £1,200) to bring an employment tribunal claim represented a huge setback for employment rights and employment tribunals. The number of employees who felt able to exercise their rights in the employment tribunal fell dramatically between 2013 and 2017.

Thankfully, in 2017, the Supreme Court overturned the law that the government had created to introduce the fees. Employment tribunals are now free to use once more and, according to the Law Society (December 2017), the number of claims being submitted to tribunals is on the increase.

Shortcomings of the employment tribunal system

While the employment tribunal system plays a vital role in upholding the rights of employees, you should be aware that – like any system – it is far from perfect. For example:

● **It suffers from chronic under-funding**

This means that delays are rife. It can take many months, and sometimes even longer, for a case to be heard.

● **The employer usually has greater resources than the employee to fight a case**

Consequently, the employee often suffers financial hardship or inequality of arms (or both) when it comes to a hearing. Employers will frequently engage several lawyers and at least one barrister to fight their case. An employee may, at most, be able to afford a lawyer and junior barrister, and will often not be able to afford to engage them to undertake the same amount of preparatory work on the case as the lawyers on the other side.

● **It's usually the employer that controls the evidence in employment tribunal cases**

The employer has access to all the documents and nearly all the witnesses called will be current employees of the employer, all of whom will most likely give evidence against you, the employee. While the employment tribunal has the power to order disclosure of evidence, it does not have the same powers in this respect as the High Court. For example, it can't hold parties in contempt of court for failing to abide by orders. Often, employers will not even disclose to their own lawyers documentation which is crucial to the employee's case, thereby putting the employee at a great disadvantage.

● **Employment tribunal outcomes are often unpredictable or unfair**

While judges aspire to impartiality and to try cases before them to the best of their ability, they are not perfect (and neither would they claim to be). The point is that when you submit your case at a tribunal for judgment, you are doing so to a human being with their own ideas, ideals and prejudices. The outcomes of a hearing can never be totally predicted and there is no guarantee that you will win, irrespective of how strong you think your case is. Furthermore, the majority of judges are from a background of private practice, and most private practice lawyers represent employers – because they have more money to pay lawyers' bills. This means that most judges have spent their previous careers representing employers. As a result, sometimes it's more difficult for them to see things from your point of view.

6.1. To claim or not to claim?

An employment tribunal claim means different things to different people. Some people just leave it on the back burner and don't think about it until the hearing date. For others, it's a year out of their lives with a huge amount of stress and upset. Either way, you are not guaranteed to win, but it could help you to achieve a settlement agreement with your employer, because it forces your employer to take notice of you. In order to assess the financial benefit of going to a tribunal, there are a few questions that you need to consider, the main ones being:

- What evidence have you got? Ideally you will have written evidence, and/or witnesses.

- Have you acted quickly enough and within the three month time limit (see below) to issue a claim?

- What is your maximum compensation? For unfair dismissal claims this is likely to be the amount of money you did not earn while looking for a new job, up to a maximum of one year's salary.

- What is the chance of you winning? This will depend on the evidence which you have, but they say that the best case in the world is only 80% likely to win. You never know what will happen in court.

- Can you fund your claim? It is very difficult to get a no-win no-fee payment agreement for a full-blown tribunal claim. At least try to instruct a lawyer to draft the initial claim and conduct the final trial.

Having said all that, it is worth mentioning that employers in receipt of tribunal claims may offer more compensation in the form of settlement agreements because they know that you mean business.

In addition, sometimes employees feel that they have been taken for a ride by their employers and they want to claim as a point of principle. Rarely does it make much commercial sense to go to tribunal. Ask yourself if you have the willpower to take this to the next level. If not, then you may think it easier just to take any money already being offered to you in a settlement agreement and move on.

You might also have legal expenses insurance which could cover at least some of the costs associated with your tribunal claim. If you're not sure whether you have this, check your home insurance policy documents or contact your insurers. Cover can often be added to your home insurance for just a few pounds a month. However it is far from fail safe and insurers do tend to try to avoid accepting your claim for tribunal expenses, by saying that you have less than 50% chance of success.

So, you should try to negotiate a settlement first, and only when you have exhausted this process should you issue a tribunal claim. Employment tribunal claims can be stressful, long, and expensive. Fortunately, this applies to your employer too. So the best way to use employment tribunal claims is to make it known to your employer that you are likely to make a claim (without overtly threatening to do so in the first instance). You may even start a claim, but aim in fact to negotiate and reach a settlement before you reach the court.

6.2. What kind of employment tribunal claim could I have?

There is a long list of claims which you might have but for our purposes here, they can broadly be broken down into the following (all of which are discussed in later chapters):

- Unfair dismissal and constructive dismissal: there is a maximum of one year's salary as compensation for this.

- Discrimination: there is technically no maximum for this but it's difficult to prove and in practice most successful claimants are awarded between £900 and £3,000 for their 'injury to feelings'.

- Breach of contract: this has a maximum compensation of £25,000 in the employment tribunal, otherwise you need to go to the High Court to claim (which is fraught with difficulties and costs).

- Other: claims could include unlawful deduction of wages for example or claims under TUPE.

TOP 3 TIPS

- Instruct a lawyer to draft the details of the claim itself as this is the most vital part
- You can withdraw the claim later if you change your mind
- Be aware of the three month time limit for issuing claims

6.3. ACAS pre-claim conciliation

Almost all employment tribunal claims require you to commence ACAS pre-claim conciliation first, and **you must start the ACAS process at least three months, less one day, from the date of the act of which you wish to complain.**

Therefore, if you have been unfairly dismissed on the 1st September, then you must commence pre-claim conciliation by midnight on 30th November. Likewise, if you have been discriminated against at work on 14th March, you must commence pre-claim conciliation by 13th June, whether you are still employed or not.

Commencing the ACAS pre-claim process

In order to begin the ACAS conciliation process, you need to visit the ACAS website and fill in an 'Early Conciliation Notification Form'.

The purpose of the early conciliation process is to enable an independent person (an ACAS 'conciliator') to act as a mediator between employee and employer and to try to broker a settlement before a full application to an employment tribunal is required. Usually this process involves the ACAS conciliator relaying information between the parties or the parties' legal representatives.

The initial period for conciliation is one month, although that period can be extended by 14 days if both parties agree to the extension. If the dispute is not resolved within this time period then the ACAS conciliator will issue a certificate to the employee that the process has been completed, and the employee will then have one full calendar month from the date of the certificate to file an employment tribunal claim.

The only exception to this is when an employee commences pre-claim conciliation with more than one month left on the usual limitation period, in which case the effect of pre-claim conciliation is that the clock stops and the employee then has remainder of the original time period to file the claim. That said, in order to avoid any confusion, our recommendation is to make a claim at most one month from the end of ACAS pre-claim conciliation.

It is a common misconception that if you are going through ACAS, then you do not need a lawyer, because ACAS will settle your case out of court for you. This is not what happens in practice. ACAS conciliators do their best for employees but they are not lawyers themselves. They also have a large caseload and no real incentive to get the best possible deal for you – they are incentivised to simply settle cases, regardless of settlement amount.

They tend to act as a go-between whereby they will go back and forth delivering offers and counter offers to the two parties. What they will not do however is to take detailed instructions from you, advise you regarding strategy and tactics, or put together a hard hitting legal letter on your behalf. They are very much neutral, and in no way are they as good for you as having a lawyer to represent you.

6.4. Understanding time limits for employment tribunal claims

As mentioned earlier, the rules on time limits in employment tribunal claims can be very strict and many an employee has come unstuck because they've failed to observe them. There are occasionally circumstances where the deadlines may be extended – as exemplified below – but these are exceptional and you should not assume that they apply in your particular circumstances.

There is a three month time limit for unfair dismissal claims. This is very strictly enforced, and the only exception is whereby it was not 'reasonably practical' to issue a claim within three months from the effective date of termination (normally the last day worked). Case law has interpreted the 'reasonably practical' test very narrowly, and found that even if the employee was ill or in hospital, they could have issued a claim within the timescale.

There is also a three month time limit for discrimination claims. The time runs from the last act of discrimination or the last of a series of acts of discrimination. That date could well be prior to the last day worked. The tribunal has a discretion to extend this time limit where it is 'just and equitable' to do so. This might be, for example, because there was a grievance process ongoing. Generally, the tribunal will need to consider the extent to which it's fair to the parties in allowing a claim to be brought outside the usual time limits. So it is slightly less strict for discrimination claims, but you still need to make sure you act within three months.

Notice of dismissal in tribunal claims generally. Whether your notice is given orally, in writing, in person or electronically, it takes effect from the day after the notice is given, unless your contract says otherwise. Even if it is served out of office hours it will take effect from the following day.

So if you have resigned or been dismissed and you are negotiating a settlement agreement, but time is slipping away, make sure that you take action to contact ACAS and take steps to submit your tribunal claim form (see below) within the prescribed time limits.

TOP 3 TIPS

- Claim deadlines are very strict
- Deadlines are normally three months less one day from the date of dismissal or last act of discrimination
- Issue a claim early not late

What to do if you are out of time

If you've missed the time limits in an employment tribunal claim you should seek advice without delay. If it is too late to bring a claim in the tribunal then, depending on the type of claim, you may be able to bring a claim in the civil courts for breach of contract, harassment or personal injury. It is mainly just unfair dismissal and discrimination claims which you can only bring in the employment tribunals (rather than the civil courts). If you are out of time to claim then you are probably going to find it difficult to negotiate a decent exit package, because your employer will be aware of the uphill struggle which you would face in court.

6.5. How to make a claim and complete an ET1 employment tribunal claim form

Once you have the ACAS certificate referred to in section 6.3., you can fill in an 'ET1', which is the name of the form used for making a complaint or claim to the employment tribunal. The form must be completed in full and sent in to the employment tribunal system in order to make (or 'file') a valid claim.

A lot of the form is concerned with general information, such as the name and address of you and your employer and your dates of employment. However, the form also allows you to set out your complaint under the heading 'details of claim' (also referred to generally as 'particulars of claim'). This is your opportunity to explain to the tribunal – and to your employer – what it is that you are aggrieved about.

It is important to set out all legal complaints in the ET1. For example, if you want to claim both unfair dismissal and pregnancy discrimination then it is important you say this – don't leave one of them out as it will be difficult to amend your claim at a later stage. You don't need to provide witness evidence or lengthy legal argument at this stage but it is helpful to include:

1. **The facts of the case** – what you say happened.
2. **Evidence** – why you say the tribunal should accept your version of events (if there is an email or a statement that backs you up – refer to it).
3. **Claims** – what kind of claims are you making? Unfair dismissal? Sex discrimination? Maternity discrimination? Unpaid holiday pay? Then say so.
4. **Legal argument** – why should your claims succeed? This does not have to be lengthy but it is helpful if you can point to any pieces of legislation or judgements that you are relying on.
5. **Remedy** – what is it that you are asking for? If you have been dismissed do you want your job back? Or are you seeking compensation?

In our view it is usually better to concentrate on points 1, 3 and 5 in the complaint to the employment tribunal. It is important to strike the right balance in your claim. Don't be too brief, so for example simply saying, 'I was dismissed on 1st May 2018. I have been unfairly dismissed and I am seeking compensation', is unlikely to be enough. On the other hand, the tribunal does not want to see pages and pages of verbatim discussions or long quotes from policies or correspondence.

A good way of testing whether a claim has included everything that it should is to ask yourself: 'If I prove everything I have set out here, will I win the case?' If the answer is yes, then it's probably good to go. If the answer is no, then you probably haven't included everything you should have.

If you are only going to use a lawyer for one thing in your employment tribunal claim, then use one to complete the ET1 details of claim. This document will be referred to again and again throughout the case, and if anything important is missing, especially a type of legal claim which you didn't think about, then you will probably find that you are out of time to add it in at a later stage – the three month time limit will probably apply. So build your tribunal claim on the solid foundation of a professionally drafted ET1.

Some examples of particulars of claims in ET1 forms are given in chapter 13.

6.6. Online ET1 employment tribunal claim form

You can choose whether to complete the ET1 claim form in hard copy and submit it by post, or online. In chapter 13 we also set out some guidance on how to complete an online ET1 form, step by step, as it's not always easy to complete. Be sure to keep a copy of your ET1 form, whether you submit it in hard copy or online, together with the details of the claim and confirmation that your ET1 form has been filed with the tribunal.

6.7. Employment tribunal preliminary hearings

When you get the response to your claim from the other side, this is the time that the tribunal will want to get things moving towards a final hearing. The next step along the way is the 'preliminary hearing'. A preliminary hearing is in essence an administrative hearing to allow a judge to begin to give the case some structure.

Although it is called a hearing, it almost always takes place by phone, which means that you dial into a three-way telephone call with the other side and the judge, so you normally need not worry about attending the court at this stage.

From the judge's point of view, the aim of the preliminary hearing is to familiarise the judge with what the case is all about; its value (i.e. how much money you are asking for in compensation or settlement), and the complexity of the issues involved.

At the preliminary hearing, both sides will have to agree the steps that will need to be taken in order to take the case to a final hearing. That means you will need to provide information about how many witnesses you might want to call to give evidence at the final hearing, as well as how and when you will send each other documents and witness statements that will form part of the final hearing 'bundle'.

The judge will also want to agree how long, and on what date, the hearing will take place. All that information will form part of an agreed timetable between the two parties involved and the judge, that you must stick to as closely as possible.

It is also an opportunity to tell the judge and the other side about any changes you want to make to the claim which you submitted. You should remember that the judge hearing the preliminary hearing is not the judge who will hear the final hearing and they can be quite helpful, especially if you don't have lawyers representing you. So it is important to be as prepared as you can, even at this preliminary stage.

Of course, it's not as simple as first meets the eye, because if you know your way round the system you can give yourself the advantage in a case by making the right kind of applications at a preliminary hearing. For example you might want to join two similar claims together, or you might want to apply for further information from the employer.

To get a better idea of things that will be discussed and need to be agreed upon at the preliminary hearing, you will be expected to complete an agenda and send it to the other side before the hearing. The agenda will normally be sent to you along with the hearing date. The current tribunal template for case management at preliminary hearings is reproduced in chapter 13, so that you know what to expect.

6.8. Witness statements in employment tribunals

This section gives you detailed advice about how to write your own witness statement/s in the employment tribunal.

TOP 3 TIPS

- Perfect the right style
- Don't repeat what's in the ET1 form
- Refer to the case documents

Witness statement style

The statement is your first person perspective account of what happened to you at work, and also what has happened since then. It should be in chronological order, with numbered paragraphs, for example:

1. On 20th March 2017, I did this or I did that.

2. On 30th March 2017, Mr Smith of the Respondent did this or that.

Use one and a half line spacing and at least 12 point font, preferably Times New Roman.

The style is important as it shows the judge that you know what you are doing, and first impressions are important in employment tribunals, as with any court. A well written witness statement can also scare the other side (the employer) into submission and act as a catalyst for negotiating a favourable settlement, for example by way of a settlement agreement, or a 'COT3'. (A COT3 is a type of settlement agreement negotiated after an employment tribunal claim has been started, but before the case gets as far as a tribunal hearing.)

Witness statement content

The aim is not to repeat the content of your ET1 claim form but instead to add additional information which the tribunal will not have seen before. Types of additional information would include:

- Comments on the ET3 (defence document).
- Details of your attempts to mitigate your loss (get another job).
- Comments on the documents disclosed by both sides (you won't have seen these at the ET1 stage).
- Comments about any documents which are clearly missing, and perhaps being withheld intentionally.
- Comments on any written answers or further information obtained from the Respondent (the employer) after proceedings started.

When you are commenting on the documents, it is good practice to refer to page numbers of the bundle, as the judge will be grateful for this time-saving exercise when trying to cross reference your statement with the paginated bundle of documents used in tribunal.

Exchange of witness statements

At the preliminary hearing, or by letter, the tribunal will set out a schedule for the case which will include a date for the exchange of witness statements. That date will generally be around four weeks prior to the hearing itself – so quite late on in the process. Normally you would confirm with the other side that they are ready to exchange statements at the same time, as you don't want to give them an advantage by sending yours over first.

If they are not ready then you can apply to the tribunal for an 'Unless Order' meaning that unless they comply then their defence will be 'struck out', and the tribunal will award a victory to you on paper, and then have a hearing to work out how much you should be awarded. As you can imagine with such a draconian remedy, Unless Orders are quite difficult to obtain.

Use of witness statements in tribunal

The actual witness statement itself will not be read out loud in tribunal, but instead it will be 'taken as read', meaning that everyone will have read it to themselves. Then you will be asked by your lawyer if you have anything to add. Then the other side's lawyer will cross examine you on it. They can also cross examine you on other matters not contained within your witness statement.

Settling at the doors of the court

It's not uncommon for cases to settle in the employment tribunal building itself prior to the trial starting, or even in an adjournment during the trial itself. This outcome saves the stress of being cross examined by the other side's lawyer and having to cross examine their witnesses yourself. It also heads off the uncertainty of the judge reaching a fair decision. So always be prepared to negotiate an exit package deal at any point during tribunal proceedings. There can also be help available in tribunal buildings from volunteer (also known as 'pro bono') lawyers or law students who may be able to take a look at your case on the morning of your trial to give you some last minute pointers.

PART TWO

Leaving employment: specific scenarios and claims

Introduction

In this part of the book, we identify common scenarios which you may find yourself in when you are having problems at work. The information will help you to identify when your employer has decided that your future is not with the business any more, and when a settlement agreement is the most likely outcome.

We also look at the different kinds of legal claim that arise from these scenarios and suggest how you could best negotiate in those particular exit situations. (See Part One for a wider discussion of negotiating.) The scenarios outlined in this section are:

- **Unfair and constructive dismissal: an overview**
  - Performance management
  - Role erosion
  - Mergers and acquisitions
  - Changes to contract
  - Bullying and harassment

- **Redundancy and TUPE**

- **Discrimination: an overview**
  - Pregnancy and maternity discrimination
  - Disability discrimination
  - Age discrimination
  - Long term sickness absence

- **Whistleblowing**

- **Restrictive covenants**

Chapter 7

Unfair, constructive and wrongful dismissal

7.1. Overview

In this chapter we look at some of the most common scenarios in employment law, which are categorised as unfair and/or constructive dismissal. In unfair dismissal, you are actually dismissed by your employer, whereas in constructive dismissal (which is shorthand for constructive unfair dismissal) you feel forced to resign, because of your employer's conduct, rather than actually being dismissed by your employer. There is also another situation called 'wrongful dismissal' that we also mention at the end of this overview.

There are many different permutations of unfair and constructive dismissal, but we address some of the most common ones later on in this chapter. They are performance management, role erosion, mergers and acquisitions, changes to contract, and bullying and harassment.

7.1.1. Unfair dismissal

If you have been dismissed and want to know whether your dismissal was legally fair, you need to look at the reason given for the dismissal. The three most common legally acceptable reasons are:

- Capability
- Conduct
- Redundancy (see chapter 8)

If the reason given to you for your dismissal was not one of the above, the chances are that you were unfairly dismissed. For example, if you were dismissed because you're friends with the old CEO, who has been fired, this is not a fair reason.

If you've been given a potentially fair reason, the next thing to look at is the procedure. If a fair procedure was not followed, then you can still claim for unfair dismissal (or use this information to negotiate an exit package). Any compensation won at a tribunal would be reduced to reflect the chances that you would have been dismissed had the correct procedure been followed (and the same goes for any amount you could negotiate). Exactly what is a fair procedure varies depending on the size and administrative resources of your employer. The bigger the company, the more hoops they have to jump through.

As a guideline, in a capability dismissal, you should be given warnings and chances to improve. You should have a fair hearing, with the chance to bring a colleague. You should also have a right of appeal to a higher level of management (or a different manager if it's a small employer). The ACAS Code of Practice is used by the employment tribunals to measure whether a procedure was fair.

In a conduct dismissal, the main question is whether the conduct in question was 'within the reasonable range of responses' available to the employer. A tribunal won't put itself in the shoes of the employer and ask what it would have done in that situation. This use of a 'reasonable range of responses' as a measure of fairness, as opposed to a fixed objective test, means that employers have quite a wide discretion to take the action which they want to take. Again, this affects your negotiating position too – the more blatant the unfairness, the more you should try to negotiate.

Proving that the reason given was not the real reason for your dismissal

This is always tricky: you may have been given a fair reason, and the procedure was fair, but you may still be able to successfully claim for unfair dismissal if you know – and can prove – that there was another underlying reason, and that the whole dismissal procedure was a sham exercise. This argument should be used with some caution: tribunals are part of the establishment and are not readily persuaded by conspiracy theorists.

Two years' service qualifying period

In order to make a claim for unfair dismissal in the employment tribunal, you need to have worked continuously for your employer for at least two years. If you have less than two years under your belt, then unfortunately it means that it is very easy for your employer to dismiss you (even if it feels blatantly unfair), and face no legal consequences. For example an employer can dismiss you without giving a reason. They don't have to mention your performance, a company restructure or any reason at all, although often they do give a reason anyway. This is simply a tough fact of life in employment law at the moment.

It is, however, possible to obtain some kind of settlement in these situations by negotiating, regardless of the legalities of the situation. The closer the termination date is to the two years' service, the stronger your argument would be. You would be surprised at how it can be possible to negotiate an exit package even where the legalities are not obviously on your side.

There are some exceptions to the two year rule. If the dismissal is for one of the 'automatically unfair' reasons below, there is no two year qualifying period:

- Discrimination
- Health and safety reasons
- Asserting a statutory right
- Trade union membership or non-membership
- National minimum wage reasons
- Refusing to exceed the 48-hour working week
- Whistleblowing

So if you don't have two years' service, you are not automatically barred from bringing one of the above claims. For example if the dismissal is related to discrimination on grounds of sex, race, age, disability, sexual orientation or religious belief, etc. (see chapter 9) then the two year requirement doesn't apply.

Tactics for negotiating

If you have been dismissed already then you can start negotiating by writing a without prejudice letter setting out how the dismissal was unfair and outlining a suggested settlement amount. Your tactics could include setting out how your employer acted outside the reasonable range of responses. In other words, you would be making it clear that no fair minded employer would have dismissed you for that reason. Your other angle could be to put forward evidence that the stated reason for dismissal was not the real reason. This is hard to prove however.

If you are about to be dismissed, but haven't yet been (for example disciplinary or redundancy procedures have been commenced), you can start negotiating early and possibly avoid the dismissal all together. This is a good time to negotiate because it saves your employer from having to make the decision and gives them a peaceful and pain free way of ending the employment relationship.

If you are not being dismissed, but you feel like you're being forced out by your employer's conduct, that is constructive dismissal which is explained in 7.1.2. below.

TOP 3 TIPS

- You normally need to be employed for at least two years in order to bring a tribunal claim for unfair dismissal
- You only have three months to submit an unfair dismissal tribunal claim
- An unfair dismissal claim financial award would be more if you were out of work for a long time than it would be for a short period (see chapter 4)

If you've been dismissed and reinstated on appeal, can you still get a settlement agreement?

The problem with this scenario is that, because your dismissal has 'vanished', your bargaining position has all but gone. However, depending on the circumstances surrounding the original dismissal it may be worth entering into without prejudice negotiations with your employer to see if you can agree an exit package. It may be that although your employer knows that they cannot fairly dismiss you, they may well agree a termination package as in practice it may be difficult to continue with the employer/employee relationship.

It may be arguable that your employer has breached your contract of employment, for example, by the way it conducted the disciplinary process. If that's the case then you may have a claim for constructive dismissal, or if there has been discrimination, this is likely to be a breach of contract, entitling you to resign.

If you are reading this and have been dismissed and are considering appealing, but you don't want your job back, this is a tricky negotiating situation. You may be able to make clear in your appeal that you want to clear your name but you are not seeking reinstatement. Or you could put in a basic appeal without too much information, so that you are seen to be going through the correct procedural motions, but are not actually trying to get your job back.

─────────────────────────────── **TOP 3 TIPS** ───────────────────────────────

- If an appeal is successful it may be difficult to negotiate an exit
- If you want to leave it is usually still best to appeal
- Consider negotiating an exit and settlement during the appeal process

7.1.2. Constructive dismissal

Remember, constructive dismissal (short for 'constructive unfair dismissal') is when your working life has been made so difficult, because of your employer's conduct, that you feel you have no choice but to resign, rather than actually being dismissed by your employer.

If you claim in the employment tribunal for constructive dismissal, you need to prove that your employer fundamentally breached your contract of employment and that you resigned in good time as a result of that breach. If you are successful in proving that, then you are treated the same by the tribunal as if your employer had dismissed you.

It can be difficult to prove constructive dismissal in employment tribunals because they believe that it's only in limited circumstances that someone feels forced to leave employment. The classic extreme examples are not being paid your wages, or being physically assaulted by your boss. There are many permutations of what could constitute constructive dismissal, but they all involve having your working life made so difficult that you truly believe that you have no option but to resign and leave your employment.

Two year qualifying period

As with normal unfair dismissal, in order to make a claim for constructive unfair dismissal in the employment tribunal, you need to have worked continuously for your employer for at least two years. To illustrate this important point, if you have less than two years' service, then your employer could simply ask you to leave out of the blue with no reason at all – or just say they have decided to terminate your employment.

The exceptions to this two year rule are exactly the same as with unfair dismissal cases (as already listed on page 144). If you are being forced out of your job because of these exceptional reasons, then the two year qualifying period would not apply (you have these rights from day one of your employment).

Evidence needed for constructive dismissal claims

Only a small percentage of claims of constructive dismissal succeed in the employment tribunal. The main reason is that tribunals decide that there is insufficient evidence to show that the employer's conduct was so bad that it was a fundamental breach of contract, instead of, for instance, a breach which falls short of being fundamental. An example of this lesser type of breach would be paying wages late, but not very late.

Another big killer of constructive dismissal claims in tribunals is when the judge deems the employee to have 'affirmed' or accepted the employer's misconduct. In practice this means that you left it too late to resign, or you acknowledged that the breach of contract was accepted by you in some other way, and by so doing you tacitly accepted the mistreatment. For example, your employer significantly changes your working conditions (such as your hours or job description) without consultation. They impose the changes on you and you comply with them for a period of time without objecting, even though the changes make your life really difficult and are actually in breach of the terms of your contract. (See also chapter 7.5. for more on changes to your contract.)

The employee normally makes the first move in a constructive dismissal negotiation

In a constructive dismissal scenario, it is normally the employee who needs to make the first move. Your employer might not be aware of the situation, or, if they are aware, they probably aren't planning to have a protected conversation with you. Instead, they will try and keep the situation calm and hope the passage of time means that you will either leave, or that any claim you may have will fall away (i.e. because you will be regarded as having accepted it by putting up with it for so long).

How to start a claim for constructive dismissal

Normally you should start your claim by putting together a without prejudice letter. In that letter you should set out the fundamental breaches of contract that you consider your employer to have committed. This might be one big breach – such as the failure to pay a contractually due bonus – or lots of separate breaches that together make up a breach of trust and confidence.

Remember, you are trying to prove your employer has breached your contract to the extent that they have effectively dismissed you, so you need to show exactly how they have done that by using the wording in your letter and any evidence that you have collected.

Negotiating a settlement in a constructive dismissal case

Technically, a case for constructive dismissal does not crystallise until you have resigned: it is only then that you actually have the legal right to sue for constructive dismissal. In the same vein, it is only once you have been dismissed that you have the right to claim unfair dismissal.

Therefore, in your without prejudice letter, you will be explaining to your employer that you have 'a case of constructive dismissal should you choose to act upon it'. What you are effectively saying is, 'if you do not resolve this to my satisfaction, then I will resign and sue you'.

Because of this delicate balance, negotiating in a constructive dismissal case can be a bit of a roller coaster ride: if your employer 'calls your bluff' and refuses to negotiate, then you will be put in the position of having to resign or to return to work. It is advisable, therefore, that you time your letter correctly to coincide with the worst breach of contract, or at the end of a long chain of breaches. There is no point in firing early in this particular duel. Remember, you also cannot leave it too long after the last breach of contract to write to your employer, or to resign – your timing really is important here.

When to start negotiating

Our advice differs depending on the type of constructive dismissal case you have. In a case where your employer has committed a sole and fundamental breach of your contract, for example they have failed to pay you according to your terms of contract, then the time to act is as soon as possible as there is no merit in waiting. You have your fundamental breach and now is the time to commence negotiations.

Whereas in the case of lots of smaller breaches, which when taken together add up to a fundamental breach of trust and confidence for example, you have to use your judgement a little more. There is no point in starting to negotiate after the first minor breach as you don't yet have a potential claim, nor do you have sufficient facts to negotiate with – so when is the correct time?

Our view is that once there is a pattern in the minor breaches that, when taken together, appear to be serious and that an outside observer would categorise as extremely bad behaviour by an employer, that is the time to start negotiating. If you think your employer will commit more breaches, and therefore strengthen your case, then you can wait for this to happen if you like; however, we would recommend waiting no more than two months from the latest incident before starting negotiations. After three months, there is a real risk that – if you haven't resigned – a judge could decide that you have affirmed (i.e. accepted) the breach and you would lose any case you brought. Which means, of course, that any negotiating position you have would be weakened.

Timing your resignation

As mentioned, the question of when to resign is a difficult one and not a decision to be taken lightly. The thing to remember in a constructive dismissal scenario is that if you are being badly treated, yet you choose to stay in your job, then you can be taken to have accepted that mistreatment; so you can't then resign and claim constructive dismissal at a later date.

But by and large, the best tactic is to put off your resignation and stay employed. This way you suffer no financial loss, you can be a constant thorn in your employer's side, and they are likely to pay you more in a settlement agreement just to get you out of their hair.

If you do resign, try to word your resignation letter correctly. Specify your last day of employment. If you plan to work out your notice, then you can still do this and claim constructive dismissal – you don't have to resign and walk out on the spot. It's a tough one to gauge correctly, but in any case, the three month time limit for claims can start to run from the last day you are actually employed, regardless of your official resignation date.

TOP 3 TIPS

- Write a without prejudice letter
- If that fails to get results, write a grievance letter
- Make sure you time your resignation right

7.1.3. Wrongful dismissal and gross misconduct

You may have come across the term 'wrongful dismissal' and wondered what it means. It's a misleading phrase, and one not to be confused with unfair dismissal. In essence, it means that your employer has dismissed you in a way that breaches your contract of employment.

For example, let's say that your contract of employment stipulates that your employer has to give a month's notice to terminate your employment. However, your employer tells you that you are dismissed and you should go home immediately, and that you won't be paid your month's notice. This is an example of wrongful dismissal, because your employer has not complied with the terms of your contract when dismissing you. If something like this happens to you, then you could have a claim in the employment tribunal – or preferably a potential settlement agreement to negotiate.

Gross misconduct is the most common form of wrongful dismissal claim in the employment tribunal. It is when the employer argues that you were guilty of gross misconduct, but you argue that you were innocent. You see, in gross misconduct scenarios at work, the employer is entitled by law to dismiss you without paying your notice pay. That is because by committing your actions you have effectively torn up the contract of employment, and therefore your entitlement to notice pay goes with it.

Extreme examples of gross misconduct include punching the boss or being caught with your fingers in the till. More common examples can include, for example, being caught working for your company's clients on the side, or being spotted on social media in the Caribbean when you're supposed to be tucked up in bed with the flu.

If you have already been dismissed for conduct issues (e.g. for gross misconduct), then the chances are that the time to negotiate has already passed. You will probably have to start ACAS pre-claim conciliation, commence proceedings and try to negotiate while fighting a claim. Maybe your employer will want to save money on legal fees and they will often make an offer on this basis – so you do have a chance – but the money you receive may not be as much as if you had negotiated at an earlier stage.

Misconduct claims are difficult for employees to win in tribunals. The employer only needs to show that they acted reasonably and that their decision to dismiss for misconduct was within the 'range of reasonable responses' open to them in the situation, and they will win the case. Therefore, if you are accused of misconduct and your employer is threatening dismissal as one of the options open to them, that's a good time to negotiate.

Suggest a protected conversation or without prejudice meeting

If your employer has not offered a protected conversation/without prejudice meeting, you should suggest it. In misconduct cases, it is often better to talk things through with your employer in a without prejudice meeting, rather than commence written correspondence. This is because people have a tendency to defend themselves in correspondence, or accuse their employer of acting improperly, and in a negotiation where misconduct has been alleged, this is not the way to go about things.

Consider admitting to doing something wrong

If you have done something wrong at work then it can help your negotiating cause to admit to it. It is never easy to admit to ourselves that we have done something wrong, messed up or acted improperly, but it may be the only way of negotiating a settlement package. Although you don't necessarily have to agree that what you have done is as serious or as extensive as your employer suggests.

Sometimes an apology and a promise to work hard to make things right would mean that your employer may not even dismiss you at all. So, if you don't want to leave and the misconduct you have committed is not something so terrible that it can never be forgiven, contrition and an apology may save your job.

Closing your gross misconduct negotiation

In summary, you should arrange a without prejudice meeting, potentially admit some culpability in what has happened, apologise, but explain that you have taken legal advice and you don't think that your employer has reason enough to dismiss you. Then say that you understand that, in the circumstances, your employer may wish you to leave and, if that's the case, then you would be willing to consider leaving for a reference, your notice, and a number (which you will specify) of months' salary.

Believe us, your employer will appreciate this approach – they don't want to go around sacking people and then dealing with the consequences. They may wish you to leave, but they will sincerely appreciate your behaviour in the without prejudice meeting and will more likely than not engage with you in negotiations.

Rather than you fighting the case against you, being dismissed, and then calling a lawyer who will tell you that you do not have sufficient prospects of success to win an employment tribunal, this way you will have a reference, your notice pay and a sum of money to see you through to your next job.

7.2. Performance management

Introduction

One of the most common scenarios which leads to a settlement agreement is the commencement of performance management procedures, aka 'PIPs' or performance improvement plans. If an employer has sufficient concerns about your performance to the extent that they are willing to engage you in formal procedures, then they most likely want you to leave.

Being told that you are going to face performance management is often like being punched in the gut. No one likes being told that their work is viewed as inadequate, but what's worse is toiling away hoping for promotion, a pay-rise or even recognition in a company that doesn't appreciate you and in an environment which probably isn't doing your mental health any good.

You may think that your performance is more than adequate and you could well be correct. It could just be that your employer has taken a dislike to you for some reason and sees performance management as a way of letting you know you are no longer wanted.

Sometimes, your employer may be justified in undertaking performance management, but you struggle to see their point of view – which is understandable given that you have probably worked hard for many years and given the job your best efforts.

HR departments do not take the commencement of performance management procedures lightly: they take up a lot of management time and HR resources and are often undertaken in a hostile atmosphere (what employee likes being told that their employer doesn't think that they are up to the job?). So, in those circumstances, you can bet your bottom dollar that your employer feels strongly about the matter and if that's the case, then they are almost certainly looking to move you out of the company and replace you.

Performance processes mean commitment and risk for your employer too

In a performance management scenario, your employer has committed to you being in employment for at least another three to six months while the performance process is completed, and this means they will need to pay your salary for that time. They have also committed to resourcing this procedure and using HR and management time to undertake what can often be quite a complicated process. They have also taken on a risk: a risk that they will make a mess of the procedure and end up dismissing you unfairly, and also a risk that you will pass the procedure and they could be stuck with an employee they don't want.

Performance management can be an opportunity for settlement

This is therefore an ideal situation to negotiate a settlement. Even if your employer takes you through a successful process and wants to dismiss you, they will still have to pay you your notice and are likely to want to do that by a payment in lieu of notice. They will probably be wanting you to sign a settlement agreement in any event and in doing so, to give up your right to sue them at a later date.

So, if you have just been told you will face performance management, or have been offered a settlement agreement as the alternative, don't worry unduly. Think of it as an opportunity. You are in a prime position to negotiate some money, get paid your notice, agree the form of wording for a reference and then go and do something better with your life.

What to do if you're facing performance management procedures

The first step for you is to accept that the writing is on the wall and that it's time to move on with the best possible financial start to a new job. Alternatively, you can stay and fight for your current role.

Our advice would be to think long and hard about whether you have a future with that particular employer. How many employees

subject to performance management survive the process? How many are happy in their role even if they do survive? How many go on to achieve a pay-rise or promotion?

The trust often goes between employer and employee once performance issues are raised, and with that, goes the future of the relationship. Of course many employees do pass performance management procedures, and many go on to remain with the company for months, even years, and if that's what you want to do then we would always encourage you to stand and fight, bearing in mind the above caveats.

The reason why this scenario is often the best in which to achieve a settlement is that both parties want a deal. The employer at the very least recognises that there is a problem and wishes to resolve it one way or another, and you recognise it may be time to move on rather than face performance management. Therefore, you have the ideal basis for an agreement: two willing parties.

It is increasingly common for an HR department to invite the employee into a meeting to commence performance management procedures, and then have a without prejudice or protected conversation to offer a settlement agreement before the procedure has actually commenced.

HR departments have to be careful about doing this, however. That's because, in certain circumstances, if you are unaware of any pre-existing issues and no performance process has started, there is a possibility that the offer will not be afforded protection (i.e. the without prejudice conversation will lose its protection and be on the record). If that's the case, you will be in a stronger negotiating position as you can allege that the result of any performance management procedure is a foregone conclusion and therefore that a dismissal is potentially unfair.

Most employers get it right, however, and it is often legitimate for them to offer you an 'either/or' scenario: either take the money and leave now with a reference, or face the uncertainty of the procedure.

The employer usually makes the first move

When you are facing performance procedures, the employer usually makes the first move in a negotiation. This will probably be in the form of a meeting to discuss your performance followed by the implementation of performance procedures and may, or may not, also include a protected conversation or without prejudice meeting or letter.

If your employer has a protected conversation with you and makes an offer to terminate your employment rather than going through performance procedures, then you can respond to that offer in writing. If, on the other hand, your employer wishes to commence performance procedures, but you think this is the time to leave and you want to negotiate a settlement, then you should consider initiating action by putting together a suitable without prejudice letter yourself.

Short-circuiting the performance process

What if you approach your employer with a solution to their problem? Remove the risk of a tribunal claim, use your resignation as a negotiating tool and offer to remove yourself from the organisation, thereby reducing the management time already committed. All they have to do in return is pay you the money they would have had to pay anyway to take you through these procedures.

This sounds ideal, and is how you should be pitching it to your employer. You should be asking for your notice paid in lieu, a reference (this is an important reason for you to settle a performance case) and the money they would have spent on your wages during the performance procedure – paid gross as an ex gratia payment.

Your argument should go something like this: 'You, my employer, are going to take six months to conclude an uncertain process, at the end of which you have to pay me notice and I will retain my rights to sue for unfair dismissal, so we should conclude this now by you paying me six months' gross salary, my notice and giving me a reference.'

Your employer may not accept your proposals, instead saying that the performance procedure will more likely be three months. If that's the case, then they will often settle at between four and five months' gross salary, leaving you to move on to another job with enough money to see you through until that time.

7.3. Role erosion

Introduction

Role erosion can happen to anyone and without warning. You may be engaged in the role you have held for years, blissfully unaware that your employer has decided to get rid of you.

Rather than tell you what the problem is, or simply explain that things are no longer working out, the employer instead begins gently to remove your role without you even realising, until, one day, you become aware of what's occurring. By this time, it's too late and you're being made redundant because you no longer have any duties to perform.

Role erosion is not in any way obvious or dramatic. In fact, it can seem almost benign at first. An employer attempting to remove you in this way moves at a glacial pace, biding their time, employing the 'death by a thousand cuts' method, ensuring that you can't point to any single reason as an example of a breach of contract in support of a constructive dismissal claim.

The cunning employer will aim to take away almost all of your role and responsibilities without you knowing about it and then declare you redundant and pay you off with the pittance which the state allows employers to pay in cases of redundancy (i.e. a statutory redundancy payment).

Other signs of role erosion

The most obvious sign of role erosion is the company employing someone to manage you with a suspiciously similar job title and description. For example, if you are the Commercial Manager and report to the Managing Director, and the company has just decided to appoint a 'Commercial Director' who doesn't actually sit on the board, and who also reports to the Managing Director, then you can guess what's down the road for you.

The appointment of someone above you, especially if you are in a management position, is usually a good sign that your employer is trying to remove you without a fuss (or without you realising). There is nothing unlawful or even apparently objectionable about employing someone to manage you, but it's a potential warning sign that things are not looking good.

The second most obvious sign usually accompanies the first, and that is that your roles and responsibilities are gradually prised away from you and given to either the new manager with the suspiciously similar job title, or to your colleagues. This often happens over a period of months, so that you can't object too quickly, and the employer has a litany of convenient excuses to fall back on, most of them encompassing waffly 'corporate speak', such as the word 'synergies'.

If you suddenly find yourself twiddling your thumbs for four hours a day, retrace your steps and look at how that happened, because if it's not an obvious downturn in business, then it's likely that other people are doing what should be part of your role. The heavy footsteps approaching your office are not the board with a bottle of champagne and a fat bonus cheque, but the hobnailed boots of the HR manager carrying a thin letter containing an even thinner figure – the dreaded statutory redundancy payment.

How to react to role erosion
The key in this scenario is for you to recognise what is going on at an early stage and to make the employer's life as difficult as possible – to the extent that the employer recognises that if they want to get rid of you they will have to pay you off, rather than continue down the route they had initially envisaged.

You need to wise up and act quickly. Don't let them get away with it! Let them know that you know what's going on. And when they know that you know, then they will know you won't take this lying down.

Object to each decision to reallocate your work to another employee in the strongest, but politest, terms. Always do this in writing and keep records of the emails. This way you are building up a record of your objections and increasing pressure on your employer not to take another step. If you suspect foul play (for example if Andy from accounts has just told you that he's now responsible for something that you used to do), then demand answers and explanations in writing. If you're getting nowhere you could make a subject access request.

If you keep up pressure on your employer, they are likely to get sick of you and approach you with a settlement agreement. If not, then after the third or fourth incident you can set out your case in a without prejudice letter (referring to all those emails you have kept) and seek a settlement agreement as a compromise to your potential claim of constructive dismissal. If this doesn't bear the fruit you want, then move to using the next tools in your arsenal including a grievance letter, a subject access request and an employment tribunal claim.

7.4. Mergers and acquisitions

Introduction

Mergers and acquisitions were once famously called 'murders and executions'. There was a reason for that: the results are not pretty! Jobs are lost, lines of reporting are changed, promotion prospects are squashed and redundancies imminent.

Sometimes a larger company acquires another because it sees a model of efficiency and simply wants the business to continue running and expanding naturally. This is rare given one company has to buy the shares of another – often at an inflated rate – or make a global offer for 100% of the shares and assets, as is usually the case in a private limited company.

This will cost a lot of money and in order to realise an investment sooner, the purchaser may try to make 'efficiency' savings (i.e. job cuts, pay cuts, bonus cuts, streamlined structures, fewer promotions or not replacing staff who are leaving etc.). This leads to a difficult, if not terrible, working environment.

So, if you are an employee in these circumstances and the consequences of a merger or acquisition are likely to affect you negatively, you may want to think about starting the negotiation ball rolling and bargaining your way out of your job before the axe falls.

The prospects facing employees in mergers and acquisitions
If you are facing the consequences of a merger and/or acquisition, you will generally fall into one of three categories:

1. Employed by the company which is taking over another.

2. Employed by a company that is merging with another to create a partnership of equals or other symbiotic relationship.

3. Employed by a company which is being taken over by a larger or more powerful concern.

If you are in category 1, you are usually going to be fine, unless your employer dislikes you and sees the change as an opportunity to oust you, in which case it's a good time to start negotiating.

If you are in category 2, you are vulnerable to new economies of scale and role-overlap, but this usually takes between six months and a year to begin to make itself known and therefore you are often better off remaining in post until the situation looks like it may lead to redundancies.

If you are in category 3, you are the most vulnerable. You are now at the mercy of a larger business, of managers who do not know you, who have no relationship with you and, when they have to make a decision, are likely to prefer their own staff over you.

When to raise the prospect of leaving your employment?

If you are facing the scenario outlined above (in category 3), and believe your job is going to be adversely affected, then this could be an opportune time to raise the prospect of leaving.

It could be that some of your role is being given to someone else without you having been consulted. It could be that your clients (which you have had for years) have suddenly been given to another employee. You might find that decisions that you usually take are being taken by someone else. These things almost always happen following a merger or acquisition, and taken together, or on their own, these instances may amount to constructive dismissal and/or a breach of the TUPE regulations (see chapter 8).

If this has happened then it's time to send a without prejudice letter offering to leave employment under a settlement agreement, in return for your notice and an ex gratia payment. If that doesn't achieve the result you deserve, then ramp up the pressure with a formal grievance, a subject access request, and – as a last resort – an employment tribunal claim.

7.5. Changes to your contract of employment

Introduction

Sometimes employers will attempt to alter your contract of employment without offering you a fair pay rise or other benefits in return. These changes could include:

- Increasing your hours.
- Decreasing your pay.
- Increasing your targets.
- Changing your commission structure.
- Taking powers out of your hands.

There is an almost unlimited number of different ways for employers to change your employment contract unfairly, and it could be that you are entitled to resign and/or ask for a settlement agreement as a result. It is difficult to determine exactly whether a specific step taken by your employer warrants asking for a settlement agreement – each case is different. It is necessary to review the contract of employment document itself, together with other contractual documents such as the company handbook as well as considering the broader context.

─────────────── **TOP 3 TIPS** ───────────────

- Except in rare circumstances, employers are not permitted to change your contract without your prior agreement
- If you continue to work too long after your contract changes, you can be deemed to have accepted the change
- If you don't accept the change, put it in writing

What to look out for in your contract

If the contract of employment contains a clause stating that the employer is entitled to vary any of the terms of the contract itself, then such a clause may well be invalid because it is so 'wide' that it is in effect an unfair term. If, however, it contains a narrowly defined clause, such as the ability for the employer to change the location of your work, then it is likely that they are entitled to rely on such a clause.

By and large, basic salary is not something which the employer can decrease without very good reason. Or, more accurately, it is not something which they are legally entitled to do (although niceties such as legal rights and obligations don't always bother some employers unfortunately).

Discretionary bonuses can be changed with impunity but contractual commission schemes and contractual bonus structures are normally legally protected.

Where your employer has tried to alter your bonus structure or commission scheme, if you can produce the statistics to show that you are in real terms being asked to take a pay cut, then you have the basis of a potential claim for constructive unfair dismissal.

The situation is less clear cut where the change relates to changing your responsibilities.

What to do about changes you are unhappy with

The key is not to be seen to accept the change, by only carrying on working under protest. Flag the matter up informally at first, but if this doesn't work you may decide you want to leave. In that case send a without prejudice letter setting out how much you are asking for as an exit package. If that doesn't work then your protest might take the form of submitting a grievance, and then proceeding to the next steps which include a subject access request and finally an employment tribunal claim.

Alternatively, you might say that you are willing to try the new system but only for a trial period and that you suspect that you will be worse off, but you are willing to give it a go before taking further action.

7.6. Bullying and harassment

Introduction

According to a study undertaken by ACAS (2016), bullying and harassment in the workplace is worryingly common, with 75% of participants saying they had been the victim of, or had seen others being subject to, bullying and harassment at work. It has impacts on the health and wellbeing of the victims and their loved ones, and has a negative effect on the economy, with millions of working hours being lost through sickness absence for work related stress. So if you're one of those unfortunate people who are being bullied at work – what can you do about it?

What is bullying and harassment?

The first thing is to understand how bullying and harassment are defined. The ACAS guide for employees on bullying and harassment at work defines bullying as: 'Offensive, intimidating, malicious or insulting behaviour, an abuse or misuse of power through means that undermine, humiliate, denigrate or injure the recipient.' It provides the following examples of bullying:

- Spreading malicious rumours or insulting someone by word or behaviour; copying memos that are critical about someone to others who do not need to know.
- Ridiculing or demeaning someone – picking on them or setting them up to fail.
- Exclusion or victimisation.
- Unfair treatment.
- Overbearing supervision or other misuse of power or position.
- Unwelcome sexual advances.

- Making threats or comments about job security without foundation.

- Deliberately undermining a competent worker by overloading and constant criticism.

- Preventing individuals progressing by intentionally blocking promotion or training opportunities.

Legal options to combat bullying and harassment

You may be surprised to learn that there is no single law directly prohibiting bullying and harassment per se in the workplace in the UK – to a large extent, bosses are legally allowed to bully their staff. We obviously do not agree with the law here, and it also makes negotiating settlements that bit more difficult in practice.

Harassment is regarded as a civil wrongdoing rather than a criminal offence. Therefore, unless harassment relates to discrimination, it is not actionable in the employment tribunal. It can be settled via a settlement agreement, but in the civil courts – where it can be tried – actions for harassment between employee and employer are rare, mainly because the civil courts are a cost-shifting jurisdiction. As mentioned in the book introduction, this means that for claims over a certain value, the losing side pays the costs of the winning side, and these can be very high. The same is not true of the employment tribunal, where each side bears its own costs save for in exceptional circumstances.

Bullying per se is not an actionable case either, either in the employment tribunal or the civil courts. Rather, it is a common definition of bad behaviour by one person towards another. Bullying may be harassment, but not always.

Limited legal protection exists in other laws, the main ones being:

- **Discrimination:** if the bullying or harassment is based on grounds of race, sex, disability etc., then you may have a potential claim for discrimination. As already mentioned above there are strict time limits to bring your claim, with the deadline being three months less one day from the date

165

of the discrimination to commence the process to pursue legal action in an employment tribunal. The deadline applies regardless of whether you have submitted a grievance or other internal complaint.

- **Personal injury:** if you have suffered a physical or mental injury and you can medically prove it was caused by the bullying and harassment, and has led you to suffer financial loss e.g. loss of income while being on sick leave, you have a potential claim for personal injury. It is difficult to prove 'causation' meaning that your employer caused your injury. You will need an expensive medical report for this.

- **Breach of contract:** there are numerous obligations implied into every contract of employment regardless of whether or not they are written into the contract, such as the duty of trust and confidence, the duty to deal with grievances without undue delay etc. If your employer breaches these duties in relation to the bullying and harassment which leads you to suffer financial loss, then you have a potential claim for breach of contract. As usual, this would be difficult to prove in tribunal but a lot easier to use as ammunition when negotiating an exit package.

- **Unfair dismissal:** if you feel that you have no choice but to resign on the back of being bullied and harassed at work, or in response to your employer's failure to address it, then you could potentially have a claim for constructive dismissal, so long as you have your two years' service.

- **Health and Safety/Protection for Harassment Act**: this is complicated legislation which you could claim under but it's a real technical minefield. You may be able to claim against the individual who is harassing you, as well as the employer. There can even be criminal implications for the perpetrator.

How to negotiate in bullying and harassment situations

As bullying and harassment is in itself not actionable in the employment tribunal, it may not always be straightforward to negotiate a decent settlement agreement for it. However, as already discussed, bullying and harassment may also be related to other claims.

Therefore, if you were to commence negotiations on the basis that a) you have been bullied/harassed, b) this constitutes a civil claim for harassment, and c) this also constitutes a constructive dismissal claim (or one of the other kinds of claim mentioned above), then this puts you in the strongest possible position for negotiating a settlement agreement.

Alternatively, many employers, particularly larger ones, will have a written policy against bullying and harassment and you could make a complaint under such a policy, or raise a grievance under any grievance policy.

Either way, you should set out in detail what action or behaviour you are complaining about, when it occurred, who was involved, how it makes you feel and what you want your employer to do about it. You should gather your evidence carefully and contact any witnesses to provide supporting statements to corroborate your account.

Sometimes a formal written complaint or grievance can lead to the employer dealing with the matter and putting things right. However a lot of employers will string out the grievance process but have no intention of upholding the complaint nor do anything to address it – other than to consider how to manage you out of the business or get rid of you in some other way. You can read more in the chapters on negotiating, evidence, and grievances.

Fighting for your rights

You may want your employer to openly admit their guilt. However, staying in your job and fighting for your rights in the face of being bullied and harassed is not for everyone, especially when your employer is failing to address the problem. It can have a negative impact on your health and you will need a lot of resolve. It is in some senses like a war of attrition where there is a prolonged period of conflict, during which each side seeks gradually to wear down the other by a series of small-scale actions. For example, it could involve multiple grievances and counter-grievances and the end result is never certain. If the bullying and harassment consists of unfair performance management, then your decision to stick it out may be short lived in any case, as your employer may plan for this to lead to your dismissal at some point. Hence the reason why a negotiated settlement is often the best outcome that you can achieve in practice.

Chapter 8

Redundancy and TUPE

Introduction

A redundancy situation does not always lead to a settlement agreement. If your employers are confident that they have conducted a fair process (see below) they may decide simply to proceed to dismiss you without any kind of exit package. If the redundancy is fair, employers need not pay any more than statutory redundancy pay unless a contractually binding policy is in place which sets out the amount to be paid.

However, many employers offer a settlement agreement with an enhanced redundancy payment in order to ensure your smooth exit from the business, and also to protect themselves against any claims.

There is a lot of variety in such circumstances. Some employers offer large amounts even though they don't have to, especially to high-earning employees. Some offer little more than statutory payments, but enough to make you accept, if your situation is hopeless.

What is important to understand is that, quite often, the ex gratia payment is negotiable. If it isn't, then you can focus on other areas such as bonus payments, the termination date, share options and holiday pay as points of negotiation to increase your overall exit package.

Redundancy law

Many redundancies are carried out incorrectly by management to the point where they amount to unfair dismissal under the Employment Rights Act 1996. If you can identify the errors then that will be the key to negotiating a better redundancy package.

It is supposed to be the role itself which is identified as being redundant first, and then the employee is identified afterwards. All too often though, managers will select those people who, perhaps for personal reasons, they would like to see made redundant. In these 'fake' or 'sham' redundancies, your employer may even build a seemingly objective redundancy selection process which just happens to select you, when the whole time it was a foregone conclusion.

A lot of redundancy packages will take into account the element of doubt about the objectivity of the process, and will offer an enhanced amount, over and above the statutory minimum. Obviously the more your employer is offering you, the less useful it is to point out the holes in the process itself.

Is there a genuine redundancy situation?

In order for the redundancy to be fair, there has in fact to be a genuine redundancy situation. A redundancy situation occurs when a business or workplace closes or when there is a 'diminished need for work of a particular kind'. The latter is often broad enough to cover the situation where an employer restructures the business.

For example, your employer might decide to merge two roles into one or divide the work among other staff. However, if you are dismissed for 'redundancy' and then your employer recruits someone else to do the same job that you were doing, then that doesn't look like a genuine redundancy situation. (The exception being where that person is on significantly less money than you were, which is a legally acceptable reason to make you redundant.)

An employment tribunal will not get involved with whether a decision to make redundancies was sensible, only whether it was genuine, and whether the selection process was objectively fair. You might think that the decision to make you redundant is really bad for the business and will result in lost revenue, but that is not the test for the employment tribunal unfortunately. Employment tribunals will not 'put themselves in the shoes' of the employer for this.

Is the selection pool for the redundancy fair?

One of the ways that your employer can come unstuck in a redundancy dispute is in relation to who they decide is at risk of redundancy, in other words, choosing the 'selection pool' for redundancy.

If there are other people doing the same job as you then they should also be in the redundancy selection pool. It becomes more complicated when there are people who are not doing the same job but where the roles are interchangeable or the skill sets for the jobs are similar. In those circumstances you should be arguing that the selection pool should include those roles as well. Obviously, the bigger the selection pool, the less likely it is that you will be selected for redundancy.

In addition, in some circumstances in a redundancy dispute, an employer should consider what's commonly referred to as 'bumping'. This means making a more junior employee redundant and you taking their job instead.

Were the selection criteria objective and fairly applied?

If there's a number of people in the selection pool for redundancy, your employer has to set selection criteria for determining who should be made redundant. These could be things like attendance, punctuality, skills and experience.

Facts about attendance can be checked against HR records and so are easily verified. Questions about skills and experience are more subjective and are often based on the opinion of the person scoring you. In those circumstances, your employer should be able to back up their scores, for example, by looking at past appraisals or peer reviews. If your employer has no basis for their scores, then your redundancy may be easier to prove to be unfair.

Sometimes employers will hold interviews to decide who will be made redundant. They are allowed to do this, but again they should be able to back up their interview scores objectively and the interview panel should be impartial and free from bias.

You should also consider whether your selection for redundancy is discriminatory. For example, if you have been absent from work due to maternity-related sickness or due to a disability, and are scored down for attendance as a result. In such cases the dismissal may be unfair and in breach of discrimination legislation.

Were you consulted about the redundancy?

If you are in a redundancy process with your employer then they do have to consult you about the proposals. They should meet with you to discuss the rationale behind the decision to put you at risk of redundancy and allow you to put forward alternatives. They should also consult with you about what other roles might be available to you in the business. The duty to consult with you is much more onerous if 20 or more people are at risk of redundancy.

For consultations with individual employees, there should be at least one meeting with the employer and they should give you written notice in advance of the meeting. They should also give you the chance to bring a colleague to accompany you. A colleague can ask questions, but can't answer questions on your behalf. At the meeting they will have to say to you quite clearly that they are going to discuss your redundancy. It will be a serious meeting where you can have a long chat and you can raise any and all issues that you have.

If you are a member of a trade union you can take your union rep to the meeting. Normally trade union reps actually work for your employer and are not trained lawyers either, so they are not always the best people to fight your corner in terms of negotiating you the highest reasonable amount for an exit package.

If you have some potential claims to bring against the employer this meeting may be a good time to mention, on a without prejudice basis, that you would consider entering into a settlement agreement.

Did your employer consider alternative work for you?

In a redundancy situation, your employer should consider alternative roles for you within the business or any group company. This should include, for example, sending you lists of all available vacancies. Often this will depend on the size and resources of the employer. It is important to note though that your employer does not have to create a role in the organisation for you where none exists.

You will be in a much better position to argue that your redundancy was unfair if you apply for lots of roles but are not successful, than if you do not apply for anything at all. It is also worth remembering that if you are offered an alternative role you are legally entitled to a four-week trial period, and if it doesn't work out in that time you can still claim your redundancy pay.

--- **TOP 3 TIPS** ---

- Ensure that there is a genuine economic need to make you redundant
- Consider whether the selection pool and criteria were fair
- Consider whether you were consulted properly about your role and if your employer offered you suitable alternative employment

Statutory redundancy pay

To qualify for a statutory redundancy payment, you must have been continuously employed for at least two years. Statutory redundancy pay is calculated with reference to your number of completed years' service. You get:

- 1.5 weeks' pay* for each year in which you were 41 years old or above.
- 1 weeks' pay* for each year in which you were over 22 but under 41 years old.
- 0.5 weeks' pay* for each year in which you were under 22 years old.

* Unfortunately, a weeks' pay is subject to a maximum figure of £508 (from April 2018). The maximum number of years which may be counted is 20. Even if you have been somewhere for 20 years, from the age of 41 to 61, you would be entitled to only (20 x 1.5 x £508) = £15,240. Redundancy payments up to £30,000 are not taxable. Any money above the statutory minimum is usually offered in exchange for you agreeing not to sue your employer.

Can you negotiate a better settlement than what's already on offer?

Redundancy situations can be one of the hardest situations in which to negotiate a better settlement package, especially if there are multiple redundancies being made. This is because if there are many people going to be dismissed for redundancy, the situation is plainly genuine. Additionally, the more people going, the greater the cost, and the less likely the employer is to make an exception in an individual case and increase the amount of compensation they will pay out to you.

One way of negotiating a better deal in a redundancy situation is if the pool is small (i.e. only two or three of you) and your employers are looking for voluntary redundancies, or are targeting you unfairly. Or, if there is a large pool and you have evidence that you should not have been selected – either through a mistake in the scoring, or the pooling, or if there is alternative employment available within the company which you were not offered.

Once you've identified the weaknesses in your redundancy process, then you can go about making the case to your employer for negotiating a better payment.

Redundancies can take many months to determine

Redundancies involving several people, especially in larger companies, take many months to determine. The first you hear of it may be at a management consultation meeting, but your employer may have been discussing it for months. They know who is in the pool, who is likely to survive and how much they are going to pay over the statutory redundancy amount to ensure that people leave under a settlement agreement, and protect the company against legal action. In many cases these days, the decision has not even been taken in this country if the company is a large one with overseas offices, so negotiating with your employer in such circumstances is more difficult.

Participate fully in the redundancy process

At the same time as negotiating on a without prejudice basis, you should be running an 'open' position whereby you attend all the consultations and go through the appeals process, flagging up where you think they have gone wrong. Be aware that sometimes it can be best not to point out these errors before you actually get made redundant, as your employer would then have a chance to correct them before making you redundant. That assumes that by now you don't actually want your job back because you feel so aggrieved with their unfair treatment, or you're sure they will select you anyway.

Ask questions about the redundancy process

Ask for disclosure of documents, especially scoring criteria. Demand to know who rated you against the criteria and why, and ask to see any evidence which the managers referred to, such as absence records or disciplinary records. You should also ask to see the scores of the other employees in your redundancy pool. By this stage your employer may start to get nervous and offer you an increased package. This is when a grievance can also be a good way to go (see chapter 3) as it forces them actually to consider your arguments rather than just fobbing you off.

Should you offer to resign before you're made redundant?

There is one tip which applies to all redundancy pay negotiations, whether you have a decent legal case or not. If you are sure that you are going to be made redundant, then you could offer to resign voluntarily first, on the basis that your employer pays you a sum of money which recognises the amount of time and effort saved by short circuiting the redundancy process.

For example, you might save them a month of HR and management time, so you could ask for a month's salary plus say another month to take into account their time and effort. It's attractive from their point of view as they won't have to carry out any kind of fair process or give you a right of appeal.

Don't forget to appeal

If you are finally made redundant, then you should make sure that you appeal against the decision, pointing out any defects with the procedure as set out above. This can be useful evidence if you do end up challenging the decision in an employment tribunal, and more importantly it gives you that additional firepower for a negotiation.

TUPE

Can I be made redundant if my employer changes hands?

TUPE is the acronym for an obscure law called Transfer of Undertakings (Protection of Employment) Regulations 2006. Don't worry if you haven't heard about it; it's not exactly dinner table conversation! A TUPE transfer could be, for example, a purchase of one company by another company. TUPE is designed to protect employees against the buyer company making them redundant just because of the transfer.

TOP 3 TIPS

- TUPE is a technical minefield
- New management often tries to sidestep TUPE legislation
- Your new contract should be just as beneficial as the old one

---

TUPE applies not only to simple takeovers, but also to more complex situations, for example, regarding big clients moving between companies. If a group of employees or contractors are working exclusively for the client at company A, and then that client decides to use company B instead, those contractors can insist on joining company B if they want to. If company B refuses to employ them, the contractors will have a claim for unfair dismissal and a claim under the TUPE legislation.

When a TUPE transfer takes place, the employees of the old company should remain on the same contractual terms as they were on before. Even if the new company makes them sign new contracts, those new contracts are not valid in the eyes of the law if they are less beneficial than the old ones, and, legally, the contracts would carry on as before. The new company can get round this by offering the old employees more money or other 'considerations' such as improved benefits. So they can offer to pay everyone a lump sum of money or a pay rise in exchange for accepting the new, less beneficial, contractual terms.

Consultation with the employees should take place where it is a fairly large company. As with normal redundancy, it may be possible for the new company to offer the employees alternative employment. This may be on another site far away from where you live, but of course you have grounds to refuse any such offer. Employers often use this loophole to avoid the effects of the TUPE legislation.

Another exception to TUPE protection is where there is an 'ETO' reason for dismissals/redundancy. ETO stands for an economic, technical or organisational reason. Examples include reasons relating to:

- The profitability or market performance of the buyer's business (i.e. an economic reason).

- The nature of the equipment or production processes which the buyer operates (i.e. a technical reason).

- The management or organisational structure of the buyer's business (i.e. an organisational reason).

So where these ETO reasons apply, the new company can legally make you redundant or offer you less beneficial contract terms. They are actually quite wide reasons which could well apply in a lot of corporate takeovers. As you can probably by now begin to appreciate, TUPE really is a bit of a technical minefield, but it's one in which a specialist lawyer would be able to help you navigate.

Chapter 9
Discrimination

9.1. Overview

Introduction

The Employment Tribunal Services publish regular statistics that tell you how difficult discrimination claims are to win. What those statistics don't tell you is that in reality discrimination cases are usually agreed through an out-of-court settlement rather than won in court. Establishing discrimination to the tribunal's satisfaction may be difficult but that doesn't mean that discrimination within the workplace doesn't exist – it most certainly does!

Some employers will often see the considerable benefit of settling any potential claim long before it gets to the tribunal but others will deny their wrongdoing, and at times even lie, to avoid dealing with the uncomfortable truth that they employ managers who engage in unlawful and discriminatory conduct.

Time limits in discrimination at work claims

On the plus side, there is no minimum period of employment before you can make a claim in the employment tribunal for discrimination. Unlike unfair dismissal, you do not have to wait two years before you have the right to bring a claim. Your rights not to be subjected to less favourable treatment begin even before you become an employee. For example, you could claim discrimination because you were denied an employment interview due to having a 'protected characteristic' (see below).

The rules on time limits for making a tribunal claim for discrimination are complicated, and as a rule of thumb, you only have three months to commence an employment tribunal claim for discrimination. This process will start with notifying ACAS through the Early Conciliation Notification form, as explained in chapter 6.

The clock starts ticking after the discriminatory incident or course of events in question (unless you can show it was reasonable in all the circumstances to wait). If you miss the time limit, the tribunal can reject your claim, unless they decide that it is 'just and equitable' to accept it. You need a really good reason for waiting more than three months to make a claim.

For this reason, your employer will be less likely to offer you a decent settlement agreement if you have missed the deadline. Employers will often try to string out any grievance procedure to take you over the three month time limit for issuing a claim!

Proving a discrimination claim

Discrimination claims can be difficult to prove as there is normally no written evidence and of course the perpetrators are likely to deny all knowledge. However if you can prove that you have been put at a disadvantage because of discrimination, then you may be able to successfully negotiate a settlement agreement, or to make an employment tribunal claim.

─────────────────── **TOP 3 TIPS** ───────────────────

- Get witnesses
- Keep a diary
- Gather relevant statistics

Who can be discriminated against?

Under the Equality Act 2010, discrimination may apply to individuals who have one or more of what are called 'protected characteristics', as follows:

- **Age:** a person of a particular age or belonging to an age range – for example: people of 18-30 years, or employees over the age of 55.
- **Disability:** a person has a disability if she or he has a physical or mental impairment which has a substantial and long-term adverse effect on that person's ability to carry out normal day-to-day activities.
- **Gender reassignment:** a person who is transitioning or has transitioned from one gender to another.
- **Marriage and civil partnership:** the legal union between a man and woman or between a same sex couple.
- **Pregnancy and maternity:** pregnancy is the condition of being pregnant or expecting a baby. Maternity refers to the period after the birth, and is linked to maternity leave in the employment context.
- **Race:** refers to a group of people defined by their race, colour, and nationality (including citizenship), ethnic or national origins.
- **Religion or belief:** religion has the meaning usually given to it, but belief includes religious and philosophical beliefs including lack of belief (such as Atheism). Generally, a belief should affect your life choices or the way you live, for it to be included in the definition.
- **Sex:** a man or a woman.
- **Sexual orientation:** whether a person's sexual attraction is towards their own sex, the opposite sex or to both sexes.

If you want more detail about these protected characteristics, the Equality and Human Rights Commission website (www.equalityhumanrights.com) is a good place to start.

Types of discrimination

1. Direct discrimination

This is when you are treated differently and badly, or worse than others, because of age, sex, race, sexual orientation, or other protected characteristics.

Unfortunately, not all unfair treatment will be unlawful discrimination under the Equality Act 2010. The reason why you are being treated differently – or less favourably – is important. In order to prove discrimination, you must show that it is because of a protected characteristic. In reality, this is difficult. Few people who discriminate do it explicitly.

In rare cases, we see an employer who might reveal their hand by saying or doing something which would amount to direct discrimination. Most often it is difficult to get to the truth, and a long road of grievances and, potentially, tribunal proceedings, may be the only option to take to uncover the discriminatory conduct. Examples of direct discrimination are:

- **Direct race discrimination**
  The arrival of a new CEO. As soon as they take up office, they are wanting to employ people of the same national origin as they are, or they make comments about other nationalities being workshy, and staff of other nationalities start to find themselves being put on performance improvement plans.

- **Direct sex discrimination**
  A woman is interviewed for a new role and is asked if she plans to have children soon. She says she does, and does not get the job.

- **Direct religious discrimination**

  Refusing to employ a woman because she wishes to wear an hijab.

2. Indirect discrimination

This is when an employer treats everyone the same but the effect of the treatment subjects you to a disadvantage because of your protected characteristic. For example:

- **Indirect sex discrimination**

  An employer which has a policy requiring all staff to work full time is likely to place a woman at a disadvantage. This is because more women than men have primary child care responsibilities so it would be more difficult for them to work full time than it would be for a man.

- **Indirect religious discrimination**

  An employer who insists that all staff must work on a Sunday may cause a disadvantage to someone whose religious observances require them to refrain from work on a Sunday. Employers have a defence if they can show there is an 'objective justification' (in other words, a very good reason), for the requirement. This is a complicated area of law, and the appeals courts have to give regular guidance on the principles of objective justification.

3. Harassment

This is when there is unwanted conduct related to a relevant protected characteristic, which has the purpose or effect of violating an individual's dignity or creating an intimidating, hostile, degrading, humiliating or offensive environment for that individual.

4. Victimisation

This is when you are treated badly because you have done a 'protected act' (or because it is believed that you have done or are going to do a protected act). A protected act is making a complaint of discrimination or offering assistance to someone else in their discrimination claim. So victimisation is essentially retaliation for complaining about discrimination.

Discrimination financial awards

The question of how much money you should get in discrimination cases is considered further in chapter 4. We'll just mention two related things here.

Firstly, if you want to understand a bit more about how much to ask for in your discrimination agreement, it's necessary to put it into context by considering how a discrimination claim would be dealt with in an employment tribunal. Why? Because most employers will ask their lawyers the question: 'If this went to tribunal what would happen?' They would then base any settlement agreement offer on their lawyer's answer.

Secondly, we'd like to emphasise that the very large payouts that get reported in the media are often due to financial loss because the discrimination meant that the individual could not work again.

If, for example, you were earning £40,000 per year, and you are 65 years old, you might be able to claim five years' salary totalling £200,000, only if you can show that you are highly unlikely to find another job. Or if the discrimination really set you back psychologically, and you have medical evidence to support this, you may be able to claim for years' worth of compensation.

We wouldn't want you to think, just because you read about very large payouts, that the same always applies to discrimination claims It doesn't!

Negotiating in discrimination cases

Being discriminated against, i.e. being treated less favourably or harassed because of a protected characteristic, is a serious claim to be made at an employment tribunal. It is taken very seriously by a judge and by society at large. Discrimination claims can be valuable, but also delicate and complicated, so any negotiations must be conducted carefully in order to have any chance of success.

Some key points in negotiating a settlement agreement for discrimination

The first thing we would say is that it's important for you to get your facts and allegations exactly right. You need to know what and why you are claiming, and how to prove it. Sometimes, this will not be readily apparent; therefore, you need to find out more information from your employer.

This is where the 'questions procedure' (previously known as discrimination questionnaires) under the Equality Act 2010 comes in. It is a formal, statutory procedure that you can use to ask questions about your employer; and your employer must answer, or 'adverse inferences' may be drawn. Adverse inferences means that any judge would be entitled to find that the employer was up to no good.

Commencing the questions procedure is a good negotiating tactic, as once your employer has a copy of your questions, they know that you mean business, and that you have fair technical knowledge – which means that you might be able to win a tribunal claim. It's sometimes a good idea to start the questions procedure and then commence without prejudice negotiations at the same time – this allows your employer the option of not having to investigate the questions, and therefore offers them the chance to keep the issues confidential.

If you simply want answers from the questions procedure, or want to wait tactically for the answers, as you believe this will put you in a stronger position, then wait for your employer to answer the questions and then use the answers, or the lack of answers, as the basis for your without prejudice letter. Remember, be strong but professional in tone, and try to support your allegations with evidence.

For more details on the questions procedure, see chapter 2 on evidence and also the ACAS booklet: *'Asking and responding to questions of discrimination in the workplace'* which you can download from: www.acas.org.uk

Make a claim while you're still in employment

With discrimination claims, if you're still employed then you can make a claim while your employment continues. This is a good negotiation tactic too, as it puts huge pressure on your employer: one of its employees is suing them and they are remaining in the company! The first instinct is to get rid of that employee, but they can't do this without victimising them, and thus increasing the likelihood of having to pay compensation. This is the perfect time for you to write a without prejudice letter and offer termination of employment in return for a good settlement package.

Discrimination claims can damage an employer's reputation and business

Being accused of, or found culpable of, discrimination is worrying for an employer. It can lead to a bad reputation and the possibility of further claims. If, using evidence and your knowledge of the law, you can show to your employer in correspondence that you have a case that has prospects of success in an employment tribunal, then your employer will probably want to settle the case.

What to do if discrimination negotiations become deadlocked

If negotiations become deadlocked when negotiating in a discrimination case, now is a good time to submit a grievance, a subject access request, and/or a questions procedure. If all of those have failed to secure the outcome you wanted, issue a claim in the employment tribunal or commence ACAS pre-claim conciliation. It will show your employer that you are serious and this often leads to an improved offer.

If you previously decided not to instruct a lawyer, now may be the time to consider instructing one if a deadlock has been reached.

To sum up: factors to consider

- Was this a one off event or has this been going on for months/years?

- Has anyone witnessed it?
- Have you complained about the treatment/asked that it should stop?
- When did it happen? (Consider tribunal time limits.)

9.2. Pregnancy and maternity discrimination

Introduction

Maternity and pregnancy discrimination is a very real issue experienced by women across the country. A shocking report published by the Equality and Human Rights Commission in 2017 found that 77% of mums felt that they had been discriminated against at work. Of this 77%, only 28% raised this with a manager, only 3% submitted a grievance and only 1% pursued it in an employment tribunal.

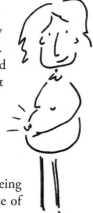

Legally, this type of discrimination is defined as being treated less favourably than other employees because of being pregnant or being on maternity leave.

It may become evident in any workplace circumstance, for example, during the recruitment process, in promotion exercises, training opportunities, selection for redundancy, or other types of dismissal.

Discriminatory or unfair treatment of a woman who is also pregnant or on maternity leave may also occur at any time during her pregnancy or maternity.

If you have been discriminated against or treated unfairly on these grounds and have the evidence to back it up, then you can use it to negotiate an exit settlement agreement if you decide you want to leave your employer. Alternatively, if all else fails you can bring a case against them in the employment tribunal.

What are your rights?

The legislation protecting women and new mothers in the workplace is extensive. However, for the purposes of identifying and making a claim against your employer, we will just focus here on the rights that tend to be most commonly breached by employers.

When you're pregnant

Employers are required by law to carry out adequate health and safety assessments. They should assess any risks that a pregnant woman may be exposed to in her working environment.

All pregnant employees also have a right to paid time off for antenatal care.

When you're on maternity leave

In total you are entitled to 12 months maternity leave. The first six months of your maternity leave is known as 'ordinary maternity leave'. The second six months is known as 'additional maternity leave'.

After your ordinary maternity leave you are entitled to return to your job. You can return to the job in which you were employed before your absence and on no less favourable terms. Your seniority and pension rights must be the same as if you had not been absent.

If you take additional maternity leave you are still entitled to return to your job. If you take between six and twelve months maternity leave you have the right to return to the same job, unless it is not reasonably practical for you to do so. If that's the case, then you have the right to return to another job which is suitable and appropriate for you in the circumstances. You're also entitled to return on terms and conditions that are no less favourable than those which would have applied had you not taken maternity leave. Your seniority, pension and other similar rights should also all be treated as if you had not been away.

Statutory paid annual leave continues to accrue. During both ordinary and additional maternity leave your paid annual leave continues to accrue.

If you are made redundant while on maternity leave you must be offered any suitable available vacancy. The terms and conditions (including capacity and place of work) must not be substantially less favourable than if you had continued in your old role. If you are put at risk of redundancy while on maternity leave your employer is still under a duty to consult with you and act fairly. If they do not, then the dismissal for redundancy could be unfair as well as discriminatory.

It's illegal for your employer to withhold benefits just because you are on maternity leave. If you're entitled to benefits such as pay rises, promotion or bonuses, it's illegal for your employer to withhold them as a result of your maternity leave.

What to do if your employer has breached your pregnancy/ maternity rights

Despite the low opinion in our society of employers who fail to uphold a woman's pregnancy/maternity rights, statistics show that discrimination and unfair treatment in such circumstances are quite common. However, as mentioned, many women simply don't raise any breaches with their employer, as their employer's poor treatment of them may well mean that they would simply rather not work there any more. Instead, they would prefer just to move on and start afresh with an employer who places greater value on working mums.

If that is your experience, we would encourage you to at least approach your employer inviting them to have a without prejudice discussion about a settlement agreement.

TOP 3 TIPS

- In general, you have the right to return to the same job after maternity leave
- If you do face discrimination try to negotiate a settlement agreement before moving on
- Ensure any settlement agreement does not require the repayment of any enhanced maternity pay

---

Negotiating a settlement for pregnancy and maternity discrimination

New mothers who take a year out of the office often return to find that they are no longer wanted by their employer, or that they are to be made 'redundant'. If this were to happen to you, it could have significant adverse financial, career and other implications.

Also, if your employer wants you to leave, they are highly likely to suggest a settlement agreement while you're still on maternity leave. That is, of course, a time when you probably have neither the time nor the energy to participate in protracted negotiations.

In order to substantiate any claims you may make about maternity discrimination, you can also follow the advice we offer in chapter 2 on how to collect and present supporting evidence, and also in chapter 1 on how to construct a without prejudice letter – which you will need if and when you commence negotiations.

Remember, discrimination on the grounds of maternity is common, and yet is also seen as one of the worst things an employer can do. The last thing your employer wants is to be held to have discriminated against a pregnant woman, or new mother, as this looks bad to the general public, customers, clients and, most importantly, the rest of its workforce.

The reason that very few cases of maternity discrimination end up in the employment tribunal is not because such discrimination is not rife (it is), it's because employers almost always agree to settle.

Tips for negotiating a settlement agreement

- **Consider if your employer paid you an enhanced rate of maternity pay.** If your employer paid you an enhanced rate, is it repayable if you don't return to work for a certain period of time after your maternity leave ends? If so, make sure there is a clause in the settlement agreement which says that you do not have to repay the enhanced package.
- **Make sure you keep all documentary evidence.** Do you have an email from your manager saying that your duties have

been allocated to someone else? Has HR confirmed a change in job role? If so, then make sure you keep records of this.

- **Submit a formal grievance to your employer.** This creates a paper trail and puts on record your complaints of maternity or pregnancy discrimination. In addition, if your employer treats you badly because you sent a grievance, then you may be able to also claim that you have been 'victimised' as result of raising concerns about maternity discrimination.

- **Emphasise to your employers the impact that their treatment has had on you.** In discrimination cases you can claim compensation for 'injury to feelings'. The greater the impact of the discrimination, the more compensation you should be entitled to.

- **Be willing to compromise.** Aim high, but you may have to compromise in order to do a deal and reach a settlement with your employer.

9.3. Disability discrimination

Introduction

The law requires employers to make 'reasonable adjustments' to accommodate employees who have a disability. There are three types of adjustments:

1. To property and premises e.g. installing a lift in the office.
2. To provide auxiliary aids e.g. provision of alternative equipment such as an ergonomic chair.
3. To practices and policies e.g. changing the employee's job description to vary duties.

What is 'reasonable' when it comes to making reasonable adjustments is not defined in law and will depend on the circumstances of the case such as the nature of the adjustment, the costs involved, the size and resources available to the employer etc. Each case will be different and what is reasonable for one employer in one set of circumstances is not necessarily the same for another employer.

Advice for disabled employees needing reasonable adjustments

The first thing to do is to ensure your employer is aware of your disability. If your employer is not aware of your condition they can't be held responsible for not making reasonable adjustments. Not every condition will constitute a disability. The legal definition under the Equality Act 2010 is 'a long term physical or mental impairment which has a substantial and adverse impact on the employee's ability to carry out day to day activities'.

The next thing is to assess what difficulties you are facing in your job or workplace due to your disability and consider the options as to what changes would alleviate those difficulties.

For example it could be that you have a condition which makes it difficult for you comfortably to use existing office equipment such as the desk and chair provided, and that you need specially designed ergonomic equipment.

Another example could be that you have more absences than non-disabled colleagues due to your condition and you want your employer to make an adjustment to the attendance policy to relax the attendance requirements/targets in your case, so that you are not subject to the same process as that which would apply to other colleagues. In a recent case (see below) the employee could not perform his job role any longer due to his disability so was offered another role within the organisation.

Once you have identified your disability and proposed any solutions to your employer, it will then be for the employer to make a decision. A good employer would refer the matter to an occupational health assessor for a medical opinion on the disability and what steps would constitute a reasonable adjustment.

In the event that your employer does not seek a medical assessment, or the outcome of the assessment is not one you agree with, then you could source a medical opinion to support your position yourself, for example from your GP. In the event that there is conflicting opinion between two medical assessments, then your employer will have some leeway to choose which opinion to follow.

You could also seek out support and guidance from organisations, such as Disability Rights UK and the Equalities and Human Rights Commission, which can provide useful information and signposting. Access to Work is a scheme under which employees can secure specific funding to help employers make reasonable adjustments subject to assessment.

Reasonable adjustments to job roles and pay protection: new case law

Is an employer who moves an employee to a new post, due to the employee's disability, required to pay that employee the same salary as for the old post even if the new post has a lower salary (called 'pay protection')? In a recent ruling, the Employment Appeal Tribunal decided that an employer who had moved an employee from a job he could no longer perform due to his disability, to another less skilled and lower paid role, should have continued to offer pay protection to that employee, and that it was therefore disability discrimination to have implemented a wage cut.

The tribunal said that there was no reason in principle why pay protection could not constitute a reasonable adjustment. However the tribunal did not say pay protection had to carry on permanently. The matter had to be judged according to the circumstances of the case at any given time and changed circumstances might mean the adjustment ceased to be a reasonable one which the employer was obliged to make.

These kinds of intellectually complicated results in tribunal hearings are exactly the sorts of reasons why it's better for everyone to reach a negotiated settlement rather than run the gauntlet of the court system.

If you are having problems at work due to your disability

If your employer is not acknowledging or addressing your situation, you should in the first instance raise a grievance formally setting out your complaints (see chapter 3 on grievances). Most employers will have written grievance and equalities policies that outline the correct complaints process.

In the case of a failure to make reasonable adjustments, the deadline for submitting an employment tribunal claim is three months less one day from the date the employer made the decision not to offer the reasonable adjustment to you. This deadline will not be suspended just because you are raising a grievance about the situation, so legal action must not be delayed even if you have started an internal complaint.

9.4. Age discrimination

Introduction

As the working population ages, due to longer lives and later retirement ages, age discrimination is becoming more prevalent and so it's even more important to be aware of the motivations behind your employer's actions. An increased focus on digital processes and a demand for a younger, cheaper workforce could both be seen as factors leading to age discrimination.

The Equality Act 2010 protects everyone against age discrimination in the workplace. Age discrimination at work which results in termination of employment would count as unfair dismissal as well as discrimination.

Types of age discrimination at work

Age discrimination can be experienced in several ways, and is most common in older employees, but can be experienced by anyone. As mentioned earlier in this chapter, the Equality Act 2010 states that discrimination can come in any of four forms, namely: direct and indirect discrimination, harassment and victimisation. In what follows, each of these categories is applied to age discrimination.

Direct age discrimination

This is when an individual acting on behalf of an employer is treating someone less favourably than others because of their age, and is unfortunately a behaviour that is still surprisingly common in the workplace. A situation to be aware of, for example, would be if a younger employee is promoted ahead of you even though you have an equal track record. This could be direct age discrimination if it is based partly or purely on the ages of the employees.

For this type of age discrimination to be present you have to be able to compare yourself with colleagues who are similar in characteristics/experience, but who differ in age. Unlike any other type of discrimination (such as race, sex or religion), direct age discrimination can legally be 'justified' by your employer, but only if there are good objective grounds for the age discrimination. This can be difficult for your employer to prove and so they will often offer a settlement agreement to you if you can put forward a good case and negotiate well with the facts at your disposal.

Indirect age discrimination

This is when an employer or individual is putting rules or arrangements in place that apply to everyone, but that put someone of a certain age at an unfair disadvantage. An example would be only to offer a certain training programme to employees who are within three years of graduating, as this is likely to discriminate against older employees.

It is irrelevant whether the discrimination was intentional or not. It is again necessary to compare your situation with colleagues who are similar but who differ in age. Indirect age discrimination can also be objectively justified by your employer. An example of this type of justification is as follows:

You are in your early fifties and want to apply for a job which you're well qualified to do. The only problem is that the job description requires applicants to have a degree, which you haven't got. Because of changes in higher education policy in recent years, you are much more likely to have a degree if you are under 40 years old than are people over 40. So this is potentially an example of age discrimination. It could be justified by an employer if they needed to recruit more staff with degrees in order to meet funding criteria.

Age discrimination: harassment

This describes unwanted behaviour linked to your age that violates your dignity, or creates a hostile, intimidating or degrading environment for you to work in. The unwanted behaviour could be classified as offensive, intimidating, or distressing. Common examples of age harassment at work could include age-related derogatory nicknames (e.g. 'Grandad'), or comments about natural signs of ageing such as wrinkles, grey hair etc.

An employee experiencing age discrimination in the form of harassment at work might be excluded from meetings or social events because of their age. Pressure to retire could also, dependant on other circumstances involved, be seen as age discrimination.

An important update to the Equality Act 2010 is that it has been extended to include age-related harassment not only by other employees at your place of work, but also by clients, customers or suppliers. If you make an official report/complaint of these behaviours to your employer and they take no action after at least three occasions (all which have been reported by you), they may be liable for age discrimination.

Age discrimination: victimisation

This is when you are treated unfairly by your employer, or by an individual acting on your employer's behalf, because you have previously complained about discrimination or harassment (or it is believed by others that you made a complaint). The complaint or grievance that you may have made about age discrimination needn't have been about yourself for you to experience victimisation. This area is slightly different from the others above, as when assessing your treatment, the law does not compare how you have been treated in comparison to other similar colleagues.

Can age discrimination at work ever be justified?

With direct, indirect and harassment age discrimination, any behaviour from your employer or colleagues based on your 'perceived age' can also count as age discrimination.

As you can see, it's possible for your employer to objectively justify various types of age discrimination. This, however, does not mean that their justification will stand up in legal argument. This is where the advice of an employment lawyer can make a world of difference.

Although the Equality Act 2010 is rightly in place to protect employees against age discrimination, the law in the UK also recognises that in some instances it is necessary and justifiable to discriminate on the basis of age either directly or indirectly. On the UK government's website, www.gov.co.uk, the reason for this is explained as follows: 'The ban on age discrimination is designed to ensure that the new law prohibits only harmful treatment that results in genuinely unfair discrimination because of age. It does not outlaw the many instances of different treatment that are justifiable or beneficial.'

In the case of age discrimination at work, an employer would have to prove that there was objective justification (see 9.1.) for the differential treatment. The employer would have to prove that discriminating against you because of your age was a 'proportionate means of achieving a legitimate aim'. This however can be very hard to do, so the odds are in your favour.

A difference in the treatment of an employee due to their age is also counted as lawful if it was a 'positive action measure', for example providing access to certain training. Though if this is the case with you then it's unlikely that you would want to take action against your employer!

Still at work? Correct process for dealing with age discrimination

It can be tricky to prove the acts and also the effects of age discrimination, but if you have the evidence and are prepared to negotiate with your employer along the lines set out earlier in this book, you could be well on the way to achieving a settlement. Make sure that you keep as many records as you can of all events (see chapter 2 on collecting evidence) and put together a robust without prejudice letter in the first instance. If that doesn't work then you can 'up the ante' with a grievance letter, discrimination questions procedure and/or a subject access request.

Are you being forced out of work because of your age?

There is no national retirement age at which your employer can require you to retire. In some circumstances your employer may be able to justify having a retirement age for their employees but this can be difficult to do. Even if your employer has a retirement age they are likely to be nervous about whether or not they can justify it.

If you are being asked to retire in accordance with your employer's retirement age you may still be able to negotiate an ex gratia payment because your employer will not want to risk a tribunal finding that their retirement age is not justified. If your employer does not have a retirement age there is no basis for them to ask you.

If you have had your employment terminated, and think that this is because of your age, then, in addition to a discrimination claim you could make a case for unfair dismissal.

Your rights if you are over 65 years of age

If you are over the age of 65 and are employed, you are still covered by the protection of the Equality Act 2010. Even after you have reached your employer's normal retirement age for your position (if they have one), you retain the right to make a claim for unfair dismissal.

You likewise still have the right to claim the statutory minimum redundancy payment if you are made redundant. Employers are also not allowed to discriminate in respect to the benefits they provide for employees over 65, except to the extent this can be objectively justified.

─────────────── **TOP 3 TIPS** ───────────────

- Age discrimination can occur at any age
- Age discrimination can sometimes be justified, so seek legal advice to assess your position
- You can't be forced to retire at any age unless your employer has a justified retirement age

9.5. Long-term sickness absence

Introduction

Instances of long-term sickness absences from work, including for example absences due to mental health problems such as stress, depression and anxiety, are increasing and have been doing so for many years. This has inevitably led to more negotiations in circumstances where you are absent from work for weeks or even months, and want to know how to bring the situation to a conclusion in the best possible way – both financially and with the least possible stress.

In these circumstances, the first area you should look at is your sick pay. How much is there left, and at what rate (full or partial pay)? This is the most important factor for you to consider, because if you have a long time left to go on full pay, there is less rush to commence negotiations at this stage. On the other hand, if you are about to run out of company sick pay and go onto statutory sick pay, you need to open negotiations now or risk losing out financially and missing a good opportunity.

Timing is critical

It is vital to act at the right time in these sorts of cases. Remember, while you remain on company sick pay and don't work, you are a financial burden to the company and the company will want to end this situation as soon as possible. However, as soon as your company sick pay runs out, you are no longer a financial burden and the company can simply bide its time and dismiss you under performance/absence procedures. So, the question of when to start negotiations is key in these cases.

Ideally, you want to commence negotiations when you have been absent from work for sufficient time for your employer to contemplate that you might not be returning to work, but have enough company sick pay left for them to see you as an ongoing budgetary liability.

If your employer has secretly decided that you are not coming back, and has in effect replaced you with someone else, this is also an ideal time to start negotiations. Your employer does not want you back as you do not fit into their plans. The prospect of you returning therefore causes problems for them, and so your employer is much more likely to open its wallet to make you an ex gratia payment for leaving. This is not only more convenient for them, but it also removes the need for them to change their plans or admit that there is actually no longer a place for you in the company.

So, timing is hugely important, and also the prospect of you returning to work is often a key motivating factor for your employer to offer a settlement agreement. That said, it is often the case that an employer will not make the first move regarding settlement negotiations when an employee is on long-term sick leave, as the employer does not want to be accused of disability discrimination.

Does your employer have insurance to pay your salary while off sick?

Your employer may well have taken out insurance against your absence, in which case an external insurer will often pay around 70% of your wages once you have been absent for a certain period of time. If this threshold has been reached, then often you will effectively be negotiating with the insurer, who has taken over liability for your wages, although your employer will actually be dealing with the insurer directly, not you. So, you may not realise it, but it will be the insurer, behind the scenes, who is making the decisions about how much to offer you.

In these cases, the insurer will sometimes make a global offer of compensation to terminate your employment as it reduces their liability and gets you off their books. This sum will then be paid to you by your employer, who will receive it from the insurer. You may also be able to negotiate an additional sum from your employer, as well as your notice and accrued holiday pay, and so leave with a good exit package.

Making the first move in negotiating a settlement agreement

The first move is often for the employee to make, which is why it is you who needs to get the timing correct. Sometimes, your employer will mention the possibility of a settlement agreement in a welfare meeting, but not always, so don't wait for them to make the first move or you may miss your chance to secure the best possible deal.

You should write a without prejudice letter to your employer suggesting that the time is probably right for you to move on given the circumstances, and that you would welcome a discussion or correspondence about a settlement agreement.

In these circumstances, you may not want to suggest a figure for an ex gratia payment. Instead, merely suggest that you want to open negotiations and let your employer make the first move in terms of figures. That way, your employer will feel in control of the situation, even though it is you who is making the first move. You can then negotiate upwards from the figure that they suggest.

If you have serious medical issues, and especially serious mental health issues, your employer is more likely to ask you to instruct a lawyer, as it would not want to be seen as taking advantage of you, and therefore discriminating against you.

Mental health absence

Mental health is one of the most challenging issues of our times, accepted by parliament and the NHS to be a national (and indeed global) epidemic. Yet, if you take time off for stress or depression or reveal any other sort of mental illness, doors will quickly slam in your face in the workplace. Many employers dislike mental health sickness because they cannot see the problem and therefore doubt whether it actually exists.

While all but the most heartless and unscrupulous of employers would allow an employee to take time off following a cancer diagnosis, support them through the treatment, and welcome them back to work, the same cannot be said for issues of mental health.

Regrettably, a significant number of our clients over the years have fallen ill because of stress, usually stress at work. They have found that their employer's reaction, while paying lip-service to the usual requirements (so as not to fall foul of disability discrimination) has in fact been far from supportive, leading to the employee being marginalised and stigmatised.

If you are reading this and are currently signed off work with a stress related illness, or with anxiety or depression, we realise that this is not the sort of thing you want to hear. However, while some employers deal with their employees' mental health issues very well, the majority do not.

Some think the employee is imagining it or even manufacturing the issue, in order to take time off or to try to obtain an exit package. Others simply cannot countenance an employee with diagnosed mental health issues returning to work and working in a business where a mistake could cost money.

Obtaining a settlement agreement because of mental health issues

In these circumstances, it's vitally important for you to ensure that the link between your illness and the offer of a settlement agreement is clearly recognised by your employer. HR professionals are wary of being accused of disability discrimination and having to go to an employment tribunal and justify their actions. Often the company will settle any claims or any threats of a claim well before this is necessary. There is arguably a premium to be paid by the employer if it offers a settlement agreement to someone who has diagnosed mental health issues, and you should not let your employer under-settle any claim you have.

Chapter 10

Whistleblowing

Introduction

Whistleblowing is one way of making sure that your employer's malpractice comes to an end. At the same time you can leave your job and hopefully receive a settlement agreement to tide you over until you find a new role. Blowing the whistle is a noble effort, and there is nothing wrong with getting something in return, but the path of a whistleblower can be fraught with difficulty.

It is surprising how many employers would rather take their chances with bad publicity than pay off what they regard as a 'troublesome' employee with a settlement agreement. We explore below some of the theory and legal dimensions of whistleblowing, along with strategies and tactics for how to blow the whistle and negotiate a settlement agreement. Financial compensation for whistleblowing, along with all other types of exit package, is discussed in chapter 4 on how much you should get in your settlement agreement.

What is whistleblowing?

In UK employment law, whistleblowing is 'making a protected disclosure' under PIDA (the Public Interest Disclosure Act). This act itself amended the Employment Rights Act 1996, so it is the ERA 1996 which you may also find yourself referring to.

In essence the disclosure needs to be in the public interest, and be something dishonest or unreliable which people should know about. It is not just restricted to criminal activity, such as fraud, but it can also be a breach of regulations or civil law, such as discrimination in the workplace, or health and safety breaches.

In most instances, once you have blown the whistle on malpractice, your employer will take steps to put right the wrongs which it has committed. So although you are not exposing them to public scrutiny (e.g. through the media) at least you are stopping the wrongdoing from occuring.

TOP 3 TIPS

- You can only 'blow the whistle' about matters in the public interest – not about your own mistreatment
- No minimum length of service is required to bring a whistleblowing claim
- Seek legal advice – it is a complicated area of the law

Whistleblowing and constructive or unfair dismissal

Often, once you have become a whistleblower, you are mistreated by your employer to the extent that you feel forced to resign, or, more rarely, you are actually dismissed. Most employers guilty of mistreatment will not go as far as to dismiss you because that would look too obvious, and of course they will deny any mistreatment should you bring a claim for constructive dismissal. But it is quite a difficult legal test to fulfil in a tribunal, so the detriments must be fairly serious in order to justify your resignation.

Suffering a detriment, bullying or harassment

Being mistreated, bullied or harassed by your employer, or even by your colleagues, because you have blown the whistle, is a breach of s.47B of PIDA, which is designed to protect whistleblowers. This means that you are able to claim compensation for such mistreatment, even if you haven't been forced out of your job. So you can issue an employment tribunal claim for victimisation while you are still employed, exactly like with discrimination claims. Staying employed while running a tribunal claim against your employer is very handy for negotiating an exit package.

The meaning of a 'detriment' is a very wide one: it is any treatment which would objectively make you feel that, in continuing your employment, you are being disadvantaged. It could be anything from being told off and ostracised, to being passed over for promotion or frankly anything at all which could be construed as a disadvantage.

Minimum length of service

The normal length of service requirements don't apply in a whistleblowing case, so where you would normally have to be employed for two years in order to claim constructive or unfair dismissal, in a whistleblowing case there is no minimum service requirement. This is very helpful to get you over that two years' service rule in a negotiation (or tribunal). However:

- **If you've been employed for under two years**: you may have to prove that you resigned (or were dismissed) as a detriment following on from blowing the whistle. In other words, if you report a wrongdoing and then the employer genuinely corrects their behaviour, without subjecting you to any detriments, then you won't be entitled to resign and claim constructive dismissal.

- **If you have more than two years' service**: you are entitled to resign in disgust at the behaviour of the employer and then claim constructive dismissal, regardless of whether you have actually been victimised as a result of whistleblowing or not. Even in this situation you will be expected to have blown the whistle before you step down.

Whistleblowing and protected conversations

Under s.11A(3) of the Employment Rights Act 1996, whistleblowing is an exception to the rule about protected conversations (see chapter 1).

In a normal unfair dismissal case, your employer has immunity from revealing in court any discussions with you about leaving your job in exchange for a pay-off contained within a settlement agreement. In whistleblowing claims however, this additional protection for the employer goes out the window, and the only way they can keep such discussions away from the judge's ears (if the case ever gets to court) is to claim that they were without prejudice.

Essentially this means there has to have been an existing dispute, such as a disciplinary or grievance process being instigated. If the employer comes out of the blue to offer you a deal in exchange for leaving quietly, there's every chance that a good employment lawyer could use this to your advantage.

Evidence

Evidence will be a key feature if you are to stand any chance of winning. The employer will often be armed to the teeth with lawyers so you can do no better than be armed with hard evidence of the wrongdoing. Nowadays a lot of business is done by email so you might be able to get together a portfolio of documentation to support your claim. Other possible forms of evidence that you could use are discussed further in chapter 2 on how to build a case using evidence.

Unscrupulous employers can make threats of legal action against whistleblowers, including claims over documents disclosed to third parties, and these strong-arm tactics can be difficult to stand up to.

But the Public Interest Disclosure Act, referred to earlier, provides that if an employee obtains confidential documents, this will not be counted as a breach of their contract of employment so long as the documents are disclosed to an appropriate person and/or used in a whistleblowing employment tribunal.

When it comes to witnesses, you'd be lucky to have any step forward, but that kind of luck can be just what you need to win your case. Sometimes there are two or more whistleblowers, or in big companies there may be other employees who are unhappy at work and can provide vital background, or even direct, experience of the type of wrongdoing reported.

Dealing with the media

This can be a very daunting experience and frankly very difficult to handle. A reputable employment lawyer will have good connections with the press, from tabloid and broadsheet, to websites and magazines, and might be able to use these connections to threaten media attention and help bring about a solid settlement agreement in your favour.

Often just the thought of you going to the press can be enough to influence the employer to sweeten the deal. At other times it can be necessary to get the media involved in the first place, either to ramp up the pressure on the employer or to do some investigative journalism and actually dig up evidence to help in your claim. Unfortunately it is quite common for the employee to think that they have a very newsworthy story but journalists, and even the employer, don't take much interest in it at all.

Dealing with the authorities

You are probably considering whether to report the foul play to the authorities in order to make sure it doesn't happen again and also to clear your own name from any involvement. This is certainly something your lawyer will want to consider carefully with you. It could be a useful exercise to understand more about what kind of evidence you would need to prove significant wrongdoing. It may also be that any settlement agreement negotiations could be affected by such a move. While it may be preferable to report matters to the authorities, you may prefer to get your employer to admit that they're wrong, by agreeing to settle your claims, and leave it at that, taking no further action. At least that way the wrongdoing has stopped and you have moved on swiftly.

Gagging clauses in settlement agreements

Settlement agreements won't expressly stipulate that you can't report your employer to the authorities, but effectively that would be the compromise which you would be entering into if you decided to accept a payment from them in return for leaving quietly. This is a difficult point to understand and to implement in practice. Basically an employer never has any guarantees that you won't report them, even after you sign a settlement agreement. They would not be allowed, for example, to claim the settlement money back because you reported their fraud after you received your settlement payment. Therefore there has to be an element of trust involved when settling a whistleblowing claim. For that reason it's even more important not to burn your bridges.

Negotiating in whistleblowing cases

Whistleblowing is a complex and technical area. For example, compiling sufficient evidence to demonstrate detriments or dismissal for whistleblowing and then ensuring that this evidence fits the highly-complex legal tests is very difficult. It therefore follows that to negotiate in circumstances in which whistleblowing discrimination has been alleged, is also very hard. Even getting your employer to understand your case can be difficult, because the law in this area requires evidence to be set out in a certain way.

It is important to put together a strong and accurate ET1 (employment tribunal claim form) and particulars of claim document for use in whistleblowing employment tribunals. This is the document which starts off your claim. It is necessary to identify the 'protected disclosures' made (when you reported the wrongdoing) and also the 'detriments' (any victimisation you suffered as a result). Additionally it's important to set out which laws have allegedly been broken by the employer.

What's called a 'Scott Schedule' (a type of table usually used to present the allegations) is used. This usually takes the form of an spreadsheet setting out:

1. A list of the illegal activities, with specific reference to which section of PIDA has been breached in each instance.

2. A list of the protected disclosures; meaning the time, date, place and how you reported it and who to. This list should refer back to the list of illegal activities.

3. A list of the detriments; meaning the instances of victimisation which you suffered, by who, where and when. This list should refer back to the list of disclosures – you have to specify which detriments were done to you in relation to the above disclosures.

Chapter 11

Restrictive covenants

Introduction

Restrictive covenants are a common feature in contracts of employment and to a lesser extent in consultancy contracts. They may also be referred to as non-compete, non-solicitation, non-poaching and confidentiality agreements or clauses.

They restrict you from doing certain things after the termination of your employment. As a result, restrictive covenants often feature in settlement agreements, when your employer will ask you to reaffirm the restrictions which already apply to you. They may even want to insert new ones at this late stage in the employment relationship.

What restrictive covenants prevent you from doing

Restrictive covenants tend to relate to poaching and prevent you from taking the following with you when you leave:

- Clients
- Suppliers
- Colleagues

Where you have access to particularly sensitive confidential information, restrictive covenants can also prevent you from working for a competitor for a very limited period of time.

Believe it or not, the common law position (that's the position which would exist if your contract was completely silent about restrictive covenants) is that you are allowed to take clients, suppliers and colleagues with you.

This is not what corporations would have you think, but in fact we live in a free market economy in which the individual is perfectly entitled to take business away from other companies, because such choice is good for the consumer. In fact there are EU directives banning anti-competitive practices like monopolies.

While you are still employed, however, you are prevented from doing the above activities by the common law, which implies a duty of loyalty into the employment contract, also known as a duty of trust and confidence. Once the employment contract is over (i.e. if you resign or are dismissed) then these duties fall away, and that is why any restrictive covenants will operate after the effective termination date (EDT).

When restrictive covenants may be unenforceable

Restrictive covenants which are too restrictive, or 'too wide', will tend to be viewed as unenforceable by the courts and tribunals. The definition of 'too wide' varies from case to case but here are a few pointers:

- **Industry-wide restrictions**: any clause which seeks to prevent you from working in the same industry is highly likely to be unenforceable unless you have access to particularly sensitive confidential information.

- **Restrictions which last too long**: generally three to six months would be an acceptable restriction length (assuming that the other criteria listed here are met) and anything over a year would be too much. A year would be quite a long time and may be unenforceable.

- **Your own contacts**: companies often place restrictions on you when it comes to contacts with people you have met while working for them. If, however, the contact was your own prior to your working for them, then they can't easily restrict you from dealing with that person.

- **Confidential information**: this is generally retained by the company whether there is a restrictive covenant in the contract of employment or not. The company has common law rights that it can assert in order to protect its confidential information. There are some grey areas however, for example the contact numbers stored in your phone. Also if someone contacts you (rather than you contacting them) then you can't be said to have used confidential information to get hold of them. Other examples of confidential information include:

  - Lists of clients
  - Prices lists
  - Business plans

But businesses cannot stop you using what's stored in your head!

TOP 3 TIPS

- If the restriction is for more than six months, it may be invalid
- Clauses which effectively stop you from working also tend to be invalid
- Restrictions on dealing with clients and suppliers are quite standard – check your contract

---

Practical tips for employees on restrictive covenants

If you're thinking of leaving your employer and either setting up on your own or joining a competitor, you should firstly review your employment contract for restrictive covenants. The last thing you need when starting a new venture is a claim against you. The costs and time spent in defending an application for an injunction and subsequently trying the issues can be exorbitant – and certainly large enough to curtail or even prevent your career plans – so ensure that you comply with the restraints. (See the example on the following page of what's likely to happen if you get served with an injunction.)

If you think the covenants in your contract are too wide or likely to make it too difficult for you, take legal advice. Don't breach the covenants without expert advice on what the consequences of doing so might be.

Some key dos and don'ts

Don't assume that communications via text, Skype and WhatsApp will not be traced. Any written record may be recovered so don't put anything in writing that you wouldn't be happy to have read out in court.

Don't be tempted to take any confidential information from your employer.

Do expect your phone records to be reviewed and be careful about who you are phoning and texting.

Do keep a clear record of all the steps you have taken to set up your new business so you can show you did not breach your restraints.

Do take legal advice to ensure your new venture gets off to the best possible start.

Restrictive covenants and High Court injunctions

If you breach the restrictive covenants in your contract of employment and your ex-employer really doesn't like it, they might decide to apply for an injunction in the High Court. This is scary stuff for you because you will receive a letter essentially threatening you to stand down, failing which you will be sued, and all within an extremely short time frame.

If this happens, then you need to contact a good employment lawyer immediately, because in the world of High Court injunctions, things can happen very fast.

Here is the process set out for you, with some example timings (actual timings may vary):

Day 1: You leave your job and breach your restrictive covenant/s.

Day 2: Your ex-employer writes to you and sets out how, in their opinion, you have breached the restrictive covenants in your contract of employment. This is normally by taking either clients, colleagues, or lists of data.

Day 3: You instruct your lawyer to write to your ex-employer. Often this has the effect of ending the matter, because a good lawyer would point out the ways in which you are not in breach of your restrictive covenants and/or ways in which the restrictive covenant clauses themselves are drafted too vaguely or too widely so as to be unenforceable or not applicable. However if this doesn't work then the matter moves to the next stage.

Day 5: You give 'undertakings' to the other side assuring them that you won't breach the restraints or use any property which you have allegedly taken (client lists etc.) until an interim injunction hearing.

Day 12: The interim injunction hearing takes place in the High Court. At this hearing a judge will decide whether or not to impose restrictions on you pending the full hearing of the matter. This hearing may not be necessary if acceptable undertakings can be agreed between the parties.

1 month later: Often the High Court judge will order that a second hearing is required after the interim injunction hearing to ensure that orders have been complied with and that any restrictions imposed continue to meet what's called the 'balance of convenience' test. This is particularly the case involving urgent applications on short notice at which the judge has made wide-ranging orders.

3-6 months later: The full trial takes place at the High Court. This will decide whether to release you from the restrictions imposed or to keep them. In practice, by this time the actual restrictions themselves will probably have worn off because they were only stated to last six months in the first place. So a lot of the point of this hearing is to determine, with hindsight, who was right at the interim hearing six months previously.

If you were right then your ex-employer will have to compensate you for the money you lost by having the restrictions placed upon you and for your legal fees. If you lose then you will now have to pay the legal fees of your opponent and any damages that you are found to have caused your ex-employer by acting in breach of your restrictions.

At any time: These cases can settle at any time during the above process. The negotiations themselves take place throughout the process, in the background, and are normally concluded by signing a type of settlement agreement.

Unlike the other employment exit scenarios outlined in this book, the way to negotiate an exit package in restrictive covenant cases is not always the way set out in Part One. In some restrictive covenant scenarios you are trying to negotiate yourself a deal – in much the same way as outlined in Part One – and you're using your restrictive covenants as a bargaining chip. Whereas in other restrictive covenant situations, you may be defending a claim made against you, rather than trying to negotiate a deal for yourself.

PART
THREE

Case studies and examples of documents used in negotiations and employment tribunals

Introduction

To conclude the book, we offer a selection of examples of letters and other documents used in negotiating a settlement agreement and also in making a tribunal claim. (Additional examples are provided on our website.)

We also present two case studies based on real cases that we have undertaken. The point of including these is to illustrate the progress of negotiations from the time that you start negotiating through to achieving your goal of a settlement agreement. You can track this process in the case studies along with the relevant letters and other documents that were exchanged during the negotiation.

Chapter 12

Examples of letters and documents used in settlement negotiations

12.1. Without prejudice letter examples

We present below four examples of 'without prejudice' letters written by our lawyers on behalf of employees in disputes with their employers (suitably anonymised of course). The examples given deal with: unfair redundancy; performance; unfair dismissal/end of secondment; and race discrimination.

Without prejudice letter: example 1
Unfair redundancy

[Lawyer email address]

To [HR Manager]
[Company]

By email only
[Company email address]
[Date]

Without Prejudice

Dear Sirs,

Re: Our Client: [Employee]

We represent your employee, [Employee].

We are aware that the company is making redundancies in certain areas; however, we remind you that in order for a dismissal to constitute a redundancy, the company must either be no longer undertaking the work that the employee undertakes, or the company's requirement for the employee to perform work of a specific type has ceased or diminished.

As you are aware, [Employee] is presently Director of [Specialism] for [Company]. He is therefore a unique employee in the sense that no other employee is currently employed in a similar or equivalent role. His role and responsibilities include [summary of key roles and responsibilities].

We are instructed that, although revenues have struggled significantly over the last financial year across the business due to a challenging trading environment, [Employee's] division corresponds to more than half of the company's revenue. While we have no information on the company's plans, those plans not having been divulged, we contend that it is highly likely that [Employee's] roles and responsibilities will continue to be performed in a substantially similar manner and within a similar role moving forward.

Given that [Employee] occupies a unique role and it is likely that his duties will continue at the company, we are surprised that no information relating to the proposed company structure after [Employee's] proposed termination has been provided to enable him to assess his situation and respond accordingly. We respectfully suggest, therefore, that the company's proposition is not so much the result of a redundancy exercise or a proposed redundancy exercise that would result in the elimination of [Employee's] role and responsibilities, but a proposed termination of his employment for other reasons. We note that performance issues have not been raised with [Employee] in any official capacity during his employment, nor has [Employee] been subject to any disciplinary allegations or any other process that may result in his fair dismissal from employment.

Given there has been no consultation and no divulgence of any information in relation to company structure or the redistribution of [Employee's] work, we are not in a position to advise [Employee] as to whether the offer of a settlement agreement is in his interests or not.

That said, our client understands that if it is the decision of the board that his time at the company has come to an end then, for practical purposes, he must face the reality of the situation and look to move on with his career elsewhere; however, in the circumstances, the offer by the company of less than two months' salary in addition to his three months' notice by way of compensation for the termination of his employment is far from adequate.

Our client is effectively prevented from working in his chosen field for four months by clause 9 and the appendix to the terms of his contract. Furthermore, the present state of the industry in [Location] and the four-month restriction period mean that [Employee] will be unemployed for a significant period of time immediately after his termination date, causing him to miss out on employment opportunities and exacerbating the likelihood of significant losses during the first year of his unemployment.

Regardless of the four-month restriction period, it is going to take a significant amount of time, most likely up to a year, to finally obtain suitable alternative employment in [Location]. The recruitment consultants that [Employee] has consulted have confirmed this to be accurate. It is highly likely that any salary [Employee] manages to achieve will be substantially less than the salary he presently enjoys, meaning that he will have a substantial ongoing loss as a result of the decision to terminate his employment.

Were the company to move to dismiss [Employee] for reasons of redundancy at this stage, we would respectfully contend that, on the information presently available to us, the dismissal would likely be held to be unfair by an Employment Tribunal. Given [Employee's] salary, it would only take a period of four and a half months of unemployment in the next twelve months, or a longer period of employment on a significantly lower salary, for his losses to reach the statutory cap. We note that notice does not apply to the statutory cap. Given the uncertainty in his future employment and the lack of information available in relation to the continuation of his role, it is not currently in [Employee's] interests to accept the present offer of less than two months' salary by way of compensation for termination of his employment.

By way of an alternative offer, we would propose the following:

1. A Termination Payment of £80,000.
2. PILON to be made as per the company's original offer.
3. A Termination Date of 30 June 2017 and the swift conclusion of all outstanding matters.
4. That [Employee's] telephone number is assigned to him.
5. That [Employee] retains his laptop and phone.
6. That [Employee] keeps his health insurance for 6 months.

7. That the company and [Employee] agree an external announcement regarding him leaving (to be released at a date of [Employee's] choosing but no more than two months after the Termination Date), and an internal announcement to be made on the Termination Date.

8. In respect of future awards, [Employee] would like for the company to undertake to give him due credit for the work undertaken on the following projects: [List of projects.]

We understand that it is plainly in the interests of both parties to come to an agreement in relation to the termination of [Employee's] employment that is both fair to [Employee] and enables him to adhere to his restrictions in his contract of employment and seek work in a challenging environment without financial pressure, and enables the company to move forward in the manner it so choses without committing further time and resources to this matter over time.

We look forward to hearing from you.

Yours faithfully,

[Lawyer]

Without prejudice letter: example 2 Performance issues

Note that the example below is quite a technical legal letter, but sometimes that's what it takes to succeed. You would probably need the help of an employment law specialist to successfully argue a case such as this.

FAO [HR Manager]
[Company]

By email only

[Company email address]

[Date]

Without Prejudice

Dear Sirs,

Re: Our Client: [Employee]

We represent your employee, [Employee].

[Employee] was surprised to be informed last Friday (15 September) that his employment was to be terminated with effect from 22 September and, furthermore, that unless he accepted the offer to terminate his employment set out to him over the telephone and later confirmed in the settlement agreement produced yesterday, the company would proceed to terminate his employment without any further payments other than contractual notice. Specifically, the [Director] told [Employee] that his last day would be 22 September and that the offer on the table was non-negotiable. [Employee] wasn't told any further options were available to him, simply 'this is what is happening'. [Employee] was asked by the [Director] on Monday to 'draw up hand-over notes' for him and give them to him 'before he left the company this Friday'. [Employee] was further told to work from home this week.

We believe that the reason given for this decision was that the company no longer had faith in [Employee] to undertake his duties.

While we are sure you are aware that s.111A, ERA affords employers some degree of protection when entering into negotiations to terminate an employment contract, it is not a termination-at-will mechanism. Indeed, there are several protections set out clearly in the legislation and the ACAS Code of Practice in relation to settlement agreements and s.111A which specifically limit the ability of an employer to threaten unilateral termination of contract in the event of a settlement agreement not being entered into.

S.111A, ERA provides:

> "111A
> *Confidentiality of negotiations before termination of employment*
>
> *(1) Evidence of pre-termination negotiations is inadmissible in any proceedings on a complaint under section 111. This is subject to subsections (3) to (5). [.......]*
>
> *(4) In relation to anything said or done which in the tribunal's opinion was improper, or was connected with improper behaviour, subsection (1) applies only to the extent that the tribunal considers just."*

Turning to the ACAS Code in relation to the question of what constitutes "improper behaviour", the Code provides as follows:

> *"17. What constitutes improper behaviour is ultimately for a tribunal to decide on the facts and circumstances of each case. Improper behaviour will, however, include (but not be limited to) behaviour that would be regarded as 'unambiguous impropriety' under the 'without prejudice' principle.*
>
> *18. The following list provides some examples of improper behaviour. The list is not exhaustive:*
>
> *[......]*
>
> *(e) Putting undue pressure on a party. For instance:*

(i) *Not giving the reasonable time for consideration set out in paragraph 12 of this Code;*

(ii) *An employer saying before any form of disciplinary process has begun that if a settlement proposal is rejected then the employee will be dismissed;"*

For the completeness, paragraph 12 of the Code states as follows:

"12. Parties should be given a reasonable period of time to consider the proposed settlement agreement. What constitutes a reasonable period of time will depend on the circumstances of the case. As a general rule, a minimum period of 10 calendar days should be allowed to consider the proposed formal written terms of a settlement agreement and to receive independent advice, unless the parties agree otherwise."

Up to this week, no formal concerns had been raised with our client in respect of his performance or any other aspect of his work. No performance process had been initiated, nor had any initial letter setting out performance concerns been sent. Our client had no opportunity to assess and address performance concerns, or improve his performance with guidance from the company. [Employee's] last appraisal in June raised no concerns regarding his performance whatsoever, and all his scoring was either three or four out of five. In short, no process had begun, and yet the company informed [Employee] that if a settlement proposal was rejected then he would be dismissed and "this is what is happening". This is a flagrant breach of the ACAS Code and lifts the ostensible protection afforded by S.111, ERA, meaning that an Employment Tribunal is fully entitled to consider the company's actions in a claim of unfair dismissal as the company's behaviour is "improper". The company's behaviour is a textbook example of "improper behaviour", following as it does the exact scenario envisaged and prohibited by the Code.

Furthermore, in giving our client seven calendar days to seek legal advice and consider his position, or face unlawful unilateral termination, the company has committed a second act of "improper behaviour", again breaching not only the spirit, but the actual wording of the Code (see also Lenlyn UK Ltd v Mr H Kular UKEAT010816D). This too would permit an Employment Tribunal to go behind S.111A protection and view the company's behaviour as evidence during a claim of unfair dismissal.

The Offer of Settlement

Given the above, and that it will take the company at least six months to undertake a fair performance assessment (not that fair consideration of [Employee's] performance could now be made given the events of this week and last – and that these events are admissible as evidence were the company to dismiss [Employee] at the end of such a process); and, furthermore, given that at the end of such a process [Employee] would be entitled to leave employment with notice and all his rights in-tact, there is simply no incentive for [Employee] to agree to terminate his employment for two months' gross salary.

[Employee] has had no notice or indication that he would be made suddenly unemployed and he has made no preparations to seek alternative employment. Given his career specialisation is [specialisation], his potential employers are limited to organisations in [Location] and its environs who are large enough to be able to have need for such a role, and are currently recruiting into that specific role. As you and the company will be aware, the uncertainty over the UK's trading arrangements post-2019 is causing many companies in [Location] to limit investment and recruitment. This, naturally, means that far from there being a plethora of opportunities awaiting him, the employment pool has shrunk in recent months and alternative employment opportunities are simply not in existence. We anticipate [Employee] being out of work for anything between nine months and one year.

Given the above, [Employee] rejects your offer of settlement.

Counter-offer

As set out above, [Employee] now has an extremely strong case for constructive and/or ordinary unfair dismissal. The company's actions mean that, whatever it does at this point short of settling the claims under a settlement agreement, it will be liable to compensate [Employee] for his losses moving forward. As such, if the company wishes to terminate [Employee's] employment then it must compensate him for his losses for terminating his employment unfairly, which, as set out above, is likely to be around 12 months' salary.

We therefore propose the following by way of settlement:

1. Notice to be paid in lieu and subject to PAYE and NI in the usual manner.
2. A payment equivalent to 12 months' gross salary (£71,000), the first £30,000 of which will be paid free of tax.
3. Outplacement paid by the company as presently set out in the agreement.
4. An agreed reference.

We look forward to hearing from you.

Yours faithfully,

[Lawyer]

Without prejudice letter: example 3
Unfair dismissal end of secondment

FAO [HR Manager, company and address]
By email only

[Full email address of addressee]

[Date]

Without Prejudice

Dear Sirs

Re: Our Client: [Employee]

Thank you for your letter of [Date].

With respect, the reason given for the termination of [Employee's] employment, in the company's own words on [Date], was her "management style". This is a matter related to performance, not "some other substantial reason". If the company had concerns about [Employee's] performance, then it had ample opportunity to raise these concerns and initiate performance management procedures; it cannot unilaterally terminate [Employee's] employment without warnings or opportunities to improve. The wording of the letter of [Date] referred to above makes it plain that the reason for termination is performance and that is why the company has purported to serve notice of termination, not the end of a "secondment" because [Employee] had failed a "trial period".

The agreement of [Date], which purports to be a secondment agreement, mentions nothing about the appointment of [Employee] to a role in a different store being a "trial period", which if she failed would render her employment liable to unilateral termination. Your letter of [Date] referred to above is the first time a "trial period" has ever been mentioned to [Employee].

If this is the reason for the termination of her employment then it is plainly an unfair dismissal.

As you are aware, and as the agreement [referred to in previous paragraph] acknowledges, [Employee's] employment with the company commenced in 2012 and is not of a fixed-term nature; it is employment in perpetuity – subject to termination via the provisions of the Employment Rights Act 1996 section 98 – and the agreement [referred to above] contains nothing within it to change the nature of the employment relationship to a fixed-term contract. A secondment within the same company is not a fixed-term contract replacing the original employment contract and the end of a secondment does not mean the employee's employment terminates automatically. Even if the company did somehow create a fixed-term contract via the [later] agreement, which is denied, the termination of that contract is still subject to section 98 as [Employee] has more than two years' service.

We understand that the company has created several new roles at [Employee's] level at the new store at the same centre where she presently works. We understand that employees, [Employee] included, were not given the opportunity to apply for these roles and merely informed that they were moving. Furthermore, we understand that several roles at [Employee's] level were filled by external candidates without the positions being advertised internally. There is presently a role being advertised, that of Head of Finance and Operations, which [Employee] is qualified to do, yet there has been no consultation with [Employee] about this role. On your own case, you were aware that [Employee's] "secondment" was coming to an end and failed to consult with her about the new roles and possible opportunities which is a behaviour outside the range of reasonable responses open to an employer in this situation, especially considering there was a total lack of consultation about any perceived performance issues. Therefore, even on your own case, the dismissal is unfair.

Finally, to terminate [Employee's] employment, the company is required to provide three months' notice as per her original 2012 contract of employment. There is no clause in the [later] agreement which supersedes the contractual notice provisions in the 2012 contract of employment.

We suggest that the company gives serious consideration to the settlement of this matter given that after [Date], [Employee] will have been unfairly dismissed without notice and will have no option but to commence Employment Tribunal proceedings against the company.

Yours faithfully,

[Lawyer]

Without prejudice letter: example 4
Race discrimination

FAO [Managing Director]
[Company name and address]

By email only [Addressee's full email address]

[Date]

Without Prejudice

Dear Sirs,

Re: Our Client: [Employee]

We represent [Employee] who is employed by [Company] ("the company") as Management Accountant for [Subsidiary of the company].
In this letter we raise serious issues regarding the behaviour of

[Director], towards [Employee]. It is alleged that over a period of six months, [Director] has subjected [Employee] to a sustained campaign of racial discrimination and harassment, bullying and threatening behaviour, commencing with an overtly negative and hostile performance review in July and culminating in the decision by [Director] to undertake formal capability procedures against [Employee] in November. Between these two dates, [Director] has admitted to deliberately targeting [Employee] alone in the finance team, admitted to not liking her alone in the finance team, treated her differently to her colleagues in the finance team in the manner in which he interacts with her, scapegoated her when problems have arisen and, harassed her and subjected her to unfair treatment which has been motivated by her race.

Prior to [Director] joining the company as Director, [Employee] was subject to positive feedback in terms of her role, positive performance reviews and was given a pay rise, and bonus due to her performance. All these events took place under the previous Director, [Previous Director].

[Director] joined the company in March 2017. By July 2017, at the time he held [Employee's] appraisal, he had a little over three months' experience of working with her. Rather than take a professional approach and decide that working with [Employee] for such a short amount of time was insufficient to form a balanced view of her performance and give a broadly neutral appraisal, [Director] decided to deliver an almost entirely negative view of [Employee's] performance, despite [Employee] meeting her KPIs for the period. Instead of focusing on the fact that KPIs had indeed been met, [Director] instead focused on what he describes as [Employee's] perceived lack of "commercial awareness", suggested she should be working longer hours and raised very minor day-to-day issues as being examples of problems relating to [Employee's] performance.

[Employee] disagreed with [Director's] assessment, and has a great deal of objective evidence that demonstrates that the issues raised by [Director] in the performance review in July were not, in fact, failings on her part at all. This raises the question as to why [Director] chose to make more of these issues in the performance review than was objectively warranted. It is also of note, and concern, that there was no constructive criticism in the review, which is the purpose of an appraisal, rather the content and tone was overtly negative and critical. Furthermore, [Director] failed to even note, let alone give praise, that all KPIs had indeed been met, rather he chose simply to record "nothing to report". The implication of this comment is not that there was "nothing to report", but that there was "nothing negative to report". When taken with the overtly negative comments in the rest of the appraisal, it is clear that [Director] approached the exercise in such a manner that he was looking for only negative issues to raise with [Employee] and thereafter record in the formal appraisal. The overall scoring [Director] decided to give [Employee] was extremely poor and especially surprising given that she met her KPIs and had never been criticised for the way she undertook her role by the [previous Director] and was performing her role in the same manner under [Director's] tenure.

We will, if necessary, ask for disclosure of the appraisals of the other members of the finance team conducted by [Director] and if – as we expect given the comments [Director] has made to [Employee] about his feelings towards her personally (below) – a different tone and approach is taken by [Director] in those appraisals, we would seek to question [Director] as to why his approach was different with [Employee].

The approach [Director] took towards [Employee] in her appraisal was continued thereafter and there are numerous examples of incidents in which [Director] failed to give praise or thanks, or even acknowledgement of work [Employee] completed, whereas any perceived minor error is highlighted, raised and used to impress upon [Employee] that she is in some way underperforming in her role, which is objectionably not the case and which [Employee] has demonstrated in her fulsome rebuttal of the recent allegations of underperformance. For example, on 29 September, [Director] and [Employee] received an email awarding the [sector professional association] Best Practice (Bronze) Award to the company for work undertaken by [Employee] prior to [Director] being appointed.

The award included a cover letter which stated it recognises and awards the company for showing leadership through its reporting and building investors' confidence. [Association's] letter congratulated the team for the effort and achievement. Later in the day, [Managing Director] agreed that [Employee] should share news of the award with the finance team. Within [Employee's] email, she encouraged them to work towards a higher level next time around and copied in both [Director] and [Managing Director]. No congratulations were received from [Director], in fact, he failed to even acknowledge the award, or the important role [Employee] played in it being awarded to the company.

Another example of [Director] failing to acknowledge [Employee's] work was work she undertook for the annual report. A first draft was due by 15 November as per the agreed timetable. This was changed at short notice leaving [Employee] with one week instead of two to produce the draft. [Employee] completed the report to meet the new deadline and, far from the error-strewn work that [Director] appears to believe [Employee] produces, his review comments consisted largely of requests to remove square brackets from certain places and instead highlight the text yellow for later update. [Employee] sent the report to [Auditors] for their technical review and it came back with no errors identified and only a few minor grammatical change requests. The report was sent to Audit Committee on time. Not a word of praise, thanks or acknowledgement of a difficult piece of work that was well done to a revised deadline was received by [Employee] from [Director].

While there are numerous examples of [Director] failing to acknowledge or praise work produced by [Employee], [Director] instead regularly criticises, undermines and challenges [Employee] for perceived "errors", quoting (erroneously) that "50% of her work contains errors" in a meeting on 5 October, during which [Director] gave [Employee] a formal verbal warning for her performance which was not based on any evidence of her performance whatsoever, and instead related to a clash between [Employee] and [Director] over the format of the year-end timetable. ([Employee] wished to continue to work to the agreed template as had been decided already. [Director] wished to use a different template.) This is not a performance issue. After administering the warning, [Director] appeared cheerful. In reply to the latest attempt by [Director] to administer a formal warning about [Employee's] performance, [Employee] has compiled a detailed and comprehensive rebuttal of the allegations, and we refer the company to this document and the large number of supporting documents which demonstrate that [Employee's] performance has not been poor and that [Director] has deliberately targeted [Employee] in order to remove her from her role on the basis of minor, day-to-day issues which do not warrant the imposition of a written warning or performance management procedures. We will be seeking to adduce evidence of the work of [Employee's] white colleagues which will demonstrate that [Employee] alone has been singled out by [Director] for disciplinary action even though the standard of her work is at least the same as her colleagues and is no different from previous years when [Director] was not Director.

Far from [Employee] making errors, it is quite clear from her rebuttal to the performance allegations that [Director] has, in fact, made several errors when acting against the advice of [Employee]. For example, he drew debt of £27.1m too early ahead of the acquisition of [Name of company acquired], costing [Name of the parent company] over £10k in unnecessary interest charges. In addition, [Director] failed to understand that the VAT requirements for the acquisition of [Name of another company] were at risk of not being met ahead of completion, an oversight that could have potentially resulted in VAT of £1.73m becoming payable, plus late payment interest, and a penalty.

On 29 September, shortly before [Director] decided to impose a verbal warning upon her, [Employee] accused [Director] of bullying her. She informed him that on at least seven occasions he had given her a cold, hard stare and said "Watch what you say to me". [Director] had not done this to any of [Employee's] white colleagues, nor had he acted in an aggressive and threatening way to them. In reply to this, [Director] said [Employee] felt this way because of being challenged for perceived "errors" in her work, and that she should report the matter to the company if she felt that way. There was no apology that [Employee] had been made to feel that way, no self-reflection, rather, [Director] decided to give [Employee] a verbal warning.

When administering the verbal warning on 5 October, [Director] handed [Employee] a copy of the company grievance policy and challenged her to report his behaviour.

In the same meeting, [Employee] informed [Director] that she feels that he doesn't support the team and that he is against the team and not for it. [Director] replied that he doesn't have a problem (i.e. a personal problem) with anyone else in the team, just [Employee].

When the [Company] budget meeting was arranged, [Director] didn't seem to want [Employee] to attend the meeting, as he postponed it for a date when he knew [Employee] was on leave. [Employee] privately asked the Managing Director's secretary to do her best to re-arrange for a date that she could make, and this was then done. [Employee] overheard [Director] hounding the Managing Director's secretary to change it back to the date she couldn't make, but the secretary confirmed the diaries would not allow it.

[Director] regularly tells lies about [Employee's] performance, for example, when [Director] was chased by a [Finance company] regarding a loan agreement, [Director] lied and informed them that he was waiting for [Employee] to send him the agreement when, in fact, she had sent him the agreement and asked for his comments. This was not a mere error, but an attempt to make out that [Employee] was to blame for his failings. [Director] does not tell lies about the performance of other, white, colleagues.

[Director] treats [Employee] differently and less-favourably than her white colleagues, for example, when [Employee] was sick with stress due to [Director's] behaviour, he challenged her and then replied that this was "unacceptable". [Director] does not respond to [Employee's] white colleagues taking sick leave in such a manner.

[Director] has regularly told [Employee] to "shut up", and has done so in front of work colleagues. For example, on 21 November when

[Employee] asked to work from home in order to take her son to an appointment, [Director] challenged her request publicly, culminating in him telling her to "shut up". This was in the open plan office, in front of her team, and various other colleagues. [Director] does not behave aggressively towards [Employee's] white colleagues, or tell them to "shut up".

[Director] has regularly and unjustifiably criticised [Employee] in front of colleagues. For example, on 27 September [Director] challenged [Employee] publicly regarding the setup of rent charging periods in the property management system, based on information provided by the property team. [Director] does not criticise [Employee's] white colleagues in such a manner. Several colleagues have informed [Employee] that they are appalled at the way [Director] speaks to her in front of others. Again, [Director] does not speak to [Employee's] white colleagues in an appalling manner. [Director] sends "thank you" emails to other, white or Asian members of the finance team, but not [Employee].

On 27 November, news was announced that Meghan Markle is marrying into the Royal Family. [Director] openly stated that it "lowers the tone" which seemed to have a racial undertone. There were several witnesses to this comment.

On Friday 1 December, in a one to one meeting, [Employee] informed [Director] that she believed he was discriminating against her and that she heard his comments regarding Meghan Markle, which he then tried to blame on the other person in the conversation, suggesting he informed the other person that it was wrong to make such a comment, which was both a lie and also revealing of the racial undertone to the comment given his attempt to distance himself from it when challenged about the racial context. [Employee] informed [Director] that other people had heard him make the comment and then asked him why he treated her differently to other finance team members. [Director] explained that it is because [Employee's] work is not to standard. This is not the case. [Employee] then asked [Director] why he sends "thank you" emails to everyone else in the team except her and why he responded to her sick leave so harshly, but is empathetic towards everyone else? He could not and did not answer this question. During this exchange, [Director] mocked [Employee] and behaved aggressively towards her, backing her up against a desk, at which point [Employee] was forced to point her finger at him and then point out to him she was backed up against the desk, at which [Director] took a step back.

It is of note that since this conversation, and since being accused of racial discrimination, [Director] has sent two "thank you" emails to [Employee].

It is clear that [Director] has treated [Employee] less-favourably than her white colleagues and harassed her by behaving in an aggressive, threatening and abusive manner towards her on several occasions. [Employee] believes, and the evidence supports the contention, that this is due to her race. [Director] may claim that his behaviour towards her was because of his demonstrably untrue (as per [Employee's] rebuttal) and prejudiced perception of underperformance – which itself is less-favourable treatment on the grounds of race – but that is not an explanation of or an answer to a charge of less-favourable treatment on the grounds of race, nor is it a defence to racial harassment. While we understand that these are serious allegations, they are supported by facts and witnesses.

[Employee] has potential claims against [Director] and the company for direct race discrimination, racial harassment, civil harassment and unfair (constructive) dismissal.

Resolution

We are aware that [Employee] has been told that she must, according to company policy, raise a grievance before instructing solicitors. Given the content of this letter and the preferred outcome, we don't believe that it is appropriate at this stage to raise an open grievance, but we will do so if negotiations fail.

While [Employee] intends to remain employed by the company while this matter is resolved, she no longer wishes to work for [Company]. [Director] has destroyed her confidence and [Employee] no longer believes that the company has her interests at heart: in short, she wishes to draw a line under her employment with the company and leave the business. Given the claims that she will be compromising, we await a proposal from the company to settle these claims in return for [Employee] terminating her employment via a settlement agreement.

We look forward to hearing from you.

Yours faithfully

[Lawyer]

12.2. Subject access request examples

As discussed in chapter 2, a subject access request gives you the right to request all information that your employer holds which relates to you. It can be a valuable addition to the evidence that you need to collect in order to make a successful a claim against your employer.

Below are three examples of completed subject access requests taken from real cases (anonymised, of course). You can use these as a starting point in making your own subject access request.

Subject access request: example 1

This example is composed by one of our clients. At his request, we guided him during the negotiations with his employer, but he wanted to carry out as much as possible himself.

PRIVATE AND CONFIDENTIAL

[Employer]

[Date]

Dear Sir or Madam

Subject Access Request

I, [Employee], make the following request:

Under the General Data Protection Regulation 2018, please supply copies of all correspondence, emails, letters, instant messenger, text, Whatsapp, data and other records relating to:

[1] my performance from [Date] to [Date];

[2] my sickness absences and my health from [Date] to [Date];

[3] the decision to consider my role for redundancy;

[4] any offer to be made to me by way of a redundancy or other settlement package;

[5] any discussions between staff at [Employer] between [Date] and [Date] regarding my leaving the business;

[6] my contract of employment;

and I would like access to the following:
- My personnel file.
- Any memoranda and notes taken (including handwritten notes) at any meeting where the above was discussed.
- Emails, or any form of instant messaging or text message communication, between [names of individuals at employer] (including personal emails to the extent that they were used for work purposes).

In conducting a search, please ensure that search terms include my full name, my initials, the short name or any name or variation that might be used by any of the above people to identify me.

In the event that you do not disclose any of the documents mentioned above, I would be grateful if you could confirm that a search has been conducted and no results have been found. I may, in due course, request sight of the search terms that were used and the results of the searches conducted.

It may be helpful for you to know that a request for information under the General Data Protection Regulation 2018 should be responded to within 30 days. If you need advice on dealing with this request, the Information Commissioner's Office can assist you and can be contacted on 0303 123 1113 or at www.ico.gov.uk.

Yours faithfully,

[Signature]

[Employee]

_____

Subject access request: example 2

The following example is a subject access request sent by a lawyer (via email) on behalf of their client:

[Employer]

BY EMAIL ONLY

[Date]

Dear [HR Manager]

Our Client [Employee] – Subject Access Request

Please make all documents and correspondence available within the company's control where our Client is the data subject, in accordance with the General Data Protection Regulation 2018.

This includes all correspondence, notes (typed and handwritten), memorandum, data sheets, emails, letters, text messages, instant messaging including Whatsapp or similar and other records. We expect that you undertake a search of the following individuals' email and telephone accounts:

[Names of individuals]

The search should include private accounts to the extent that they were used for work or business purposes. The search should be comprehensive and include search terms including my Client's full name, her initials, a short name or any name or variation that might be used by any of the above people to identify her.

In the event that you do not disclose any of the documents mentioned above, we would be grateful if you could confirm that a search has been conducted and no results have been found. We may, in due course, request sight of the search terms that were used and the results of the searches conducted.

It may be helpful for you to know that a request for information under the General Data Protection Regulation 2018 should be responded to within 30 days. If you need advice on dealing with this request, the Information Commissioner's Office can assist you and can be contacted on 0303 123 1113 or at www.ico.gov.uk.

Yours faithfully

[Lawyer]

Subject access request: example 3

This is another subject access request sent by a lawyer on behalf of a client:

FAO [Name]
HR Manager
[Company]

By email only

[Addressee's email address]

[Date]

Dear Sirs,

Our Client [Employee] – Subject Access Request

Please make all documents and correspondence within the company's control available where our Client is the data subject, in accordance with the General Data Protection Regulation 2018.

This includes all correspondence, notes (typed and handwritten), memorandum, data sheets, emails, letters, text messages, instant messaging including Whatsapp or similar and other records. We expect that you undertake a search of the following individuals' email, messenger, social media and telephone accounts:

[List of names]

The search should include private accounts to the extent that they were used for work or business purposes. The search should be comprehensive and include search terms for our Client's full name, his initials, a short name or any name or variation that might be used by any of the above people to identify him.

The search should also encompass the minutes of meetings in which our Client's name has been mentioned.

For ease of reference, our Client's employee number is 12345 and his system login is 'PAWS'.

In the event that you do not disclose any of the documents mentioned above, we would be grateful if you could confirm that a search has been conducted and no results have been found. We may in due course, request sight of the search terms that were used and the results of the searches conducted.

It may be helpful for you to know that a request for information under the General Data Protection Regulation 2018 should be responded to within 30 days. If you need advice on dealing with this request, the Information Commissioner's Office can assist you and can be contacted on 0303 123 1113 or at www.ico.gov.uk.

Yours faithfully,

[Lawyer]

12.3. Grievance letter examples

As discussed in chapter 3, if you have a serious problem at work (in other words, a grievance) you might want to raise it formally with your employer. You would do this by way of a grievance letter. Here we offer you two quite different examples of grievance letters so you can get a better idea of how to write your own, if you wish.

Grievance letter: example 1

In this example, the employee was a director of a large building supplies company, and he found his package of benefits was changed unilaterally. He had to submit this grievance to get a decent settlement package. Possible claims include constructive dismissal, breach of contract and disability discrimination.

[HR Manager and address]

Dear [HR Manager]

Re: Formal Grievance

It is with deepest regret that I find myself writing this letter after a successful 17 years unblemished career with [Company]. Please institute the formal grievance procedure for the following reasons.

Background
During September [Managing Director], told me that he looked forward to working with me during the year ahead in an "Operational Director's" role grade X2. We even discussed the actual job role which was very exciting indeed. I was also given a job description for this new role which gave me encouragement and confirmation of my contributions at a senior level within the business. This was also a Regional Director's role, at the same grade of X2.

At a meeting in December [Date] in [Location] with [Employee 2], it came as a complete surprise to me that I would not be considered for this role after all, as according to [Employee 2] the company felt I did not have the qualities in that capacity. Instead I would be offered a demotion with a huge real-terms pay reduction. Also I would be expected to stay in [another location] for 3-4 nights per week. This was discussed verbally with [Employee 2] in December in some detail.

Complaints

1. As you can imagine this came as a shock to me, as this is the first time I had been given feedback like this during my career with [Company], especially as I have been written to on a regular basis on my outstanding performance. That also includes the period of time when I relocated my family in [Date] to Yorkshire for the position of Regional Director. Most recently in November I also received a 'getting it right' award.

2. I feel that after my loyal service and commitment to the company, and having been told numerous times, that "I am one of the good guys in the business", I am being stripped of so many benefits and status – why? To add to this I was informed in the December meeting, that some of this was due to *"You can not be on the same deal as the new gaffer"*.

3. I do feel that the company should have managed my expectations a long time ago on this. On January [Date] the [HR Director], mentioned that the whole process had been handled in a poor manner, which I agree with. It also alarmed me that if there were any performance issues that no one has ever discussed them with me. I do not believe there were, as I am sure they would have been addressed at the time, and maybe the offer of some coaching or training or the chance to improve.

4. I have not been placed on performance review. I have never had any negative feedback from you or been told that certain areas of my work need improving. The only time I have ever been told that my performance was an issue was at the meeting in December [Date], and that was informal and verbal. It seems to me that the reason why you are doing this to me is because of internal politics and also partly that my contract is the same as the [Multi Channel Director], who would be my new boss.

5. From having the meeting in December and receiving the letter dated [Date in December], there seems to be some communication difference which I feel is not on my side.

6. Your letter of [Date in December] states "for the purposes of clarity and as discussed and agreed" with reference to the new proposed job role for me. As you know I have not agreed anything at all, as the whole situation is far from agreed. The letter also

details entitlements which will cease and highlights what is non contractual. I also am fully aware of what is contractual. The changes which you have outlined in the letter of [Date in December] would have the following detrimental effects on me:

a) Grade – my grade has been demoted from X2 Regional Director (which is in my contract of employment) to M2 Support Functions Management, which is 4 grades below X2. You could have demoted me to [one of three other grades] below X2, but you have jumped me down 4 grades!

b) Notice – the current notice period of change of contract is six months by both parties. This is proposed to be changed to three months, which is unacceptable.

c) Temporary basis – "the appointment is initially on a temporary basis". It is to be reviewed in [Date] – this gives me no confidence that there is any job security on a permanent basis.

d) Benefits – at the meeting in December it was clearly discussed that, where there is any loss of benefit, this would be detailed in writing to me along with the new offer of appointment, and payments would be made to me of the equivalent value of the loss. This has not happened.

e) Bonus – the new bonus scheme that has been offered has certainly been a de-motivator. There was a huge concern in the December meeting on how to continually keep myself motivated in a new role. Dropping my potential earnings by 30% has certainly not helped. My old X2 level bonus enabled me to earn £24,224 p.a. above basic salary, which I actually achieved consistently in the last few years' payments. The new proposed M2 bonus would put me on a maximum of £5,318 p.a. above basic salary, being a decrease of some £18,906.

f) Shares – I would no longer be entitled to company performance share plans which are calculated at 16% of basic salary, being around £8,613. I have received this share benefit every year since my X2 appointment in 2012.

g) Company car – in a Senior Executive role, the benefit of a luxury car is a benefit. This benefit is to be lost at renewal in [Date] or sooner. This could be worth a considerable amount.

h) Death cover – reduction from 5 times to 3 times salary is of huge concern to me and my family. This is a huge £106,366 difference, if the worst should happen.

i) Permanent Health Insurance – this is completely removed, without explanation. A typical annual cost of this would be in excess of £1,200 at the age of 40.

j) Salary – I am being kept on the same basic salary and being given no standard company salary increase for [the next year]. My colleagues have all had a salary increase of minimum 2% (£1063 p.a for me).

7. This poor managing of my expectations, and a huge pay cut and demotion without warning has certainly caused me great personal concern and exacerbated my health issues recently, hence the delay in writing this letter.

8. As you know, since December [Date] I have also had to deal with my mother having radiotherapy, and it seems that she may now be in remission. These various causes of anxiety have caused me to be signed off work from January [Date] to the current time, which is the first time in my 17 years of service that I have had any extended period of time off sick.

9. Since I have been off sick you have taken the opportunity to put your proposed changes into practice, without any agreement from me or without written notice.

10. I have noticed that there has been a status downgrade on the system, my current X2 contract has already been changed on the HR computer system to M1-M2 Head Office contract. This should not have happened especially as the full notice has not been given, and I have not accepted the proposed changes.

11. Since I have been off sick, even the new proposed role has been given away to someone else – the Project Manager role which I was to be appointed has now been handed silently to another

Regional Director and kept on the same X2 grade and benefits. This shows that I could easily have been kept on the X2 grade and benefits, and by trying to demote me you are clearly trying to manage me out of the business.

12. Fuel benefit – in an email of [Date] you stated that I would lose my fuel allowance, worth £1500 p.a. but that I would be compensated accordingly in the same month's salary. This has not been paid.

13. I have been given no annual review for the coming year [Date].

14. In conclusion you are tearing up my contract of employment by trying to reduce not only my real terms salary, but by slashing my bonus and eliminating nearly all of my benefits, relocating me to a different part of the country and telling me that I am not up to the job.

15. Can you imagine how you would feel if you were told one minute that you're doing a great job, and shortly afterwards you are demoted, relocated, and effectively have your income halved? Of course I feel that the relationship of trust and confidence has been destroyed and I have no choice but to consider resigning.

16. Resigning would be a huge step for me after 17 years of loyalty and commitment, and not one I would take lightly, so I would like to give you a chance to reconsider your decision and reinstate my package as per my contract and a chance for you to formally apologise for the way that this has been handled – in which case I could consider not resigning.

I look forward to hearing from you at your earliest convenience.

Yours faithfully

[Employee]

Grievance letter: example 2

In this grievance letter example, the employee was off work with a bad back and when he returned he had been moved into a different, lesser, role. He therefore alleged disability discrimination, as well as other complaints including equal pay and victimisation due to whistleblowing.

[Employee address]

[HR manager]

[Company name and address]

[Date]

Dear [HR Manager]

I am writing to you to raise a formal grievance.

As you are aware, my employment started in July 2013. I am employed as a Payroll Supervisor.

Since October 2016, following an instruction from [Manager 1] part of my role has been to check and to double check the values being processed through the office for overtime to ensure that the correct amounts were processed, that individual employees were paid the appropriate amount and to ensure that where appropriate, overtime was charged to our relevant clients. As part of this task, and more generally as my role of Payroll Supervisor, naturally I have access to the payroll details for all employees. I can see at a glance the hourly rate of my colleagues and myself.

The reason I was allocated this task, which I have completed on a monthly basis since October 2016 is that I identified problems and errors with the overtime payment. In fact, most recently, in September 2017, I again identified some errors, which had to be corrected because the wrong person was paid some overtime. I was following reasonable instructions given by my superiors. At no point have I done or accessed any documents which I did not have permission to. In order to check the correct overtime payments were being made I looked at a spreadsheet which would include the following information in relation to my colleagues:

- Salary;
- Hourly rate;
- Amount payable;
- How much was being paid for the overtime (e.g. x1.5, x2 or x3); and
- Whether that amount was chargeable or rechargeable to clients.

I have always been able to see whether the hourly rate for other employees was greater or less than my hourly rate, as I know that my hourly rate is £14 per hour.

On 10 December 2017 you accused me of accessing this information for my own personal financial gain, which I strongly deny.

I was on paternity leave in November 2016: I had two weeks off. When I came back from paternity leave I was moved, without my consent, to a different role. This amounted to detriment for having taken paternity leave and it was a unilateral variation of my contract of employment.

The role that I was doing before paternity leave was to supervise a team of 18 to 20 staff in the payroll team; when I returned from paternity leave I covered another colleague's maternity absence. This involved managing a new smaller team involved in a higher profile piece of work. This team was performing poorly and it required a lot of work to get into shape. Between about May 2017 to August 2017 I was required to work excessive hours and I in fact worked 349 hours of overtime during that period.

Between May and August 2017 my team and myself were regularly working from 7am until 11pm. In addition, I was also required to travel a lot and I spent a lot of time in the office. Because of the company's need to have me working such long hours I started to experience lower back pain. I have never had a risk assessment or workstation assessment and the length of time I was sitting at my desk working caused the pain. The company is responsible for this injury as it was caused as a result of the company's negligence, failure to take care of my health and safety at work and breach of the Working Time Regulations 1998 by making me work excessive hours.

During that period on numerous occasions I raised verbally with my direct manager [Manager 2] and with another manager [Manager 3] that both my team and I were suffering and that I was concerned about my well-being and health. On numerous occasions I told both [Manager 2] and [Manager 3] that my team and I could not carry on as we were because working such long hours was putting a serious strain on my health and my team's health. On more than one occasion I felt obliged to send my entire team home early because they were so tired and exhausted, having not had adequate rest breaks and being required to work such long hours.

I have never had back problems before but eventually my doctor signed me off work and I was diagnosed with a slipped disc. My doctor said that this was work-related back pain because of the amount of time I'd had in the office. I had to have an operation and I was off work for two weeks from 27 August 2017.

When I returned to work on about 15 September 2017, I still had lower back pain that is ongoing and my doctor does not know whether it will improve or not. I had painkillers injected which are supposed to sit in my spine for between three to six months. In most afternoons I feel pain. I consider myself to be disabled for the purposes of the Equality Act 2010.

When I went back to work after my back operation I was taken into a meeting room; I was told by [Manager 1] that I was no longer required to supervise or manage staff because of the risk of recurrence of my back pain and because of the high-profile nature of that role. I was replaced by a female employee who is less experienced than me. I did not agree to this variation and I objected. I asked to speak to [Manager 2] who did agree to meet me and who told me directly that that the "*issues with your back have given us the opportunity to move you*". This was less favourable and unfavourable treatment because of my disability.

There was no change to my job title or to my pay. I was still the most senior payroll supervisor operating for the company and aside from removing my direct reports, my duties were the same, including carrying out the monthly overtime check, which I have set out above.

In each October, employees are normally awarded pay increases. I realised that my pay had not increased in October 2017. I spoke to colleague and friend at work, [Employee 2], in October 2017 about this, I realised that she and other female colleagues had been awarded a pay rise whereas I hadn't. [Employee 2] told me that she was now on £27,500 a year. I am paid £26,000 a year. All of the other payroll supervisors are female and all of the other payroll supervisors were being paid more than £26,000 per year. I am led to believe that they have been paid more than I have for the last 2 years.

After [Employee 2] had told me that my female colleagues had all been awarded a pay rise in October 2017, I spoke to my other colleagues face to face in October and November 2017. They all confirmed that they had indeed been awarded a pay rise.

At 11am on Monday 8 December 2017, I requested to meet with [Manager 2] to ask why it was that I had not been given a pay rise. I suspected that I was being discriminated against, possibly because of my disability or possibly because of my gender.

Before that meeting could take place, due to the lack of [Manager 2's] availability and on 8 December 2017, I carried out the overtime checking task that I do on a monthly basis (a little earlier than usual as payroll was to run earlier in the month so that staff could be paid before Christmas). I was not looking for confirmation of the pay rises: I had no need to as my colleagues had already verbally told me that they had been awarded pay rises of various amounts. However, I accept that if I had wanted to get confirmation from the figures, I would have been able to do this during the overtime checking task, as I have access to all employee's hourly rates of pay, and always have had such access. I finally met with [Manager 2] on 9 December 2017 and asked why I had not been awarded a pay rise, whereas my female colleagues all had. I asked him whether he knew of any reason as to why I had not been given a pay rise. I asked whether it was because of the move I had to make following the birth of my daughter when I returned from paternity leave. [Manager 2] agreed that he would speak to [Manager 3] and come back to me. Instead of this, I was summoned to an investigation meeting.

I explained the above in detail to [Manager 3] at an investigation meeting on 12 December 2017.

Of the disciplinary process:
- I was not informed what the investigation was about before the meeting on 12 December 2017. I was then told that the matter was about a breach of data protection, which it is clearly not as I have always had permission to access the payroll information of my colleagues as part of my job as Payroll Supervisor.

- It is of note that I was not suspended during the investigation and I was required to carry on with the job I carry out, which involves accessing and checking the overtime spreadsheet which contains all individuals' salary details.

- The investigation timeline is wrong in several respects and [Manager 3] has lied.

- [Manager 3] was not independent and should not have been the investigating officer, as I had brought my complaint to him in the first place.

- The statements taken from all employees were written for them and they were forced to sign them at their manager's request, as [Manager 3] confirmed.

- I was alleged to have committed a "serious breach of data protection act" in regards personal information (but it is not clear what personal information other than salary details which I am entitled to access as part of my role, or how this is a breach of the data protection act).

- I was alleged to have committed conduct which causes loss of faith in my integrity and a "serious breach in trust and confidence".

- The allegations made against me are trumped up charges presumably to punish me for raising a complaint about my pay, or for trying to protect my own health and that of my colleagues, or for having a disability.

- I was summoned to a disciplinary hearing on 18 December 2017, which [Manager 3] chaired. In that hearing I pointed out that I was protected under the Equality Act 2010 and was entitled to ask about my pay and why I had not been awarded a pay rise.

- The disciplinary hearing outcome was that [Manager 3] was "unable to draw any clear conclusions in relation to the allegations on the basis of the investigation process completed". Instead of dismissing the allegations at this point, which he clearly ought to, he ordered that there be another investigation, to be carried out by an impartial manager.

- I was suspended at this point, despite the allegations not being proven and the fact that I wasn't suspended in the first place.

I am still suspended; however, the company has taken the remarkable step of asking me to terminate my employment in exchange for £1,856.00. If I don't accept the offer, I am told that the disciplinary investigation will proceed, which will no doubt lead to my dismissal. I do not accept that this offer is properly "without prejudice" nor do I accept that it amounts to a "pre-termination negotiation" and it is a clear indication of the company's intention to force me out of my job.

My complaints:

1. **Breach of contract:** The company has fundamentally breached my contract of employment by the actions I have set out above. I reserve all my rights in this regard and this letter is very much a last hope that the company will do the right thing and to compensate me and apologise for the appalling way I've been treated. Otherwise I feel I have no option but to resign.

2. **Personal injury:** The company has caused me to suffer a back injury which has left me disabled.

3. **Working Time Regulations:** The company has breached the working time regulations by making me work excessive hours, without adequate rest breaks and has subjected me to detriments (see below) for having complained about this.

4. **Whistleblowing:** The company has subjected me to detriments (moving roles, taking away my team, not awarding me a pay rise and subjecting me to a disciplinary investigation and hearing on trumped up charges which did not comply with the company policy or the ACAS code of conduct, and was not impartial, suspending me without reason and not dismissing the allegations when it became clear that they could not be proven) because I have blown the whistle and informed my managers about the dangerous working hours and the threat to health and safety of myself and other employees.

5. **Health and Safety:** The company has subjected me to detriments (see above) because I was in serious danger and took or proposed to take steps to protect myself or other people from danger

6. **Equal Pay:** The company has paid me less than my female colleagues who carry out like work or work of equal value. I would like to have my pay backdated to whenever the discrimination started. There is no justification for the pay differential.

7. **Disability discrimination:** I have been subjected to less favourable or unfavourable treatment (see above) because of

my back condition. This might also be why I was not given a pay rise. No adjustments were made to allow me to continue to do the role which I was in before my sick leave.

8. **Unpaid holiday pay:** I have not been paid holiday pay for the additional overtime I worked. I am entitled to £601 in additional holiday pay for the 349 hours (12.07% pay rate x £14.29 = £601).

I look forward to hearing from you and would invite you to lift my suspension immediately, to award my pay rise, to compensate me for the above treatment and to allow me to return to work.

Yours sincerely,

[Employee]

12.4. Settlement agreement example

Although every settlement agreement will be different, this is a fairly standard example which is likely to suit people with straightforward cases. It is up to date and compliant with relevant legislation (July 2018). In two places, clauses have been omitted which mostly list employment legislation. We have indicated where they have been removed.

If you would like to see another kind of settlement agreement, have a look at the one which concludes case study 1 in chapter 14.

THIS AGREEMENT is made on [Date]

BETWEEN:

(1) [EMPLOYER NAME] of [ADDRESS] (The **"Employer"**); and

(2) [EMPLOYEE NAME] of [ADDRESS] (The **"Employee"**).

BACKGROUND

A. The Employee has been employed by the Employer since [Date] her last post being as a [Job title].

B. It is intended that the Employee's employment will terminate on [Date].

C. The purpose of this agreement is to settle all claims which the Employee has or may have against the Employer and any of its employees, workers, officers, agents or Members arising out of the Employee's employment or its termination, whether or not any such claims exist or are known to exist or contemplated by the parties or are recognised by law at the date of this agreement.

D. The Employer and the Employee intend this Agreement to be an effective waiver of any such claims and to satisfy the conditions relating to settlement agreements contained in the relevant legislation.

IT IS AGREED AS FOLLOWS:

1. Termination of employment

1.1 The Employee's employment with the Employer will terminate by mutual agreement on [Date] (the "Termination Date").

1.2 The Employer enters into this agreement and makes the payment referred to in clause 2 of this agreement without any admission of liability whatsoever by the Employer.

2. Termination payment

2.1 In the period from the date of this agreement to the Termination Date, the Employer will pay the Employee's basic salary, subject to normal deductions for tax and employee national insurance contributions. Subject to this agreement being signed by the Employee and her Representative, with the completion of Appendix 1 of this agreement the employer will pay the final salary payment and the compensation payments referred to in clause 2.2 within 28 days of receiving this agreement duly signed by the Employee and her Representative or within 28 days of the termination date whichever date is the later. The Employer will provide the Employee with a Form P45 within 28 days of the termination date.

2.2 Subject to and conditional upon the Employee's obligations under this Agreement the Employer shall in consideration of the termination of the Employee's employment but without any admission of liability pay the Employee the sum of [£xxx] being the "Termination Payment" subject to the deductions referred to in clause 2.3 below. The Termination Payment consists of:

(a) [£xxx] as a payment in lieu of the Employee's contractual notice period;

(b) [£xxx] as compensation for the termination of employment (loss of office);

(c) [£xxx] in respect of y days accrued but untaken holiday entitlement.

2.3 Payment of the Termination Payment is conditional upon the Employee's agreement under clause 7 below and compliance with the warranties under clause 8 below.

2.4 The Termination Payment shall be subject to the following deductions:

(a) The Employer shall deduct from the sums listed at 2.2 (a) and 2.2 (c) the income tax and employee's national insurance contributions for which the Employer is liable to account to HM Revenue and Customs in respect of the Termination Payment in accordance with the Income Tax (Pay As You Earn) Regulations 2003 ("PAYE Regulations");

(b) The Employer and Employee believe that the first £30,000 of the sum referred to in clause 2.2 (b) can be paid without deduction of income tax or employee's national insurance contributions. [The balance of this sum shall be subject to the deduction of the income tax which the Employer is required by law to account to HM Revenue and Customs in accordance with the PAYE Regulations.]

Any further liability to income tax and/or employee's national insurance contributions on the Termination Payment and on any other benefits provided to the Employee pursuant to this Agreement shall be the Employee's alone.

2.5 With effect from the Termination Date the Employee's benefits, whether contractual or otherwise, will cease. For the avoidance of any doubt the Employer shall cease to provide any Employer's contributions to the Employee's pension with effect from the Termination Date.

3. Tax Indemnity

3.1 The Employer makes no warranty or representation as to whether income tax or employee national insurance contributions are lawfully payable in relation to the payments made under this Agreement.

3.2 The Employee shall be responsible for and shall indemnify the Employer against, and shall on written demand forthwith pay to the Employer any further income tax or employee national insurance contributions (and interest, costs, penalties or expenses relating to any tax assessment) that the Employer is required to pay or account for in respect of the payments made by the Employer to the Employee pursuant to this Agreement in excess of any amount deducted at source. In this regard the Employer shall be deemed to be obliged to pay any such amount if it receives a written demand from HM Revenue and Customs.

3.3 The Employer will give the Employee reasonable notice of any demand for tax which may lead to liabilities on the Employee under this indemnity and shall provide the Employee reasonable access to any documentation the Employee may reasonably require to dispute the claim (provided that nothing in this Clause shall prevent the Employer from complying with their legal obligations to HM Revenue and Customs).

4.   Restrictions

4.1   The Employer makes the compensation payment referred to in clause 2 above in consideration of which, the Employee agrees and confirms that the Employee:

(a) has not disclosed or made use of and will not at any time after the date of this Agreement disclose or make use of, for the Employee's own or any other person's benefit, any trade secret or Confidential Information concerning the business, finances, affairs, products, services, processes, equipment or activities of the Employer or any of its or their respective customers, agents, suppliers or clients except with the consent of the Employer or where required to do so by law;

(b) has not and shall not directly or indirectly disclose to any third party the terms of and the circumstances surrounding the conclusion of this Agreement, save where such disclosure is required by any competent authority or to comply with any statutory requirement or is otherwise required for the purpose of enforcing any of the provisions of this Agreement. This clause does not prevent the Employee disclosing the terms of this agreement to the Employee's professional advisers and spouse provided that the Employee agrees to take reasonable steps to prevent further disclosure by such individuals to any other persons;

(c) has not and shall not directly or indirectly make, publish or otherwise communicate any disparaging or derogatory statements, or encourage any other third parties to make such statements, whether in writing or otherwise, which are intended to or which might be expected to damage or lower the business or professional reputation or financial standing of the Employer or any of their respective present or former officers, partners, directors, agents, customers, consultants, workers, employees or Members;

(d) has not and shall not communicate to any third party including the press about any matter concerning the activities or financial position of the Employer and/or hold her self out as an employee or representative of the Employer following the Termination Date;

(e) In the event that the Employee breaches this Clause 4 and without prejudice to any other remedies the Employer may ask for the payments the Employee has received under this agreement to be repaid to the Employer immediately, in full, on written demand; and

(f) In the event that the Employee issues a claim in breach of Clause 7 of this agreement relating to her employment or its termination against her Employer, or their Officers, Employees, Agents or Members whether in the Employment Tribunals, the High Court, or otherwise, other than for the purposes of enforcing her rights under this agreement the employee agrees that full account will be taken of the payments that she has benefited from under this agreement.

(g) Upon receipt of a reference request for the Employee, the Employer will provide a reference on behalf of the Employee in the terms of the agreed reference attached to this settlement agreement Appendix 2. Unless a further request is made by the Employee this will be the only written reference provided and any oral reference given will be consistent with the terms of the agreed written reference. The reference will form part of the settlement agreement.

4.2 The Employer shall not authorise its officers, agents, Members and employees to make, publish or otherwise communicate any disparaging or derogatory statements, whether in writing or otherwise, concerning the Employee.

5. Return of Employer Property

5.1 The Employee agrees to return on or before [Date] to the Employer:

(a) in good condition and order, subject to fair wear and tear, all property of the Employer in the Employee's possession or under the Employee's control including, but not limited to all keys, mobile telephones, laptop computers, security passes; and

(b) all correspondence, books, papers, files, documents and records (whether kept in hard copy or stored in electronic or in some other form), all computer discs and tapes which belong to or relate to the Employer or any of their respective customers, agents, suppliers, clients or contacts and further agrees that the Employee will not make or retain copies or extracts of the same in any form.

6. Legal Costs

6.1 Provided that the Adviser (who is [Name] of [Name of law firm]) has, by the Termination Date, delivered to the Employer's Solicitors the Adviser's Certificate as set out in Appendix 1 and provided that the Employee has complied with the Employee's obligations under this Agreement, the Employer will pay the Employee's legal fees up to a limit of £500 plus VAT incurred solely in advising the Employee in connection with the termination of the Employee's employment and the preparation of this Agreement. The Employer will make the payment of such fees directly to the firm for which the Adviser works on receipt of a VAT invoice addressed to the Employee but marked payable (whether in whole or in part) by the Employer.

7. Agreement

7.1 The Employee agrees that the terms of this Agreement are offered by the Employer without any admission of liability on the part of the Employer and are in full and final settlement of all and any claims or rights of action that the Employee has or may have against the Employer or any of its or their respective current, former or future officers, workers or employees arising out of the Employee's employment with the Employer or its termination or from events occurring after this Agreement has been entered into whether under common law, contract, statute or otherwise, whether such claims are, or could be, known to the parties or in their express contemplation at the date of this Agreement, including claims which as a matter of law do not at the date of this Agreement exist and whose existence cannot currently be foreseen in any jurisdiction and including, but not limited to, the following claims (each of which is hereby intimated and waived):

(i) for wrongful dismissal;

(ii) for breach of contract;

(iii) in respect of any right or entitlement the Employee has or may have to payment of bonuses, any benefit or award programme or grant of equity interest, or to any other benefit, payment or award the Employee may have received had her employment not terminated, save as otherwise set out in this Agreement;

(iv) for unfair dismissal and related claims, including under sections 93 and 111 of the Employment Rights Act 1996;

(v) for a statutory redundancy payment, under section 163 of the Employment Rights Act 1996 and/or any contractual redundancy payment;

(vi) for direct or indirect discrimination, harassment or victimisation because of and/or related to age, under section 120 of the Equality Act 2010 and/or direct or indirect discrimination, harassment or victimisation related to and/or on the grounds of age under regulation 36 of the Employment Equality (Age) Regulations 2006;

[A list of 20 more potential claims has been omitted here. See the introduction to this example.]

7.2 The waiver in clause 7.1 above does not apply to:

(a) any claims for personal injury other than (a) where the Employee is currently aware of any facts or circumstances which do or may give rise to the claim and (b) those which may be brought under any discrimination legislation; and

(b) any claims by the Employee to enforce this Agreement.

7.3 The waiver in clause 7.1 above shall have effect irrespective of whether or not, at the date of this Agreement, the Employee is or could be aware of such claims or have such claims in her express contemplation, including such claims of which she may become aware after the date of this Agreement in whole or in part as a result of new legislation or the development of common law or equity [or arising from events which occur after this Agreement but connected with the subject matter of this Agreement].

7.4 The Employee acknowledges that the conditions have been satisfied relating to settlement agreements under [the names of more than 20 different pieces of employment law legislation. See introduction to this example].

7.5 The Employee shall be liable for and shall indemnify the Employer in respect of any costs, claims, demands, fines or expenses (including legal and other professional expenses) which may be incurred by the Employer which arise out of or in connection with any claim (whether contractual, statutory or otherwise) brought by her or on her behalf, which, but for section 147 of the Equality Act 2010, she would have been prevented from bringing by this Agreement.

8. Warranties

8.1 The Employee represents and warrants that:

8.1.1 She has received independent legal advice from the Adviser as to the terms and effect of this agreement and, in particular, its effect on her ability to pursue her rights before an employment tribunal or other court;

8.1.2 the Adviser is a relevant independent adviser within the meaning of the acts and regulations referred to at clause 7.4 above;

8.1.3 the Adviser shall sign and deliver to the Employer a letter in the form attached as Appendix 1 to this Agreement;

8.1.4 the Employee is not aware of any claims that she may have (whether at the time of entering into this Agreement or the future) arising out of or pursuant to or connected with her employment or its termination or otherwise, whether contractual, statutory or otherwise, nor any facts or circumstances, that may give rise to such claims;

8.1.5 the Employee has been advised by the Adviser that there is in force and was, at the time she received the advice referred to above, a policy of insurance covering the risk of a claim by her in respect of loss arising in consequence of that advice;

8.1.6 as at the date of this Agreement, there are no circumstances of which she is aware or of which she ought reasonably to be aware which would amount to a repudiatory breach by her of any express or implied term of her Contract of Employment/ Service Agreement which would entitle (or would have entitled) the Employer to terminate her employment without notice or payment in lieu of notice and any payment or benefit provided to her pursuant to this Agreement is conditional upon this being so;

8.1.7 the Employee is not aware of any claim for personal injury she may have against the Employer arising out of or in connection with her employment with the Employer or any facts which may give rise to such a claim; and

8.1.8 the Employee has fully disclosed all matters which might reasonably affect the willingness of the Employer to enter into this Agreement.

8.2 the Employee acknowledges that the Employer has relied on the warranties set out in clause 8.1 when entering into this Agreement.

9.   Counterparts

9.1   This Agreement may be executed in any number of counterparts, each of which, when executed and delivered, shall be an original, and all counterparts together shall constitute one and the same instrument.

10.   Law and Jurisdiction

10.1   This Agreement shall be governed by and construed in accordance with English Law.

10.2   The parties submit to the exclusive jurisdiction of the English Courts and tribunals with regard to any dispute or claim arising under this Agreement.

11.   General

11.1   In this Agreement:

(a) a reference to any legislative provision includes any lawful amendment or re enactment of it; and

(b) the headings are for convenience only and shall not affect its interpretation.

11.2   The Appendices to this Agreement form part of (and are incorporated into) this Agreement.

11.3   This Agreement sets out the entire agreement between the parties and supersedes all previous discussions, negotiations, agreements and arrangements (if any) whether oral or in writing and whether express or implied relating to the termination of the Employee's employment by the Employer.

11.4   This Agreement, although marked "without prejudice" and "subject to contract" will when dated and signed by both parties and accompanied by the Adviser's Certificate become an open document evidencing an agreement binding on the parties.

11.5 Nothing in this Agreement shall be taken to prevent the Employee from making a protected disclosure as defined by the Public Interest Disclosure Act 1998.

11.6 The complete or partial invalidity or unenforceability of any provision of this Agreement for any purpose shall in no way affect:

(a) the validity or enforceability of such provision for any other purpose;

(b) the remainder of such provision; and/or

(c) the remaining provisions of this Agreement.

Signed for and on behalf of

[Company]
By [HR Manager name]

Signed by
[Employee]

APPENDIX 1

ADVISER'S CERTIFICATE

I have given independent legal advice to [Employee] of [Address] as to the terms and effect of the above agreement and in particular its effect on [Employee's] ability to pursue her rights before an employment tribunal. I confirm that I am a Solicitor of the Senior Courts of England and Wales holding a current practising certificate and that there is and was at the time I gave the advice referred to above in force a policy of insurance covering the risk of a claim by [Employee] in respect of any loss arising in consequence of that advice.

Signed . . . .

Address. . . . .

. . . .

Dated . . . .

APPENDIX 2

AGREED REFERENCE

Dear Sir/Madam

Reference Request

I am writing in response to your request for a reference for the person detailed below. It is the company's policy to provide a reference in a standard format. The nature of your request will therefore have determined the information provided as a response below.

[Employee]

[Job title]

[Date of commencement]

[Date of Leaving]

[Tenure]

[Scale]

[Spine point]

[Salary per annum]

The information given above is provided in confidence and good faith and is accurate to the best of our knowledge and belief. However, the information is provided strictly on the basis that no liability is accepted by, or on behalf of, either the Employer or the author, and that any risk is borne entirely by the party placing reliance on such information.

Yours sincerely

[Former Employer]

Chapter 13

Examples of employment tribunal forms and particulars of claim

13.1. Online ET1 employment tribunal claim form

On the next page we have recreated the online ET1 form and given you notes and tips on how to complete each section/question.

QUESTIONS	OUR NOTES
Claim Type	Single claim.
Does your claim relate to	Mostly the answer here is 'not applicable.'
Failure by Secretary of State	No (in 99.9% of cases).
Appeal against a notice	No (in 99.9% of cases).
Another type of claim	Generally tick this box.
Your details	Self explanatory.
Respondent's details	Employer's details.

Do you have an ACAS Early Conciliation Certificate number?

Enter your certificate number here. If you don't have one, then you need to get one, which is free. You will then be contacted by ACAS. Once they've tried and failed to negotiate a settlement, or if you tell them to issue a certificate prior to that point, they will issue you a certificate. This ensures that all claimants have at least attempted to settle out of court.

Do you wish to add additional respondents?

Probably only if your employer changes while you were employed. For example a corporate buy-out whereby one company bought your employer company.

Also in discrimination cases you can add individual respondents for managers and others who have personally discriminated against you. You also need a separate ACAS conciliation certificate for each individual respondent.

Multiple cases	Probably 'no', unless there's a group of you all suing the same employer.
Were you employed by a Respondent?	Highly likely that the answer will be yes.
Employment details	Self explanatory.
Earnings & benefits	E.g. company car, health insurance, bonus, commission.
Type of claim	Choose from list provided.

Details of claim

This is the most important section. It's advisable to instruct a lawyer to draft this part. If you want to do it yourself, there are examples later in this chapter, called 'particulars of claim', which you can modify to suit your particular circumstances and attach to your claim. If you write more than 70 lines it will all count, but they simply won't send you a copy of additional lines automatically – you have to call them and ask for a copy or you can upload a text file if you prefer.

What you want if your claim is successful	Normally you would put 'compensation only'.
What compensation or remedy are you seeking	Just enter 'damages' (this is standard and gets assessed much later).
Whistleblowing claim	Only if you were fired or treated badly for uncovering illegal activity.

13.2. Agenda for case management at employment tribunal preliminary hearings

The agenda reproduced below is used by the employment tribunal to manage preparations for a tribunal case. It is reproduced in full here (and without comment by us) so you can get an idea of the kind of information the court will want to receive prior to hearing a claim. See chapter 6 for more on the way a preliminary hearing fits in to preparations for bringing a case before an employment tribunal.

AGENDA FOR CASE MANAGEMENT AT PRELIMINARY HEARING Rules 29 - 40 and 53 - 56 Employment Tribunals Rules of Procedure 2013

It may help the efficient management of the case if you complete this agenda, as far as it applies, and send it to every other party and the Tribunal to arrive at least 7 days before the preliminary hearing ("ph"). A completed agreed agenda is particularly helpful.

1. Parties

1.1 Are the names of the parties correct? Is the respondent a legal entity?

If not, what is the correct name?

1.2 Should any person be joined or dismissed as a respondent? If yes, why?

2. The claim and response

2.1 What complaints (claims) are brought? This should be just the complaint title or head (e.g. unfair dismissal).

If any are withdrawn, say so.

2.2 Is there any application to amend the claim or response? If yes, write out what you want it to say. Any amendment should be resolved at the preliminary hearing, not later.

2.3 Has any necessary additional information been requested? If not, set out a limited, focused request and explain why the information is necessary. If requested, can the relevant information be provided for the preliminary hearing? If so, please do.

3. Remedy

3.1 If successful, what remedy does the claimant seek? This means e.g. compensation or re-instatement (where that is possible) etc.

3.2 What is the financial value of the monetary parts of the remedy? All parties are encouraged to be realistic.

3.3 Has a schedule of loss been prepared? If so, please provide a copy.

3.4 Has the claimant started new work? If yes, when?

4. The issues

4.1 What are the issues or questions for the Tribunal to decide? It is usually sensible to set this out under the title of the complaint/s.

4.2 Are there any preliminary issues which should be decided before the final hearing? If yes, what preliminary issues?

Can they be added to this preliminary hearing? If not, why not?

5. Preliminary hearings

5.1 Is a further preliminary hearing needed for case management? NB This should be exceptional.

If so, for what agenda items?

For how long?

On what date?

5.2 Is a further substantive preliminary hearing required to decide any of the issues at 4.1? If so, for which issues?

How long is needed?

Possible date/s?

6. Documents and expert evidence

6.1 Have lists of documents been exchanged? If not, date/s for exchange of lists.

6.2 Have copy documents been exchanged? If not, date/s or exchange of copies:

- for any further preliminary hearing
- for the final hearing

6.3 Who will be responsible for preparing:

- index of documents?
- the hearing bundles?

Date for completion of this task and sending a copy to the other parties?

6.4 Is this a case in which medical evidence is required? Why?

Dates for:

- disclosure of medical records
- agreeing any joint expert
- agreeing any joint instructions
- instructing any joint expert
- any medical examination
- producing any report
- asking questions of any expert
- making any concessions

7. Witnesses

7.1 How many witnesses will each party call? Who are those witnesses?

Why are they needed?

7.2 Should witness statements be: exchanged on the same date? or provided sequentially?

Dates for exchange:

- for further preliminary hearing
- for the final hearing

8. The hearing(s)

8.1 Time estimate for final hearing, with intended timetable.

Is a separate hearing necessary for remedy? If yes, why?

8.2 Dates to avoid (with reasons) or to list. Any dates pre-listed by the Tribunal?

9. Other preparation

9.1 Should there be admissions and/or agreed facts? If yes, by what date/s?

9.2 Should there be a cast list? From whom and when?

9.3 Should there be a chronology? From whom and when?

9.4 Are there special requirements for any hearing? (e.g. interpreter, hearing loop, evidence by video, hearing partly in private under rule 50) If yes, give reasons.

10. Judicial mediation

10.1 Is this a case that might be suitable for judicial mediation?

10.2 Are the parties interested in the possibility of judicial mediation?

10.3 JUDICIAL USE ONLY

Judge to consider whether judicial mediation criteria are met; if so, discuss with the parties; record/direct their responses.

11. Any other matters

13.3. ET1 claim forms: examples of particulars of claim

This type of example document is the one which you need to start an employment tribunal claim. It sets out your case and is referred to throughout the tribunal process.

Example 1: Particulars of claim for unfair redundancy and equal pay

In the ET1 below, the employee was selected for redundancy when in fact this was just a way of getting rid of her. She also found out that she had been getting paid less than an equivalent male colleague, hence the equal pay claim. The real identity of the employee, all other individuals and identifying information, have of course been changed.

PARTICULARS OF COMPLAINT

The Parties

1. The Claimant was formerly the Head of the Defendant's VAT department (the department).

2. The Defendant is an enterprise cost management company. The Defendant's website indicates that their commercial offering is to improve business performance in the following areas: tax, research and development, employers' charges, working capital and purchasing performance.

Background

3. The Claimant was employed as Director & Head of the VAT Department on 11 September 2011. Initially, the Claimant's salary was £65,000 p.a. The Claimant also benefited from a £5,000 car allowance.

4. In her role as Head of the department the Claimant was responsible for the operational, technical and strategic needs of the department and had managerial responsibility for in excess of 14 staff and generating revenue of £1,300,000.

5. In the first financial year in which the Claimant was employed (2011-2012), the department did not meet the performance targets set by the Defendant. In the period 2011-2012, all other departments failed to meet the performance targets set by the Defendant.

6. In the second financial year in which the Claimant was employed (financial year ended December 2012), the department met its targets and the Claimant received £10,000 gross of tax by way of bonus pay. The bonus pool for the period 2012 was £120,000.

7. In May 2013 the company launched a Management Buy Out.

8. In June 2013 the then MD of the UK office of the Defendant, the Head of the R&D Tax department, and the Claimant, were involved in discussions.

9. In September 2013, the Claimant acknowledged that the MBO had taken place by way of an internal email congratulating the investors and understood that neither she, nor the MD and the Head of R&D tax from the UK office had been invited. The Claimant questioned the MD who confirmed that both himself and the Head of the R&D Tax department had been invited but refused to invest.

10. The Claimant voiced a complaint to the MD with regards as to why she had been brought into discussions and subsequently not invited. He referred the matter to HR; who in turn referred the matter to the International MD as the decision maker regarding the MBO.

11. In October 2013, the International MD explained that the Claimant was a Grade 9 Director and only grade 10 Directors and above were invited to invest; but that the Claimant would be invited on the next occasion.

12. In April 2014 the Claimant was promoted to Grade 10 Director.

13. At the end of April 2014 the Claimant was invited to invest; but upon acknowledging details of the investment and exit plan, the Claimant decided not to invest for the lack of confidence in the Defendant's choice of employees to deliver on the agreed business plan for the UK business in 2014 and going forward.

14. On 23 September 2014, the Claimant was made aware that the Defendant was considering a restructuring of the management roles within the department and that there was a possible redundancy situation in respect of her role. The Defendant indicated that the department did not require staffing at a "director level" and that the business need indicated staffing was only required at "manager level" for a diminished need of advisory and compliance services.

15. At the same meeting, the Claimant was asked to make herself available on 2nd and 3rd October 2014 to hand over client matters to Miss Smith who was being transferred to the UK from the Italian office at the end of October.

16. On 25 September 2014, the Claimant had a consultation meeting with the Defendant's Human Resources department. The Claimant argued against the redundancy of her current position. In the course of the meeting the Claimant was offered the newly created "VAT Manager" role and also suggested that it wasn't suitable. The Claimant had to refuse the offer.

17. On 26 September 2014 the CEO visited the company for the routine 3rd Quarter meeting to discuss current revenue and strategy to reach target for the end of the Financial Year (31 December). This meeting was organised before 23 September 2014; everyone else was invited in a timely fashion to prepare and attend, with the exception of the Claimant.

18. On 03 October 2014, the Claimant was informed by way of a further meeting with the Defendant's Human Resources Department that her current role was redundant.

19. On 16 October 2014, the Claimant was dismissed from her employment with the Defendant.

20. On 28 October 2014, Miss Smith moved to the UK to undertake the role of VAT Manager created further to the redundancy of

the Claimant's role; and shortly thereafter she was offered the position of VAT Practice Leader, the same internal title held by the Claimant.

21. When the Claimant was dismissed her salary was £83,900 p.a. The Claimant also benefited from a £6,000 car allowance.

22. The Claimant later found out that there were two further roles available during the consultation that were not offered to her for consideration: VAT Project Leader in the UK Office (the Claimant's understanding was that the hiring for this role was put on hold indefinitely by HR in June 2014) and the Head of VAT Compliance role in the Italian Office. Both roles, albeit more junior, were still suitable to the Claimant's skills.

Particulars of Claim

Unfair dismissal

23. The Claimant was unfairly dismissed contrary to section 98 of the Employment Rights Act (ERA)1998, in that:

   A. none of the potentially fair reasons for dismissal, as contained with section 98 (4) ERA 1996, applied to the Claimant at the time of her dismissal and the Defendant held no genuine belief on reasonable grounds that such a fair reason existed;

   B. specifically, the Claimant was not redundant at the time of her dismissal on the basis that the requirements of the business to carry out work of a particular kind (namely that which the Claimant was undertaking) in the place where the employee was employed by the employer (namely London) had neither ceased nor diminished. Although a few clients were lost, these were affecting only the revenue in the VAT Recovery line of business, an area that the Defendant claims was not within the Claimant's remit; whilst the Fiscal and Advisory areas of the business, that the Defendant claims were within the remit of the Claimant, were stable in revenue compared to the previous year and in the course of business development by way of the Defendant's commitment to invest in sales for the VAT department in 2014.

C. if, which is denied, one or more of the potentially fair reasons for dismissal contained with section 98 (4) ERA 1998 applied to the Claimant at the time of her dismissal, it was nonetheless unfair for the Defendant to dismiss the Claimant for that reason;

D. specifically, if, which is denied, the Claimant was redundant within the definition of section 139 (1)(b) ERA 1996 the decision to dismiss was unfair on the basis that:

1. no genuine redundancy situation existed;

2. the Claimant was unfairly selected for redundancy in that other suitable candidates were not included in the redundancy pool;

3. the Defendant failed to offer alternative employment, namely Head of VAT Compliance and VAT Project Leader.

Sex Discrimination

24. The Claimant was subject to direct sex discrimination contrary to section 13 of the Equality Act (EA) 2010, in that:

A. in May 2013, the Claimant was, because of her sex, treated less favourably by the Defendant than Mr Jones, Head of the Defendant's R&D department, in that, contrary to Mr Jones, she was not invited to invest in the Defendant as part of a management buy out (MBO);

B. throughout the course of her employment, the Claimant was, because of her sex, treated less favourably by the Defendant than male peers, including but not limited to Mr Jones in that she was not invited to various corporate events;

C. in financial year 2012 Mr Jones was paid a larger bonus than the Claimant despite the revenue results for both departments being similar.

Equal Pay

25. A term in the Claimant's contract, namely remuneration, was less favourable to her than the corresponding term of a comparable man's, namely Mr Jones's, contract, in that:

    A. throughout the course of her employment, the Claimant was paid less than Mr Jones despite undertaking work which was the same or, alternatively, broadly similar and where there were no differences between the work done by the Claimant and Mr Jones of practical importance in relation to the terms of employment;

    B. alternatively, throughout the course of her employment, the Claimant was paid less than Mr Jones despite undertaking work which is of equal value to that done by Mr Jones.

Remedy

26. On the basis of the above the Claimant seeks the following by way of remedy:

    A. The compensatory award – £xxxx all financial losses (past and future), including expenses incurred, loss of fringe benefits, loss of pension etc., as a result of dismissal (the compensatory award to be "uncapped" due to sex discrimination);

    B. a declaration that the Claimant's contract, namely the term(s) in respect of remuneration, were less favourable than those of Mr Jones's;

    C. pay in arrears from 11 September 2011-16 October 2014 – £xxxx [the difference between the Claimant's pay and Mr Jones's for this period];

    D. interest on arrears in line with Employment Tribunals (Interest on Awards in Discrimination Cases) Regulations 1996 SI No 2803;

    E. compensation for injury to feelings in line with the Vento guidelines.

Example 2: Particulars of claim for whistleblowing

The particulars of claim set out in the ET1 below are for victimisation due to whistleblowing and are technically quite complex. The employee flagged up some problems with technical equipment being made by his employer, which was not in accordance with European standards. Soon afterwards he found himself transferred to another department and effectively demoted.

The identity of the employee, all other individuals, names of technical equipment and of companies involved in the case, have all been changed. The First Respondent has been renamed as Barmouth Jones and the Second Respondent as Nailsea Technology.

PARTICULARS OF COMPLAINT

The Claimant brings claims of unfair (constructive) dismissal, dismissal and detriments for making a protected disclosure, and dismissal and detriments for raising health and safety concerns. In particular:

1. The Claimant is a senior [Job title] engineer, initially commencing employment in October 2012. The Respondent is the United Kingdom subsidiary of a global business. The Respondent's site at [Location], where the Claimant worked, specialised in the manufacture of industrial [type of] machines.

2. The machines manufactured by the Respondent use X-rays and [other technologies] which, potentially, can be very harmful. The radiation dose the person can receive in case of an accidental exposure is potentially many times higher than a normal hospital CT scan. While the harm done by exposure to [this kind of] X-Ray irradiation is not visible immediately, it can show symptoms after some time; one of the primary symptoms is the early onset of cataracts.

3. The nature of the products manufactured by the Respondent dictates that the highest standards of safety must be adhered to at all times in order to ensure the safety of its staff in the manufacturing process, the compliance with European Union safety legislation and "CE" marking, and the safety of the end-users of its products. It is averred that the Respondent failed in these duties during the Claimant's period of employment.

4. In October 2013, the Claimant's terms and conditions were unilaterally altered without consultation or consideration. The Claimant was informed in that contract that he was employed by Nailsea Technology Limited (the Second Respondent), which the Claimant believes is a wholly owned subsidiary of the First Respondent. The Claimant considers that there may have been a transfer of undertakings between the two companies. For the ease of reference, and until informed otherwise by the Respondents, the Claimant shall refer to both Respondents in the singular throughout these pleadings.

5. On 22 December 2014 the Claimant issued notice of termination under the terms of his contract in reaction to what the Claimant perceived as continuous breaches of good health and safety practice, a serious safety-related event caused by the carelessness of one of the Claimant's managers and the consequential lack of proper reaction and corrective actions from higher management.

6. During the Claimant's three month period of notice he was approached by [Name] (Vice President and Barmouth Jones' board member). He asked the Claimant to reconsider his resignation in light of the future improvement activities he was planning to introduce. The Claimant informed [Vice President] about new safety regulations relating to the Respondent's products and highlighted the fact that the Respondent's products would soon be illegal to sell within the EU were changes not made to the manufacturing process and components of their machines. On [Vice President's] initiative, the Claimant and Respondent negotiated an improvement plan in respect of the safety and standards within the Claimant's area of activity and the Claimant agreed to stay with Barmouth

Jones to start and spearhead the *Improvement Project*. The Claimant rescinded his notice and continued to work for the Respondent. It is contended that the Respondent's actions in light of the Claimant's initial resignation strongly indicate that the Claimant was indeed correct regarding safety standards at the Respondent's site at [Location] and the viability of the Respondent's products due to safety concerns.

7. The Claimant, in effect, agreed a new role with the Respondent, that of Senior [new job title], reporting to the Director of Engineering. The Claimant's role was then amended once more and in October 2015 he was created "[Job title] Team Leader" with two engineers seconded to his team. From early 2015 up until the date of the Claimant's resignation, the Claimant was charged by the Respondent with focusing on the improvement of the safety of the Respondent's products and processes and compliance with EU product safety legislation; prominent among the latter is the EU CE marking system.

8. The CE marking system is used to ensure standards of electronic products sold within the EU. Not only does the end-product manufactured by a company need to comply with the CE marking system, but each electronic element of that product must be CE compliant. In order to apply the CE mark to a product, the engineers must sign documentation to say that the product and its component parts meet the requisite criteria. There is, therefore, a burden of responsibility upon engineers to ensure meticulous safety standards are applied to the compliance with CE marking conditions in respect of each component of each product manufactured for sale within the EU as all electronic goods potentially carry the risk of injury or death if unsafe. The Claimant contends that this is particularly the case with products, such as [type of] X-Ray machines, that are already potentially dangerous in their use and must be used only under strict safety conditions.

9. When a company manufactures a product for sale within the EU that has the CE marking label attached to it, if it is found that the components of that product are not CE compliant then the company may be prosecuted. It is therefore a legal requirement

that each product manufactured by the Respondent (and each of its component parts) for sale within the EU is CE mark compliant. It is contended that from January 2015 it was the Claimant's job to identify and rectify problems with the safety of the Respondent's products, including identifying and then rectifying problems within the manufacturing process that would give rise to failures in the CE marking process, thus invalidating the Respondent's products manufactured for sale within the EU. It is also worthy of note that some non-EU countries accept the CE mark as a satisfactory safety sign and therefore rely upon the safety process of the CE marking system.

10. On 10 April 2015, the Claimant produced a paper which was sent to [Vice President] on machines called the ABC and XYZ. The Claimant's paper demonstrated, inter alia, that the machines were not compliant with CE marking criteria yet were being shipped to EU areas and other areas that rely upon the CE marking system.

11. On 15 May 2015, the Claimant produced a presentation document which states more generally and for a broader public within the Company all the technical issues regarding a whole range of products affected including the ABC, XYZ, 456 and 789 machines. This document was sent to [Vice President] and to his team.

12. On 20 May 2015 the Claimant sent an email to [Vice President] which repeated, in detail, problems relating to safety and CE marking.

13. On 30 July 2015 the Claimant informed verbally Mr Andrew Raynor (Director of [Job title]) about products non-compliance and on 1 August 2015 informed in writing [Vice President] about this fact.

14. Between 12 and 15 February 2016, tests were run on the ABC system and equipped with the prototype of [Name of new] card which was designed by the Claimant to substitute the old [Name of old] card in use in the machine. During the tests, the system was found to have two serious failures; namely, the inability to switch off X-Rays in the event of a communications loss from the controlling computer and the prevention of

automatic X-Rays reactivation after the interlock circuit returned to a close state from a previous open state. These tests were run by [Job title] Manager, Nigel Wiggins, on the basis of issues initially raised by [Job title] Engineer, Christopher Selby, and said issues revolved around an item of hardware known as the [Name of the old] card. The Claimant had been testing a new card known as the [Name of new] card, a device designed by him but based on the original [Name of old] card. Therefore the Claimant's design assumptions were based on the original [Name of old] card. During testing it was found as follows:

(a) The X-Rays machine design in its original version relied on the undocumented portion of [Name of old] card (i.e. the machine's design was therefore not compliant with CE marking as a component of the machine was undocumented and could not be signed off for compliance purposes);

(b) Nobody in the Respondent Company knew exactly how the card worked.

(c) Placing the safety-related functions in the new [Name of new] card designed by the Claimant would also be wrong because design assumptions (not specified at all by the engineering managers at the time) for new design, while good for a normal product, were not good for a high reliability one such as this machine.

(d) The software installed on the machine's computer [Name of the software] prevented the automatic X-Rays source reactivation, but was not designed at all to be responsible for safety-critical functions.

15. The consequence of this discovery during testing was a finding by the Claimant that the management of the Respondent was potentially negligent due to a lack of a proper documentation and design process. This potential negligence led not only to a massive loss of time and resources, but to potentially dangerous situations in the use of its product. The product was not CE compliant in the expert opinion of the Claimant.

16. In compliance with the requirements of his role within the Respondent as [Job title] Team Leader and with his professional position as a qualified and experienced engineer, the Claimant produced a report on 22 February 2016. This report set out in detail the history of the problem, the Respondent's failure to comply with CE safety requirements in respect of a product that it had certified as CE compliant and had sold within the EU, and the risk to safety and the Respondent's business viability that this represented. The report was sent via email to Brian Stewart (Director Engineering), Nigel Wiggins [Job Title], Frank Jones [Job Title], David Ashley [Job title], Christopher Selby (Engineer), and to [Overseas manager], reporting to [Vice President].

17. The Respondent failed to engage with the Claimant's report. There was no discussion about the problem, no corrective measures discussed, no plan about how and where to enforce safety functions within the instrument itself.

18. On 20 April 2016, the Respondent was banned from shipping its products to geographical areas where the CE mark was required.

19. On 5 July, Brian Stewart, [Name] (Human Resources Head) and [Name, Location site manager] met with the Claimant unannounced. The purpose of the meeting from a subsequent email sent to the Claimant when they could not initially find him was to have been to "clarify the HR situation you raised [sic] in our last meeting". The Claimant had raised an issue of resourcing in a previous meeting in terms of the two engineers seconded to him. The Claimant had complained that they were not available when needed and that he had, in effect, been starved of the resources that would enable him to do his job.

20. When Brian Stewart, [Name of HR Head] and [Name of location site manager] met with the Claimant two hours after Brian Stewart sent the email referred to above, it was for the purpose of:

    (a) removing the Claimant from his role resulting in an effective demotion without consultation or even notice;

    (b) placing him back within the general engineering team, thus changing his line of reporting so that the Claimant would report to James Radlett, the manager who was forcing the Claimant to comply with what in his view were unlawful working practices;

(c) forcing the Claimant to comply with unsafe and unlawful working practices; and,

(d) informing the Claimant that he was subject to an allegation of poor performance and was soon to be subject to a poor performance procedure. It is alleged that the Respondent had no grounds for making such an allegation, failed to record, assess and communicate the Claimant's performance in any objective manner and failed utterly to comply with a reasonable procedure in making such an allegation. The Claimant was, in effect, ambushed by this allegation.

21. In respect of the events of the meeting of 5 July 2016, it is contended that the Respondent's actions were breaches of the Claimant's contract of employment, breaches of trust and confidence and, furthermore, detriments for making protected disclosures.

22. Around the same time in July 2016, the Respondent's manager, James Radlett, took the decision (without consulting the Claimant) to revert to the old, non-compliant manufacturing process for the ABC System using the undocumented and unverified [Name of old card]. It is alleged that James Radlett ignored the findings of the Claimant's report and that, in the Claimant's view, to continue to use the old manufacturing process would result in a non-CE compliant product. The Claimant would be expected to sign the documentation confirming that the component [Name of old card] was CE mark compliant despite having produced a report specifically stating that it was not. The Claimant was unaware of this decision until 7 July 2016, during a meeting held from 11:00 to 12:30 by James Radlett with a group of engineers including the Claimant. The Claimant refused to comply with this decision and communicated this refusal to James Radlett verbally at around 17:00 on Thursday 7 July.

23. The Respondent wrote to the Claimant on 8 July setting out what, in its view, was the content of the meeting on 5 July. The Claimant disputes the events of the meeting as set out in the letter of 8 July.

24. On 11 July, the Monday following receipt of the letter dated 8 July, the Claimant resigned his employment without notice as a direct result of the actions of the Respondent.

Qualifying Disclosure

25. The Claimant contends that he made qualifying disclosures within the meaning of section 43B of the Employment Rights Act 1996 in that on 10 April 2015, 10 May 2015, 30 July 2015 and 22 February 2016 the Claimant conveyed information to the Respondent that:

    (a) A criminal offence had been committed or was likely to have been committed by the Respondent; and/or,

    (b) The Respondent was failing to comply with a legal obligation to which it was subject; and/or,

    (c) That the health and safety of an individual was being, or was likely to be, endangered.

26. The information disclosed by the Claimant relates to the Respondent's initial and ongoing failures in respect of the ABC System, and other systems, which were being sold to customers in the EU and worldwide during all relevant times despite being non-compliant with CE marking, as set out above, but in particular:

    (a) The fact that the Respondent was manufacturing for sale within the EU and that had been given a CE marking a product that contained a part that was undocumented, therefore unable to be assessed for CE marking and therefore in breach of EU regulations; and,

    (b) The fact that the Respondent was manufacturing for sale within the EU a machine that failed two critical safety functions and was potentially dangerous.

Protected Disclosure

27. The disclosures were made to the Claimant's employer, in particular [Vice President] and are therefore protected under section 43C.

Health and Safety

28. The Claimant contends that in his role as [Job title] team leader, particularly when taken in the context of his initial resignation in December 2014, he was designated by his employer to carry out activities in connection with preventing or reducing risks to health and safety at work. He carried out (or proposed to carry out) any such activities, within the meaning of section 100 (1) (a) of the Employment Rights Act 1996.

29. The Claimant further contends that he brought to the Respondent's attention, by reasonable means, circumstances connected with his work which he reasonably believed were harmful or potentially harmful to health or safety; those circumstances are related to the ABC Machine referred to extensively above.

Dismissal

30. It is contended that the Claimant has been dismissed within the meaning of the section 95 1 (c) in that the Claimant was entitled to resign his employment without notice by reason of the Respondent's conduct, and that dismissal is unfair for the following reasons:

    (a) The dismissal, or resignation, was a due to the Claimant making a protected disclosure or protected disclosures as per section 103A of the Employment Rights Act and the Claimant suffering detriments as a result entitling the Claimant to resign and consider himself dismissed;

    (b) Further, or in the alternative, the dismissal, or resignation, was due to the Claimant raising serious health and safety concerns within the meaning of section 100 (1) (a) of the Employment Rights Act 1996;

(c) Further, or in the alternative, the dismissal was generally an unfair (constructive) dismissal in that the Claimant resigned due to a breach of contract and/or breach of trust and confidence by the Respondent, particularly:

    (i) The Claimant was removed from his role without consultation or notice;

    (ii) The Claimant was expected to be responsible for an input data (i.e. the design) for the CE marking process he knew was non-compliant;

    (iii) The Claimant was effectively demoted;

    (iv) An allegation of poor performance was made against the Claimant without substance or evidence presented to him;

    (v) The Respondent moved the Claimant under the management of James Radlett, a man who was, in the Claimant's express view, forcing him to operate an unlawful process.

Detriments

31. The Claimant further claims that the actions set out above at paragraph 30 (c) were detriments for making a protected disclosure within the meaning of section 47B of the Employment Rights Act 1996, and/or detriments for raising health and safety concerns within the meaning of section 44 of the Employment Rights Act 1996.

Causation

32. The Claimant alleges that there is a direct causal link between the protected disclosures he has made and health and safety concerns he has raised and the Respondent's actions in July 2016 which are set out above.

Remedy

33. The Claimant claims damages for his loss of employment and the damage to his future career.

Chapter 14

Case studies on leaving employment

14.1. Case study 1: Employee dismissed after customer complaint

Case details

In this case study our client had been dismissed for gross misconduct without any notice pay or any settlement payment at all. She had been accused of not following company procedures with documentation and invoicing. We achieved a settlement package worth around eight months' gross wages for her. This example is drawn from a real case, although all the names and exact circumstances have been changed.

- **Client name:** Ms M
- **Job title:** Operations Manager
- **Employer/company size:** Retail industry. Circa 250 employees
- **Annual basic salary, before tax:** £47,000
- **Annual expected bonuses and commission:** £9,852
- **Date of first action by Monaco Solicitors:** 15th December 2016
- **Date of case completion:** 13th June 2017
- **Initial agreed fee:** 15% inclusive of VAT
- **Original settlement offer:** There was no initial offer as the employee was originally dismissed for gross misconduct
- **Final settlement agreement amount:** £29,000
- **Final fee billed (Total):** £4,350 (inclusive of VAT)
- **Other terms:** The company rescinded their finding of gross misconduct so that the client could claim her income protection insurance which would pay a portion of her salary for the time she was out of work

What the client said:

'The Company have claimed gross misconduct and loss of confidence in view of poor performance of my duties. They have summarily dismissed me without notice or pay in lieu of notice.

'I do not believe that the company policy or ACAS guidelines have been followed with regard to my disciplinary hearing. I do not believe that the issues raised (irrespective of my guilt) warrant the severity of the punishment. I received no notice of investigation, no performance review or notification of concerns. I have been given no opportunity to rectify any issues or improve performance. I intend to lodge an appeal.

'I believe that following the sale of the company and appointment of new senior management including head of my department, my services are not seen as a good fit for the direction the company wishes to take. Over the past 18 months I have been subjected to effective demotion and systematic erosion and undermining of my management status, which has increased since the appointment of a new department manager over my head a year ago. I believe that it was hoped that this would force me to resign of my own accord. As this has not worked, the company have now resorted to engineering a scenario to dismiss me.'

Lawyer's initial thoughts:

'Based on the facts presented, it sounds as if there has been a failure to follow process and there are certainly a lot of questions about the justification for dismissal. The bar for an employer establishing misconduct is low. The employer must satisfy a two stage test. Firstly, that there were sufficient grounds to find that misconduct occurred following a reasonable investigation. Secondly, that the dismissal was within a reasonable range of responses open to the employer.

'By way of example, it is worth looking at the case of Mrs Birchall in the case of British Home Stores (BHS)–v-Burchell [1978] UKEAT 108_78_2007 which, while an old case, remains good law. Mrs Burchell was an employee of British Homes Stores and was accused of stealing. BHS conducted an investigation and concluded that Mrs Burchell had stolen company property. She was dismissed. Following her dismissal the real perpetrator was discovered. Mrs Burchell took her case to the tribunal claiming unfair dismissal and won. The Employment Appeal Tribunal, overturning the original finding in Mrs Burchell's favour, found that:

- The employer reasonably believed that there was misconduct.
- There were reasonable grounds for that belief.

'In summary, an employer may not always reach the right decision but a tribunal will give them a fair amount of latitude if they follow a fair and reasonable process.

'Getting back to Ms M, following an initial call it was apparent that some serious allegations had been made against the client regarding the performance of her duties and that the company claimed that they had suffered some significant financial losses. However, what was apparent was there was a separate agenda to scapegoat and blame her for wider departmental failures. I advised that this might be a difficult case as the employer was taking a hard line, but we would be confident when taking on the case that we would recover at the very least her notice payment and, hopefully, compensation equivalent to a decent redundancy payment.'

Chronology of case actions with lawyer commentary

'Monaco Solicitors were instructed shortly before Christmas. In the following weeks, we worked with the client to compile evidence in support of her case, including drafting the grounds of appeal against dismissal for use at the company's internal processes. The appeal is presented in the first formal letter to the company from Monaco Solicitors on behalf of Ms M dated 6th March 2017, below.'

06/03/2017: First letter to the company from Monaco Solicitors on behalf of the employee

'The appeal had to cover a lot of ground both in terms of addressing the seven allegations and findings against our client and also to explain the background to the events and how she had been subjected to a bullying campaign by her line manager which was clearly intended to put enough pressure on her so that she would resign.'

[Note: The letter setting out the appeal against dismissal is highly detailed, so in the copy below, we have edited it down a little and indicated in the letter where sections have been abbreviated.]

▶ Letter

Private and Confidential

Mr D

Managing Director

By email only

6th March 2017

Dear Mr D

Appeal against dismissal

Further to my email of [Date] notifying you of my client Ms M's appeal against the decision to dismiss her from employment. We had expected to be furnished with all the requested information prior to the submission of the grounds of appeal but in view of the delay in the provision of this information, please find set out below the grounds of appeal. Once we have sight of the additional information requested, we reserve Ms M's right to amend these grounds of appeal.

We set out below some useful context for your consideration in the appeals process and evidence which appears to have not been considered in the original disciplinary process.

Ms M was employed from 2006 as a manager for the company. At the point of her dismissal, it is noted that Ms M was due to receive her long-service award but the company failed to give the agreed long-service award. When Ms M was first employed by the company, her department consisted of Ms M and an administrator. During this time, they used independent subcontracted engineers to carry out the works on site. Prior to her appointment, servicing and repair of the product had been a hit and miss affair which only took place on a requested basis with no focus until Ms M realised the growth of this part of the business.

As this part of the business grew so did Ms M's responsibilities and, over time, she developed this side of the business with steady and sustained growth, an expanding portfolio and a core group of quality knowledgeable employees. Ms M's efforts were rewarded with regular pay increases, bonuses and an upgraded company car. Clearly, Ms M was integral to the success of this arm of the business and it is testament to her endeavours that the company enjoys the success that continues to this day.

Following the company's acquisition, Ms M was aware that there would be a period of flux and that given the business was now part of a larger group of companies there would be a time of readjustment. This was particularly evident following the retirement of Mr F and the appointment of a new managing director.

Ms M was more than prepared to move with the new challenges of the changed business and the changes that would inevitably take place. Following Mr B's arrival and appointment to the role of Senior Service Manager, Ms M asked Mr F if her title could be changed from Maintenance Manager to Operations Manager to better describe her revised role within the business. At the time, it was made clear to Ms M that her skills were best suited to the day-to-day logistics of the operations. Whilst no formal job description has ever been issued, it was understood that Ms M's core responsibilities were [outline of responsibilities].

It was widely understood that Mr B, as a more senior manager, would be taking overall responsibility for the department, concentrating on the commercial aspects of the operation and ensuring that the department developed and grew. Clearly, the responsibility for all the commercial aspects – particularly meeting sales targets, invoicing, etc. – came under the auspices of Mr B. It is apparent that the scope of Ms M's role was not properly recognised during the disciplinary process and particularly, the areas of Mr B's overarching responsibilities. On an objective basis, it is quite evident that there was a clear attempt throughout the disciplinary process to back Ms M into a corner and be identified as the *fall-guy* for any perceived failures within the department. We will discuss these issues below in greater depth.

Since his appointment last year, Mr B has waged a consistent and relentless campaign to marginalise Ms M and undermine her authority. This has seriously compromised Ms M's ability to manage her team and the day-to-day operation of the service offering effectively.

Mr B has completely failed to engage with Ms M or draw on her 35 plus years of engineering, service management and customer service experience, or her substantial knowledge and experience of Company X's history, procedures and products. He made no attempt to develop a professional and productive working relationship with Ms M. Quite the opposite, he consistently took every opportunity to undermine Ms M's authority by second guessing all decisions and approvals. He instructed staff from within and outside of the service department to refer all instructions made by Ms M to him for further approval. This was done covertly and evidently done to undermine, marginalise and exclude Ms M.

At the end of June, Ms M discussed her concerns with Ms E, the company's Human Resources Consultant, who discussed the option of raising a formal grievance about Mr B's treatment. Ms M was reluctant to bring these issues to the fore as she realised it would likely be counter-productive and thought she should follow the company's procedure to raise matters informally with Mr B directly, which she did. Ultimately, she was keen not to fracture an already difficult relationship.

Some weeks after the original conversation, Ms E spoke to Ms M and asked if she had made progress. She told her that immediately following their previous conversation, Mr B had insisted upon speaking to Ms E in an attempt to find out whether Ms M intended to submit a grievance. In hindsight, it would appear the commencement of disciplinary action was likely a pre-emptive strike from Mr B and one which was probably motivated by self-preservation.

In terms of the grounds of appeal, at its core the appeal centres on the failure to follow a fair process and one which has rendered the disciplinary decision unsustainable and unfair. In view of the fundamental failures to undertake a fair process, there is no means upon which this could be remedied upon appeal. In the circumstances, we invite you to rescind the decision to dismiss Ms M from employment and reinstate her to her previous position. In support of this contention we make the following points:

1. *Failure to appoint an independent investigator to undertake a fair and impartial investigation and disciplinary process.*

    Whilst we have not seen the company's grievance and disciplinary policy we assume that the company's general policy would be to act in manner consistent with the ACAS Code of Practice and the principles of natural justice.

    As we have mentioned above, Mr B was brought into the business to manage and oversee the Service Department and the allegations levelled against Ms M are matters which came within Mr B's remit and any departmental failures rest with Mr B and not with Ms M.

    Mr B attributed blame to Ms M for matters which came within the ambit of his own responsibilities and for that reason could not be a fair and open-minded decision maker. It is believed that there has been a deliberate campaign to deflect responsibility from himself and he could therefore not be an independent judge of the issues that fell to be considered. Furthermore, it is apparent that he went on a *fishing expedition* to find and obtain biased information which would assist in building a case against Ms M.

    It is clear from the evidence provided in support of the disciplinary action taken against Ms M that there had been a series of leading questions asked of members of staff to provide statements which were detrimental to Ms M. Ms M was not offered the opportunity to ask questions of the individuals concerned and examine how these statements had been realised. It is apparent that they were asked, presumably at Mr B's behest, to provide statements which established alleged wrongdoing. You will note the request below for all data for which Ms M is the subject to be disclosed under the Data

Protection Act 1998 [replaced in 2018 by the General Data Protection Regulation]. We believe that it is pertinent that any appeal officer should examine the correspondence between Mr B and the individuals who provided statements in the course of the disciplinary investigation and we invite you to do so.

For example, the witness statement of Ms D purports to have been written on 12 August 2016 and yet refers to events and emails received days later. Clearly the information was provided at Mr B's request and is far from an unsolicited complaint from a colleague as advanced in the disciplinary allegations of 22 August 2016.

2. *Substantive evidential failures and consideration of incorrect facts or findings of fact that no reasonable adjudicator could have found.*

As part of a decision-making process, an adjudicator should take account of the evidence provided and, in particular, the explanations offered in defence of the allegations. It is clear that there was a wholesale failure to take account of the evidence presented by Ms M in the course of the disciplinary investigation and consequently findings of fact were made that no reasonable adjudicator could have found based upon the facts presented. In respect of this ground of appeal, we break down the various allegations which were considered to be well-founded and make the following comments:

Allegation 1 – the client complaint

This complaint was not directed towards or about Ms M or the handling of this account. In fact, Ms M had a good, long-term relationship with the client who had always been complimentary about Ms M's advice and support. The material facts are as follows: the client called the Service Coordinator, Ms X (currently on probation for promotion to Contracts Manager), in response to a repair estimate submitted by her for repairs to equipment that had been damaged in one of the stores. This call came in after office hours (and after Ms M should have left to go on annual leave). Ms X sent an email to Ms M at 17:45 saying that there was a problem and asked Ms M to discuss it with her. Ms M called her immediately but received no response, so left a voicemail message asking her to call her straight back.

[Letter abbreviated here. See introductory note.]

Evidently, this [i.e. the outcome of Ms M's subsequent telephone conversation with the client] is not the conduct of an unhappy customer. It is appreciated that the basis of Mr B's argument appears to be that this matter was not escalated to him. Ms M saw no reason to do so as she was the main point of contact and having a long relationship with the customer and an in-depth knowledge of the equipment installed, evidently Ms M was the most appropriate person to follow it through. Further, Ms M was aware that Ms X had made Mr B aware of the issue so it would have been a duplicated effort had Ms M also made contact with Mr B.

Allegation 2 – Failure to submit documents

This relates to an order intake versus jobs completed analysis for 2015 which Mr B had been tasked to complete. It is appreciated that Mr B found this task difficult as he had limited knowledge of the system and history and he had made little progress. In mid-2016, Ms M offered to assist him with this by having the data reviewed and compared. Ms M tasked Mr Q, one of her team, to start this process, with Ms M's assistance. After two weeks, Ms M had a meeting with Mr B and Mr Q and reviewed the data collated so far. At that meeting, they discussed the fact that the task was about 50% complete, but was proving very time consuming and difficult, particularly with the limited staff resources and heavy workload. It was agreed they would reconvene in about two weeks to review further progress. This meeting was never called.

This coincided with two other incidents which have a bearing on the completion of the task. Ms R, the administrative assistant, who was helping with this task, was suddenly removed from Ms

M's team, without warning or consultation and transferred to another department. This obviously put the already stretched team under additional pressure. Ms M discussed the impact that this decision would have on the comparison work with Mr B. He told Ms M not to worry about it for the time being and that it could be picked it up at a later date, if necessary. Ms M asked for clarity on a couple of other occasions and the first response was "oh don't worry about that, he'll be gone soon anyway". This was a reference to Mr F's announcement that he would be retiring and a new Managing Director would be taking his place.

On another occasion, Mr B told Ms M again, not to worry about it as he would deal with it. Ms M has recently become aware that Mr B was investigating this issue and was taking considerable time away from the office, apparently working on it from home. Ms M offered to assist, but Mr B said he would not require her assistance.

In the dismissal letter there is a reference to the flowchart. This has been taken entirely out of context. At the meeting on 26 June 2016, Mr F asked about the order process and whether there was a flow chart. Ms M confirmed that there was an overall process and flow chart documented in the quality manual which had been recently updated. Ms M also went through the process and suggested some improvements and illustrated this on the flip board in his office. Ms M does not recall being asked to produce a flowchart document. Had she been asked to do so, she would have pointed out that she does not have any experience or training to carry out this task and that as part of the Company's ISO9001 accreditation, any new process document would need to be produced, approved and incorporated into the company quality manual by the Quality Manager.

Allegation 3 – Lack of control over invoicing

As we have stated in correspondence, we await sight of the specific detail as to date no evidence has been produced to substantiate the figures or responsibility.

[Letter abbreviated here. See introductory note.]

It was well-known and discussed frequently with Mr B, and the previous management, that the department was seriously understaffed and that it was necessary to employ additional staff in order to effectively cope with the volume of work and administration generated by this. Furthermore, Ms M had consistently warned that mistakes and problems would occur if this was not addressed. In November 2015, this was recognised by Mr B who sought approval to recruit an additional admin assistant. However, the recruitment process was poorly managed by Mr B and the role has still yet to be successfully filled. The administrative burden was increased when Mr B made the decision to move the Service Coordinator into a new contract management role, which meant that she could not effectively undertake her existing duties.

Allegation 5 – Failure to respond to a direct request for handover information

There is a considerable evidential dispute which is not made clear from the dismissal letter regarding this purported failure to handover information prior to Ms M's annual leave. Ms M's recollection of the events is as follows:

[Letter abbreviated here. See introductory note.]

In reality, Mr B showed very little interest in any of Ms M's projects. Prior to Mr B's holiday in the summer, Mr B sent an email to Ms M consisting mainly of a list of things that he had not done and was either asking Ms M to do them or had passed them over to another member of the team. This was in response to a meeting that Ms M had requested with him, expressing her concern with the lack of communication from him and the secrecy with which he conducts his day-to-day business on behalf of the company. Ms M frequently was required to deal with unresolved matters whilst Mr B was on annual leave.

Allegation 6 – Formal letter from member of staff outlining no support

The basis of the allegation is unfounded. The "letter of complaint" refers to the incident detailed in allegation 4 for which Ms M was exonerated and the item dismissed. This individual was a new team member whom Ms M was training up. She used opportunities to involve Mr A in addressing unusual and more complex technical issues as part of that training which was done with support from Ms M and other members of the team. By involving the trainee and encouraging him to find the answers and relay these to the client and follow through the process he is both learning and hopefully experiencing a sense of achievement and contribution to the team as a result. This is a training technique that Ms M has used to great success previously.

Clearly it is a cause for concern that Mr A felt pressurised even though he handled the tasks that he was given well. Had Ms M been given the opportunity, this was something that could have been addressed and a solution found to support him further. It is notable that there are no specific further examples given in his letter. This is not an allegation which should be the basis of disciplinary action being taken.

It is also strongly suspected that Mr A may have been encouraged or influenced to put his concerns down in writing rather than discuss it with Ms M informally as per the Company's grievance procedure. Although, Ms M is without conclusive proof (please see comments above and Subject Access Request below), this is a tactic that Mr B has used on previous occasions in order to give him an excuse to take disciplinary action against other staff members.

Mr B would have been aware that Ms M had concerns, also shared with the Service Coordinator, over Mr A's ability to cope under pressure and his lack of detailed concentration and questioned whether he was right for this demanding role.

Allegation 7 – Formal letter of complaint from Accounts

This is a case of misunderstanding and Chinese whispers. Also the statements in the letter are inaccurate. Ms M did not inform Mr P that she had issued documents to, or was waiting for them to be completed by, the accounts team. The Health and Safety consultant completed the health and safety elements of the form (including the insurance details) for Ms M on 4 August but was unable to do the accounts element. As Ms M was out of the office for two days, the consultant obtained the additional information on Friday 5 August and completed the forms.

[Letter abbreviated here. See introductory note.]

The job was subsequently completed on schedule and to the complete satisfaction of the client. The job and paperwork trail was subsequently used as an example of company procedures during an external quality audit and passed satisfactorily. Again, this seems to highlight Mr B's fishing expedition to find individuals to provide witness statement finding fault as above.

In the circumstances, there has been no lawful basis to dismiss Ms M from employment and the allegations are without foundation and the decision to dismiss Ms M in these circumstances was well outside the range of responses open to an employer in particular taking account of Ms M's lengthy and unblemished service.

We look forward to hearing from you in due course.

Yours faithfully

[Lawyer]

13/03/2017: Second letter from Monaco Solicitors to the company (without prejudice letter)

Lawyer's comments:

'Following receipt of the appeal, we were in communication with the General Manager of the company and sent him the following without prejudice letter going into some detail about the dismissal circumstances and the likely findings if matters were considered by a tribunal. We hoped that there would be engagement from the General Manager and there would be pragmatic approach adopted that would ensure that a swift settlement could be reached. The General Manager equivocated and then said he wished to let the internal process be exhausted and was not willing to entertain settlement.'

▶ Letter

<u>Strictly Private and Confidential</u>

Mr W

General Manager

[Company]

13 March 2017

<u>Without prejudice and subject to contract</u>

Dear Mr W,

You will have seen the comprehensive letter of appeal that has been submitted on Ms M's behalf. We do not wish to fetter your decision-making ability in considering this appeal but are conscious of the fact that Ms M is currently without any income and her dismissal has taken a considerable toll upon her. She has, therefore, asked me to explore the possibility of settlement before she takes the step to prepare Tribunal proceedings for unfair and wrongful dismissal.

Ms M was a long-serving and loyal member of staff who was both conscientious and diligent in her work. She has been the victim of a concerted and cynical campaign by Mr B to remove her from the business. Her employment should not have been terminated in the way that it was. The decision to dismiss her for gross misconduct is without foundation and we are confident that a tribunal would find that there was no evidence of misconduct and, even if there were (which is vehemently denied), it is apparent that the decision to dismiss Ms M from employment fell outside the range of responses open to an employer. A tribunal, on balance, will find Ms M's claims well-founded and award compensation.

If, which is not accepted, there was anything in the allegations that have been levelled against Ms M then the appropriate way of dealing with such matters would have been under a capability procedure and not as disciplinary action. In such a circumstance, the steps should have been to commence a performance improvement plan, or any other appropriate measure, under the company's capability procedure. Clearly, we do not know what would have happened if the company had followed proper process.

One would have hoped that the company would have supported Ms M to identify any areas of weakness and worked with her to continue in her role unimpeded. Had there been sufficient concerns about her performance, then the company should have commenced a formal process. This would have resulted in a series of warnings, and following on from this, had there been consistent poor performance, this would have been the juncture to consider dismissal. We estimate that this would have been between six to nine months hence.

If this matter were to proceed to trial, we would be confident that Ms M would succeed in both wrongful and unfair dismissal claims and she would be entitled to the statutory maximum award of compensation. In light of the above, and in an attempt to reach a speedy and amicable resolution, we are instructed to make the following offer:

- Rescission of the reason for dismissal being gross misconduct.
- £11,750 – three months' pay in lieu of notice.
- £35,250 – nine months' pay as compensation for loss of earnings.
- A sum of £7,185, equivalent to a basic award of compensation.
- Release from all post-termination restrictions save for confidentiality.
- All accrued holiday pay including the holiday pay that would have accrued during her notice period.
- A payment in respect of loss of pension for a period of 12 months following dismissal, estimated at £1,500.
- Honouring the gift of a long-service award which was outstanding at the time of dismissal.
- Payment of £1,437 in respect of loss of statutory rights.
- An agreed reference from Mr W.

In return for the above, Ms M will be prepared to sign a settlement agreement and compromise her right to bring any proceedings against the company relating to her employment or the circumstances surrounding her termination. She will sign a confidentiality and non-disparagement clause and would expect the company to do the same. Our fee for advising on the terms of a settlement agreement is £500 plus VAT.

I look forward to hearing from you or your appointed representative substantively.

Yours sincerely

[Lawyer]

Our next steps:

'Monaco Solicitors worked with Ms M to prepare for her appeal hearing, and considered the various documents that the company belatedly sent over by way of disclosure. We also made a subject access request for all documents where the employee had been the subject, as she is entitled to see these under specific sections of the [then] Data Protection Act 1998.'

▶ Subject access request

[Name and company]

BY EMAIL ONLY

[Date]

Dear [HR Manager]

Ms M – Subject Access Request

Please make all documents and correspondence within the company's control where our client is the data subject available in accordance with the Data Protection Act 1998 [replaced in 2018 by the General Data Protection Regulation or GDPR].

This includes all correspondence, notes (typed and handwritten), memorandum, data sheets, emails, letters, text messages, instant messaging including Whatsapp or similar and other records. We expect that you undertake a search of the following individuals' email and telephone accounts:

[Employees]

The search should include private accounts to the extent that they were used for work or business purposes. The search should be comprehensive and include search terms for my client's full name, her initials, a short name or any name or variation that might be used by any of the above people to identify her.

In the event that you do not disclose any of the documents mentioned above, we would be grateful if you could confirm that a search has been conducted and no results have been found. We may in due course, request sight of the search terms that were used and the results of the searches conducted.

It may be helpful for you to know that a request for information under the Data Protection Act 1998 [replaced by the GDPR 2018] should be responded to within 40 days [changed to 30 days in the GDPR 2018].

If you need advice on dealing with this request, the Information Commissioner's Office can assist you and can be contacted on 0303 123 1113 or at www.ico.gov.uk

Please inform us by return if you require my Client to pay a fee to cover your administrative expenses.

Yours faithfully

[Lawyer]

15/03/2017: Internal appeal made by the employee with assistance from Monaco Solicitors

'On appeal, the company upheld the original dismissal. We had anticipated that the employer might attempt to remedy their earlier failures by concluding that while there were grounds for dismissal with the misconduct being well founded, there were not grounds to dismiss without notice and accordingly pay the employee in lieu of her notice. If they would have done so, this would have put the employee in a difficult situation and her unfair dismissal claim would not have been so strong, as case law has established that an employer can remedy earlier failures on appeal.'

16/03/2017: Attempts by Monaco Solicitors to contact the company

Our lawyer recalls: 'I made various other attempts to speak to the General Manager to discuss settlement but was rebuffed. I would not be passed over to the General Manager when I called the company, and my messages were left unanswered. When I emailed the relevant representatives at the company, my attempts to discuss the appeal (and so avoid lodging a tribunal claim) were dismissed.'

2/03/2017: Tribunal claim

'The employee was left with no choice but to issue tribunal proceedings and instructed us to prepare the papers on her behalf.'

▶ Tribunal application

IN THE EMPLOYMENT TRIBUNAL

IN THE MATTER BETWEEN

Ms M

The Claimant

-and-

[Company]

The Respondent

DETAILS OF CLAIM

1. The Respondent is a manufacturer of [Products] based in [Location] and provides maintenance and servicing to residential and commercial premises, warehouses and retail outlets throughout the UK.

2. The Claimant was employed by the Respondent from March 2006 until her dismissal from employment in September 2016. During this period, the Claimant held various roles within the business and most recently was employed as Manager. The Claimant had always performed well, whilst she did not have regular performance reviews she was informally praised and received regular pay rises, bonuses and upgrades to her company vehicle.

3. The Claimant was first employed by the Respondent as a Service Manager and at that time ran the service department with the assistance of an administrator. Over time, the Claimant developed the service side of the business with steady and sustained growth and increased the turnover from £180k per annum to over £1 million over the course of eight years. The Service Department was heralded as the most profitable division of the company, the Claimant's endeavours were recognised and she was part of the senior management team.

4. In the course of 2015, the Respondent was sold to another company and during this period the former owner and Managing Director, Mr F, retired from the business and a new managing director was appointed in December 2016.

5. In July 2015, Mr F recruited Mr B and he was appointed to the role Senior Service Manager. At this time, the Claimant held the position of Manager. As a consequence of Mr B's appointment, the Claimant's duties were changed and, whilst no formal job description was provided, the Claimant's core responsibilities were to ensure that jobs being requested were fulfilled, resources (plant and materials) were equipped and qualified engineers were available to carry out the work. The Claimant was also responsible for the project management of larger jobs as well as overseeing the supporting colleagues running projects. She supervised day-to-day operations on site, resource planning, training and recruitment of engineers.

6. Mr B has overall responsibility for the department, its commercial aspects of the operation and was mandated to develop and grow the business. This included matters of financial control including meeting sales targets and invoicing.

7. Following Mr B's appointment in July 2015, the Claimant was subjected to a constant and relentless campaign where Mr B would marginalise the Claimant and undermine her authority. This seriously compromised the Claimant's ability to manage her team and the day-to-day operation of the service department. For example, staff both within and outside of the department were told to refer all instructions made by the Claimant to Mr B for further approval. This caused the Claimant considerable concern and anxiety. Departmental meetings and structural changes were made whilst the Claimant was on leave and without her knowledge. When challenged, Mr B's response was "well I didn't need to tell you as you had no say in it".

8. In June 2016, the Claimant discussed her concerns with the Company's Human Resources Consultant, who discussed the option of raising a formal grievance about Mr B. The Claimant was realistic that this would likely fracture the relationship further. The Claimant raised matters informally with Mr B in line with

the Company's grievance procedures. Mr B acknowledged his failings and for a short time following the discussion made some show of discussing department decisions with the Claimant. The Claimant did not consider that Mr B genuinely wished to involve her in future decision making but did so to placate her.

9. Some weeks after the original conversation with HR, they spoke again and HR asked if matters had improved. The Claimant expressed her concerns as outlined in paragraph 8. [HR Consultant] informed the Claimant that immediately following their previous conversation, Mr B had approached her to ask about what the Claimant had discussed and whether she intended to submit a grievance against him.

10. On 19 August 2016, the Claimant received a letter inviting her to a disciplinary hearing on 22 August 2016 regarding seven allegations. They related to a purported complaint from a customer of a key account ("Allegation 1"), failure to produce documents within an agreed timeframe ("Allegation 2"), no control over the invoicing procedure ("Allegation 3"), concern over gaps in response to customer ("Allegation 4") which was later dropped, failure to hand over information to Y ("Allegation 5"), formal letter from a team member alleging no support ("Allegation 6") and allegation of providing false statements to a prospective client ("Allegation 7")

11. The Claimant attended the meeting on 22 August 2016. Mr B was present and another took notes. The Claimant was provided with limited documentation in support of some of the allegations made but robustly defended her position and gave clear context to the allegations. Following his submissions, Mr B adjourned the meeting to undertake further investigations and wrote to the Claimant on 23 August 2016 confirming that a Sales Director would investigate this additional information.

12. The Claimant attended the adjourned meeting on 5 September 2016 and was informed that her employment would be terminated and she would be placed on gardening leave until sending out the correspondence confirming her dismissal. The Respondent later produced minutes of the meeting which did not record this conversation accurately. Following the meeting,

Mr B wrote to the Claimant informing her that there had "been a breach of trust and confidence and serious negligence on your part which causes a loss to the Company". Mr B gave no consideration of the evidence considered, failed to explain the conduct that he considered to be a breach of trust and confidence, failed to provide any or adequate reasons why he had not given consideration to the evidence and submissions made by the Claimant in the course of the disciplinary process.

13. He went on to state:

Therefore, this constitutes gross misconduct within the Company's disciplinary procedure. I have advised you that the disciplinary penalty for this is dismissal without notice and therefore, your employment with Company X is terminated with immediate effect from the date of my decision.

14. In making the decision to dismiss, Mr B failed to take account of the options available to him in consideration of an appropriate disciplinary sanction. The Claimant had a long and unblemished service history with the Respondent and in all the circumstances, the decision to dismiss came outside the range of reasonable responses open to the Respondent. The Respondent failed to take account of the material circumstances in the case to take account of the other factors at play.

15. On 3 October 2016 the Claimant submitted a lengthy letter of appeal, providing a detailed rebuttal of each and every allegation and providing the context to some of the purported complaints that had been received from the client, Company X, and the members of staff and made it clear that Allegation 3 related to problems encountered in the department as a whole and this was not the sole or main responsibility of the Claimant. In particular, she stated:

Prior to Mr B's appointment as "Senior Service Manager", his predecessor, Business Development Director, carried out this function. It was his responsibility to monitor all sales, quotations, follow-ups and invoicing via the spreadsheets and reports maintained by the team. Any anomalies or omissions would be addressed and corrected through discussion and regular communication. When Mr B took over, the Claimant went through all the spreadsheets and [Name of] the electronic service management system with him to ensure he was *au fait* with the system and able to find the information.

16. The Claimant recognised that there were problems with the invoicing system. There were various systemic problems. For example, an Order Bank or Purchase Orders were often set up prematurely prior to works being undertaken which often meant that an invoice appeared outstanding before work had been undertaken or indeed completed. One of the invoices of concern that formed the basis of the allegations against the Claimant related to work that Mr B had been responsible for and it was alleged that the Claimant was accountable for the financial loss. Further, the Claimant gave evidence about the issue relating to outstanding invoices.

Over the course of recent months, the issue of outstanding invoices had been discussed and it was apparent that work needed to be done rectify some of the historical problems. Ms M understood that this was the entire team's responsibility. In informal meetings during July-August between Ms M and Mr B, it was agreed some changes in roles and priorities for individuals would be made and at the point of the disciplinary action being taken against Ms M this was in the process of being implemented. Ms M had agreed to undertake certain process changes to ensure that the "holes" had been plugged. At no point was there any suggestion that Ms M was at fault personally, or that the performance of her duties was in question.

17. The Claimant made it clear that she had been held accountable for failures within the department that ought to have been identified as departmental shortcomings. Indeed, at the time of the disciplinary action, historical invoicing anomalies were being addressed by Mr B, the Claimant and other senior leaders.

18. The Claimant's appeal was considered by the Respondent's managing director. On 24 October 2016, the Claimant met with him to consider these points and following a delay of over two weeks he provided a short letter confirming that he upheld the dismissal. The letter demonstrated a wholesale

failure to consider the points that the Claimant had raised at both the disciplinary hearings and at the appeal. There was no reasoned consideration of the evidence available and he mirrored the partisan and flawed approach to the alleged misconduct that had been taken by Mr B in the disciplinary investigation and hearing.

Wrongful Dismissal

19. The Claimant was dismissed summarily in circumstances which could not reasonably be considered to have been gross misconduct. The Claimant is therefore entitled to receive a payment for the Respondent's failure to give adequate notice of termination of her employment.

Unfair Dismissal

20. The Respondent did not behave reasonably in making the decision to dismiss the Claimant and in the circumstances was unfair in the following respects:

   a. The Respondent failed to follow a fair process in the investigation of disciplinary action.

   b. The Respondent failed to appoint an independent decision-maker to consider the disciplinary allegations.

   c. The Respondent reached conclusions of culpability that no reasonable adjudicator would have taken in the same circumstances.

   d. The Respondent went on a *fishing expedition* to identify any of the Claimant's purported misdemeanours

   e. The Respondent treated the Claimant in an inconsistent manner.

21. It is averred that if, which is not accepted, there were identifiable concerns with the Claimant's work then this was not a matter of conduct but performance and the Claimant should have been given warnings, a personal improvement plan, a reasonable opportunity to improve/training and/or additional support.

22. As set out in paragraph 14 above, the decision to dismiss the Claimant was outside of the range of responses open to the Respondent and the decision to dismiss the Claimant summarily was unreasonable in all the circumstances.

23. The Claimant seeks a declaration that her claims are well founded and compensation at such a level as the Tribunal sees fit.

Lawyer's comment:

'We also prepared a detailed and reasonable assessment of Ms M's financial losses (see below). She remained out of work despite her best attempts to find employment. Her search was hindered by her sudden dismissal after ten years of service and with no reference.'

▶ Assessment of Losses

IN THE [.....] EMPLOYMENT TRIBUNAL

IN THE MATTER BETWEEN

Ms M

The Claimant

-and-

[Company]

The Respondent

PRELIMINARY SCHEDULE OF LOSS

Date of Birth	[Date]
Date of Commencement of Employment	12/03/06

Date of Termination of Employment	04/09/16
Annual Salary	£47,000.00
Monthly gross salary	£3,916.67
Weekly gross salary	£903.85

Wrongful Dismissal

The Claimant was dismissed summarily; she was entitled to 10 weeks' notice on termination of employment.

£826.80 x 10 weeks	£8,038.50
£122.40 x 10 weeks (car allowance)	£1,224.00

Unfair Dismissal

Basic Award

The Claimant is 52 years old and had over ten years of reckonable service. She has an annual salary of £47,000 and benefits including a Company car allowance of £6,364.80 p.a.

The Claimant is entitled to a basic award of	£7,185.00

Compensatory Award

Past Losses

Since her dismissal, the Claimant has been unable to find alternative work.

This is a period of three months; she is entitled to past loss of earning as follows:

£3,916.67 x 3 months	£11,750.01
£581.00 x 3 months (car allowance)	£1,591.20

Future Loss of Earnings

The Claimant has applied for many roles but despite relevant and appropriate skills for the roles has not been shortlisted for interview. The Claimant considers that as a consequence of the circumstances of her dismissal from employment she is significantly disadvantaged and it will take a significant time before she will be able to find a commensurate role. Even if the Claimant is able to find a role in the short to medium term, it is unlikely that it will be at the same salary and there is likely to be a significant shortfall in salary. It is estimated that she will be employed at a starting salary of circa £28,000, a shortfall in her annual salary of £15,000.

The Claimant expects that she will be unemployed until July 2017 and thereafter find employment at a salary of £28,000.

Her losses are as follows:

September 2016 to 31 May 2017, a period of 9 months:

£4447.07 x 9 months	£35,250.00

31/03/2017: Response from the company to the employee's tribunal application

'Once the case is issued, the respondent has 28 days to file a response (ET3). This is often a good opportunity to settle, but in this case the respondent instructed solicitors and submitted their ET3 at the 11th hour.

'The response did not provide a particularly robust defence and it failed to answer many of the issues that were raised in the ET1. They exposed a weak defence and this offered us greater confidence that a tribunal would accept our arguments about a flawed process and the decision to dismiss for gross misconduct was difficult to justify.'

03/04/2017: Negotiating settlement before the case reached tribunal

Lawyer's comments:

'The tribunal gives the parties a timetable for directions to manage the case before it gets to hearing. We were in the process of preparing our list of documents, when the respondent finally got in touch to say that they had an offer to settle. They put forward an offer of £3,500 which was derisory. We counter-proposed £35,000.

'Part of our terms were that the company would rescind their finding of gross misconduct as the employee had income protection insurance that provided cover if an employee was involuntarily dismissed, usually in the case of a redundancy but also in the case of an unfair dismissal. Following further negotiation by telephone, we were able to reach terms, agreeing £29,000, and the gross misconduct was rescinded as part of the settlement terms too which meant that our client could claim on her income protection insurance policy.'

10/04/2017: COT3 settlement agreement received

'We received a COT3 which is a type of settlement agreement which can only be used once a tribunal claim has already been commenced. Once this is agreed, the tribunal claim is closed and the claimant won't be able to make a future tribunal claim in those matters.'

▶ COT3 Settlement Agreement

CASE NUMBER: [XXXXX]

IN THE [Name] EMPLOYMENT TRIBUNAL

B E T W E E N

Ms M

Claimant

-and-

[Company]

Respondent

COT3 WORDING

1. Without admission of liability the Respondent will, within 14 days of receipt by the Respondent's representative of both this Agreement signed by the Claimant and the Copy Letter, pay to the Claimant the sum of £29,000 (twenty nine thousand pounds) (the "Termination Payment").

2. The parties believe that the sum listed at clause one above can be paid without deduction of income tax or employee national insurance contributions. Any tax liability on the Termination Payment shall be the Claimant's alone.

3. The Claimant will accept the Termination Payment in full and final settlement of all (if any) claims she has or may have in the future against the Respondent or against any officer or employee of the Respondent arising directly or indirectly out of or in connection with her employment with the Respondent or the termination of her employment whether within the jurisdiction of an Employment Tribunal or any other form of Court or Tribunal and without prejudice to the foregoing all claims whether at common law, under statute, pursuant to European Community Legislation or otherwise, including but not limited to her claims for wrongful dismissal and unfair dismissal against the Respondent under case number [XXXXX] (the "Claims") and any claims for breach of contract, redundancy, any form of discrimination or under Part II Employment Rights Act 1996 save for any claim for personal injury not arising from the facts currently before the Tribunal or any claim the Claimant may have in respect of accrued rights under any pension scheme of the Respondent of which she may be a member.

4. The Respondent shall upon request provide the Claimant with a reference in the agreed form set out in Schedule 2. The Respondent shall answer any oral enquiries in a manner consistent with the agreed reference.

5. The Respondent shall upon request provide the Claimant's insurers for her income protection policy with the agreed statement set out in Schedule 3.

6. In consideration of the Respondent's undertaking in this clause 6, the Claimant agrees and undertakes that the fact and the terms of this settlement shall be strictly confidential and undertakes that she has not and will not discuss or disclose the fact or the terms of this settlement with or to any third party (including the [Name] Employment Tribunal) otherwise than as required by law or to her professional adviser. The Respondent agrees to use reasonable endeavours to ensure that its current officers and employees directly involved in the termination of the Claimant's employment and/or the preparation of this Agreement, keep the fact of and the terms of this Agreement strictly confidential and agree not to disclose, communicate or otherwise make public its terms to anyone (except to its professional advisers and the relevant tax authorities and otherwise as may be required to be disclosed by law or the requirements of any regulatory authority or by the Respondent's insurers).

7. The Parties agree not to directly or indirectly publish or otherwise make derogatory or disparaging comments about the other.

8. The Claimant agrees that, she will immediately within 7 days of signing this Agreement, sign a copy of the letter set out at Schedule 1 of this Agreement to withdraw the Claims and via her solicitors, Monaco Solicitors, send such signed letter by email to the appropriate Employment Tribunal copied in to the Respondent's representative, (the "Copy Letter").

9. The parties confirm that they understand the Claims will be dismissed by the Tribunal on receipt of the copy letter and the parties believe that it is in the interests of justice to do so.

10. The Claimant acknowledges that completion of this agreement is evidence that she has abandoned irrevocably the claims referred to in clause 3 above. The Claimant has not issued proceedings before the Employment Tribunal, High Court or County Court in respect of any claim in connection with her employment or its termination other than the claim XXXXX. The Claimant undertakes that neither she or anyone acting on her behalf will issue or continue any proceedings

in respect of any claim referred to in clause 3 and if she does so, without prejudice to any other remedy which may be available, and notwithstanding this agreement an award is made, the payment in clause 1 will be set off against the award and be considered in whole or in partial satisfaction, as the case may be, of any such award.

Signed for and on behalf of the Claimant	Signed for and on behalf of the Respondent
....	....
Date........................	Date........................

Schedule 1 – Withdrawal of Claim

[Name and address of] Employment Tribunal

Dear Sir/Madam

Ms M v Company X – Claim Number: [XXXXX]

I am writing to withdraw claim number [XXXXX].

I confirm on behalf of both parties to the claim that we understand my claim will be dismissed by an Employment Judge and both the parties believe that issuing such a dismissal judgment is in the interests of justice.

Yours sincerely,

Ms M

Schedule 2 – Agreed Form of Reference

[ON EMPLOYER'S HEADED NOTEPAPER]

PRIVATE & CONFIDENTIAL

[Name/Address of prospective employer]

[Date]

Dear Sir/Madam

Re: Ms M

Thank you for your recent enquiry regarding the above individual.

We confirm that Ms M was employed by Company X from 2 March 2006 until 4 September 2016, most recently as an Operations Manager.

It is our policy only to provide references containing information as to employees' roles and dates of employment. However, this should not be seen as implying any comment about the candidate or her suitability for employment as [Position] at [Prospective employer].

This information is given in strict confidence, and should not be divulged to any third party. It is also given in good faith, but neither the writer nor Company X accepts any responsibility or liability for any loss or damage caused to the addressee or any third party as a result of any reliance being placed on it.

Yours sincerely,

Mr W

Managing Director of Company X

Schedule 3 – Agreed statement to claimant's insurers

[ON EMPLOYER'S HEADED NOTEPAPER]

Dear Sir/Madam

Ms M was employed by Company X ("the Company") until her dismissal on 4 September 2016. Following a disciplinary process, it was found that there was gross misconduct. Ms M challenged the decision to dismiss her and the finding of gross misconduct, at both the dismissal and appeal stage. The circumstances of the dismissal were the subject matter of employment tribunal proceedings and the parties have agreed confidential terms to settle.

In reaching terms, the company agreed to pay Ms M compensation and rescind the finding of gross misconduct. It was mutually agreed that Ms M would withdraw her claim for unfair and wrongful dismissal.

[Employer's representative]

Final outcome:

'We were able to secure a financial settlement of £29,000 as well as additional terms that were important to the employee. This was a very different outcome to the situation that the employee was in when she came to us for help with her case.'

Lawyer's analysis:

'As well as the satisfactory financial settlement, the employee had income protection insurance that covered her if there was a no fault, involuntary, dismissal. It was important that the finding of gross misconduct was rescinded by the employer so that Ms M was able to claim on this income protection insurance – hugely decreasing financial pressures while looking for new employment.'

Client's reaction:

'I am very appreciative of all your advice and assistance in bringing this case to completion. My lawyer presented each stage of the process to me in a very straightforward way.'

14.2. Case study 2: Excessive workload caused sick leave

In this case study our client was made to work 70 to 80 hours per week then suffered work related stress. The employer then made him an offer to leave quietly but we managed to significantly increase this offer for him. This example is based on a real case, but the names and exact circumstances have been changed.

Case details

- **Client name:** Mr F
- **Job title:** National Business Development Director
- **Employer/company size:** Travel Industry, 35-50 employees
- **Annual basic salary, before tax:** £78,000
- **Annual expected bonuses and commission:** N/A
- **Date of first action by Monaco Solicitors:** 2nd February 2017
- **Date of case completion:** 16th February 2017
- **Initial agreed fee:** 15% inclusive of VAT
- **Original settlement offer:** £26,000: consisting of 3 months' notice pay (£19,500) plus an ex gratia sum equivalent to 1 months' salary (£6,500)
- **Final settlement agreement amount:** £45,500: consisting of the 3 months' notice pay (£19,500) plus an ex gratia sum equivalent to 4 months' salary (£26,000)
- **Increase in settlement amount achieved: £19,500**
  In addition to the settlement amount, the employer also agreed to contribute £1,000 towards the employee's legal fees.
- **Final fee billed:** £1,925 (comprising 15% of the increase of £19,500 – being £2,925 inclusive of VAT – minus £1,000 which was paid by the employer towards legal fees).

What the client said:

'I realise that I have only been employed by the company for a little over two years; however, within that short space of time I have undertaken a role that is both demanding on my time and on my professional skills. Because a colleague decided that he no longer wished to work for the company and left without working his notice, I was asked to fulfil both significant aspects of his role in addition to my own while the company considered its options regarding recruitment.

'As my own role was at the level of senior management, and therefore was around fifty hours per week, undertaking a second role at the same time not only impacted upon my performance in my substantive role, but also began to take an intolerable strain on my health. I found myself working up to seventy or even eighty hours per week.

'The company failed to recruit an additional employee for a significant amount of time, which in turn led to an episode of work-related stress in mid-2015. I alerted my employer to this; however, the situation did not change and led to me taking sick leave due to stress in the autumn of 2015. Upon my return it was promised to me that my workload would be alleviated, but this was not immediate and by the spring and summer of 2016 my workload had increased once again to intolerable levels putting a significant strain on my health and family.

'I was asked to attend a without prejudice meeting and was made an offer to leave despite not having had any negative performance reviews and my having taken on significant extra responsibilities. I was made an offer of £26,000 to terminate my employment, which was made up of my notice and an ex gratia element of one month's pay.'

Lawyer's initial thoughts:

'Because Mr F only reached having two years' service in 2016 he was in an impossible position prior to this point, despite the unreasonable increase in his workload and the strain on his health. If Mr F had been employed for at least two years when he suffered the symptoms of severe stress in March 2015, he would have had a case for constructive dismissal; however, that right was only available to employees who had worked for two years or more for their employer.

'At the time Mr F contacted me, his employer had not committed any breach of contract in the previous three months; therefore there was no obvious case of constructive dismissal. The without prejudice conversation he was asked to have was what is known as a protected conversation and therefore could not be established as a breach of contract.

'Although Mr F suffered from stress, anxiety and quite possibly depression as well, the only time he had taken off work had been over a year prior to his contacting me, and there had not been a diagnosis of depression. It is arguable that he could be classed as disabled; however, there was no evidence that the company had treated him less favourably due to a disability.

'There is the possibility of a personal injury claim given the company's failure to alleviate Mr F's workload in time and the stress he has since suffered, although I do not think the case would be a winner.

'I am therefore left without much of a case to argue if we were to make a claim in the employment tribunal, and any such claim would probably fail. It is therefore my responsibility to ensure that the client maximises his settlement offer. The company has approached him and clearly wants to do a deal and the present level of settlement is not bad, being three months' notice and one months' pay. That said there is always room for negotiation, it is simply how we manage to move the ex gratia payment from one month to three or four months.

'The decision was made to write to the employer, setting out the basics of Mr F's treatment at the company's hands over the last two years and to flag up potential claims Mr F may have, but not to be too direct or forceful given the offer on the table was not too bad to begin with. This strategy allows us to keep our powder dry for the follow up letter were our initial offer to be rebuffed. We decided to ask for six months' gross salary plus notice, which was nine months' gross salary. We also decided to ask the Company to pay the majority of Mr F's legal fees given it was they who initiated this termination and also because they do not have to pay VAT on legal fees.'

Chronology of case actions with lawyer commentary

02/02/2017: First letter to the company from Monaco Solicitors on behalf of the employee

'This letter set out a sequence of events without making specific allegations in an attempt to use the goodwill in existence between the parties to get a deal done. It particularly emphasises the company's part in Mr F's ill-health, its failings in that regard and also the consequential effects on Mr F's ability to obtain alternative employment.'

▶ Letter

[Company]

FAO Ms A

[Email address]

WITHOUT PREJUDICE

02/02/17
Dear Sirs,

RE: Our Client Mr F

We represent your employee Mr F in relation to your recent offer of a settlement agreement with the purpose of terminating Mr F's employment.

We attach a sick note which was issued yesterday by Mr F's G.P. confirming that he is suffering from depression; however, it is asserted that you, as Mr F's employer, had constructive knowledge of his condition for over a year.

In the late spring and summer of 2015, Mr F's workload significantly increased. In particular he was responsible for accounts in India and the USA placing him in the centre of two separate time-zones. This meant that as well as being given additional work to do, long hours were inevitable every day.

In November 2015, Mr F took a week's sick leave. The reason specified for Mr F's absence was stress. Mr F returned after a week, but was in a clearly distressed state at work resulting in him being signed off sick for a further two weeks. Importantly, Mr F was then offered a course of counselling under the company's insurance policy from December 2015 until March 2016, and his additional workload was removed temporarily.

In late January or early February 2017, Mr F met with HR Director Ms P and Mr B. During this meeting, Mr F was informed that his workload would begin to increase again over the following months back to the levels he experienced prior to his initial stress-related absence.

Mr F, in reply, informed both Ms P and Mr B that his counsellor had recommended him taking three months absent from work with a stress-related illness. It is contended that nothing was said in reply to this comment. Indeed, further to this comment it is contended that the company has not made any enquiries into Mr F's wellbeing, nor has it held welfare meetings to discuss his workload or how his workload was impacting upon his health, which was clearly in jeopardy.

During the period November 2015 to the present day Mr F has been prescribed antidepressants and sleeping pills in order to cope with depression and anxiety. The present situation Mr F finds himself in has increased the symptoms of his depression and anxiety and, regrettably, he now finds himself contemplating whether he is able to work for the foreseeable future because of mental health issues.

We make no accusations at this stage regarding responsibility for Mr F's illness, or the acts or omissions of you, as his employer, over the past fifteen months. We believe that this would be unhelpful and hopefully unnecessary as Mr F recognises, reluctantly, that given recent events in the business both parties would be best served by reaching terms and parting ways. Nevertheless, Mr F's condition has a direct impact upon his ability to seek and obtain employment at the same level of status and remuneration he presently enjoys. He is therefore understandably nervous about agreeing to terminate his employment when his ability to work in the future is so uncertain.

We therefore propose the following by way of a termination package:

1. A termination date of 16 February with Mr F's contractual benefits and holiday pay being paid up until the termination date;

2. Mr F to receive three months PILON and a sum representing his accrued benefits, including his pension, during that period (to be calculated by the company);

3. A termination payment representing six months' salary so that Mr F may take adequate respite and then seek employment in the new year without financial concerns that could further exacerbate his illness.

4. The company to pay Mr F's legal fees of £1,500 plus VAT incurred in Mr F seeking advice on his potential claims.

There are some minor amendments to the proposed settlement agreement in terms of Mr F's reference that we wish to make, however we do not believe these amendments to be contentious in any way and we will return to these when, hopefully, we have agreed the heads of terms.

Mr F believes that there is the will present on both sides to come to acceptable terms and wishes to leave the company with good relations maintained.

We look forward to hearing from you.

Yours faithfully,

[Lawyer]

09/02/2017: Reply from the company to Monaco Solicitors

▶ Letter

To Monaco Solicitors

9 February 2017
Without Prejudice

Dear Sirs,
Re: Mr F

Further to your letter of 2 February 2017 and the subsequent certificate of fitness for work for Mr F we have reviewed the points raised in your letter and would like to respond to some of the points you have raised. Mr F was employed as a Global Account Director and as such there should always have been an expectation that he would work across a number of time zones. In early 2015 his role did include the management of a major key client account which was demanding, but in line with the expectations of the role and level Mr F was employed at.

As an employer we became aware in November 2015 that he had a number of major issues in his personal life that were causing him considerable concern and difficulty in performing and concentrating in his role. Once we became aware of these issues, and he returned to work following a period of sickness, his workload was immediately reduced in recognition of this. Following discussion with Mr F, his manager took over the management of the key client account and Mr F was left with managing the less demanding clients. This has remained the case to date.

As you mention he was signed off sick 4 November for six days and again 18 November for 11 days, we ensured he had access to the counselling service through the company employee assistance program and over and above this, funded a further six counselling sessions, however this was to support him in all the issues he was facing. In the workplace his role and responsibilities have been considerably reduced. It should also be noted that until his most recent spell of sickness there have been no absences due to sickness since November 2015.

In relation to your proposals we would respond as follows:

1. We can accept this proposal;
2. We can accept this proposal subject to calculations;
3. We have proposed one month's termination payment;;
4. The legal fees seem high and as such we would propose an increase in fees to be paid of up to £1000.

Yours sincerely,
Ms P
HR Business Partner

Our next steps:

'This was a disappointing response. The company, having admittedly made a reasonable offer, has decided to respond only to the parts of the initial letter they wish to deal with.

'Our strategy must now adapt to events. Rather than treat our letter as a polite invitation to make an improved offer because the company has created this entire situation, the company has decided to stick to its guns. The goodwill which appeared to exist clearly does not extend to an increased settlement offer. We must therefore utilise all the information we have at our disposal to increase the offer and make strong allegations that the company has caused Mr F significant injuries due to its actions. This is the only way of achieving a result from this point.'

12/02/2017: Second letter to the company from Monaco Solicitors

'This letter makes plain that the company was on notice that Mr F was struggling and did nothing about it, which is good evidence that they caused a psychiatric injury. It also alludes to the failure of the company to make reasonable adjustments and that this led to the company informing Mr F that he would be taken through a capability procedure.

'Were this to happen, this would arguably be discrimination, given that the origins of the capability concerns are related to a potential disability. The letter is designed to cause alarm and alert the company to the realities of a claim if the case does not settle. In reality, a tribunal claim would be difficult to prove in this case.'

▶ Letter

[Company]
FAO Ms P
[Email address]

WITHOUT PREJUDICE
12/02/17

Dear Sirs,

RE: Our Client Mr F

We are in receipt of your letter and subsequent emails.

The addition of a little over one thousand pounds to our client's settlement monies has done nothing to assuage our client's concerns regarding leaving employment and the points made in our first letter remain valid.

Turning to your letter, we note that you state that it was problems in our client's personal life which, you allege, caused our client's health problems in the summer and autumn of 2015. If you admit this (and for the record we do not accept that our client's health problems were caused exclusively by issues in his personal life, rather we assert that they were caused or exacerbated or significantly contributed to by you as his employer) then we contend that you were on notice with regard to these problems by March 2015 at the latest when our client informed Mr B that his daughter had run away from home. Any reasonable employer being on notice of the extent of our client's problems at home would be on notice that our client would be vulnerable to psychiatric injury himself whilst under such emotional strain.

Having been put on notice that our client was at risk of psychiatric injury, you owe a duty of care as our client's employer to ensure his working conditions did not cause or contribute to an injury. Given you purposely significantly increased our client's workload during the period April 2015 – November 2015, it is averred that you breached that duty of care and caused or significantly contributed to our client's initial psychiatric injury in the autumn/winter of 2015.

Furthermore, you were put on notice of that injury itself by way of our client being signed off sick in September, then engaging with a counsellor provided by you and, furthermore, by our client informing you in late-January/early-February 2016 that his counsellor had recommended a three month period absent from work because of that injury.

As we referred to in our previous letter, you simply ignored our client in regard to the latter notification. Because you ignored our client and failed to engage with his welfare needs, he felt unable to take the sick leave necessary to recuperate and worked through his illness. Ultimately, this has been extremely detrimental to his health.

We further note that you admit in your letter that you have been reducing our client's workload to that of what would be expected of an employee in his position. One can therefore assume that the workload was previously too high and our client was expected to perform over and above what would be expected of an employee in his position, and that this expectation was in spite of you admitting that you were on notice of his vulnerability to psychiatric injury. We are aware that this expectation continues to this day.

Furthermore, we remind you of your duty to our client under the Equality Act 2010 as it relates to disability and in particular reasonable adjustments. Our client is suffering from depression and has been for a period of time. You have constructive knowledge of that disability because, inter alia, of the events highlighted above and in our previous letter. That duty has therefore existed for a significant period of time, therefore it is contended that there has been no attempt to engage with your responsibilities under the Equality Act in this regard.

Further still, any capability procedures you wish to impose upon our client will, first, be tainted with discrimination arising from previous failures to make reasonable adjustments and, second, be subject to reasonable adjustments themselves. Therefore, if you wish to engage our client in capability procedures if and when he is well enough to attend work, you will have to make a wide range of adjustments to his role and to his working environment to comply with your obligations under the Equality Act in order for the process to be free of discrimination.

One reasonable adjustment would be, for example, to allow our client more time to complete the capability procedures given his illness. We are sure that you are aware that any dismissal following a failure to make reasonable adjustments would be discriminatory, automatically unfair and lead to a claim for direct disability discrimination and unfair dismissal in the employment tribunal.

Therefore, using your previous proposal as a platform for further negotiation, we respectfully submit that if you are requiring our client to relinquish his employment with you and forgo a lengthy period of capability procedures (before which there will be a significant period during which you will have to consider reasonable adjustments for our client), waive his rights in the employment tribunal and state that he doesn't know of any facts that may give rise to a personal injury claim, you will need to make that requirement attractive to him. Therefore, you will need to significantly increase the ex gratia payment presently on offer to a figure close to the sum of six months gross pay we proposed in our initial letter.

We look forward to hearing from you.

Yours faithfully,

[Lawyer]

14/02/2017: Second reply letter from the company to Monaco Solicitors

Lawyer's comments:

'This is the place I intend almost all my negotiations to end up: the company reviewing the matter, understanding that its position is as not as strong as it first considered and that there is risk attached to this process which needs to be mitigated against by ensuring the employee is offered a reasonable sum of money to compromise their claims. A company will very rarely admit it is either in the wrong or at any serious risk, but this is not the aim of a negotiation. The aim is to achieve a result which is acceptable to both parties. The agreement to the payment of a proportion of legal fees is also a good result as this means that the client will not have to pay for a significant proportion of his fees out of his settlement monies.'

▶ Letter

[Company Logo]
To:
Monaco Solicitors [address]
Attn of [Lawyer]

14 February 2017

Without Prejudice

Sirs,

Re: Mr F

We write further to your letter dated 12 February 2017. We note your comments and thank you for the detailed commentary, although, we would strongly dispute your assumptions and allegations.

However, in the interests of settling this matter we would be willing to increase the ex gratia termination payment to £26,000, equivalent four months' salary, in addition to the three months notice payment (£19,500) and an increase in legal fees to £1,000. We attach an updated settlement agreement reflecting.

We look forward to hearing from you.

Yours sincerely,
Ms P
HR Business Partner

16/02/2017: Final settlement agreement received

'At this stage, and given the weaknesses in the client's case, we advised him to accept the revised offer from the employer.'

If you would like to see the settlement agreement, there is a copy on our website in the case studies section.

Appendix One

Glossary

Some terms frequently used in employment law and settlement agreements

ACAS Advisory, Conciliation and Arbitration Service

Barrister A type of lawyer. Barristers typically specialise in the processes surrounding courts and tribunals, as opposed to solicitors, who are more focused on out-of-court work. Barristers do the talking in court. They also prepare court documents. They can also represent you in negotiations, although this is less common than a solicitor doing it.

Compromise agreement The old name for a settlement agreement.

Constructive dismissal When an employer acts in a manner that the employee is entitled to resign and consider themselves unfairly dismissed. The circumstances in which this may occur are wide-ranging, from breaching the terms of your employment contract such as reducing your pay structure, to acting in another way that breaches 'trust and confidence', like asking you to commit corporate fraud.

COT3 A type of settlement agreement negotiated after employment tribunal proceedings have started. They have the effect of closing the tribunal proceedings down, normally in exchange for a payment to you. If more complex terms are required to be agreed, then a settlement agreement is normally used as well.

Detriment Any treatment by an employer which would objectively make an employee feel that are being disadvantaged in continuing their employment.

Discrimination Making a distinction in favour of, or against, a person based on the group, class, or category to which the person is perceived to belong, rather than on individual attributes.

DWP The government's Department for Work & Pensions.

EDT Effective date of termination (of employment). This is often the last day worked, but if you were put on garden leave then it's the last day of your notice period.

ET1 Employment tribunal claim form, to be completed by the employee in order to start a claim.

Ex gratia payment A sum of money paid when there was no contractual obligation or liability to pay it. 'Ex gratia' is Latin for 'out of good will'.

Exit package A term sometimes used in this book to denote the main contents of a settlement agreement. Commonly also known as a severance package.

Grievance A grievance is a complaint, concern or problem experienced by an employee at work. If the employee wants to take this up formally with their employer, the process is called raising a grievance.

HMCTS Her Majesty's Courts and Tribunals Service. A government service responsible for the administration of employment tribunals, amongst other things.

Lawyer A generic term used to describe anyone who is a Licensed Legal Practitioner qualified to give legal advice. Solicitors and barristers are both types of lawyer. (See also **Solicitor** below.)

PHI Permanent Health Insurance (aka income protection insurance).

PILON Pay in lieu (i.e. instead) of notice.

PIP Performance Improvement Plan, also known as Performance Review or Performance Management.

Redundancy A redundancy situation occurs when a business or workplace closes or when there is a 'diminished need for work of a particular kind' and results in job losses. It's the role rather than the individual which can be made redundant.

Restrictive covenant   A clause in an employee's contract which restricts the post-employment activities of the employee for a limited period of time.

Settlement agreement   Successor in name to compromise agreement (see above) but in essence refers to the same thing. The terms are still often used interchangeably. It's the document which you sign after you have negotiated an exit package. Essentially it says that, in exchange for a payment, you give up rights to sue your employer.

Solicitor   A type of **lawyer** (see above) who is a qualified legal professional and who works directly with clients. A solicitor deals with all the paperwork and communication between both sides in order to resolve a case for a client.
If you have contacted a lawyer to handle your employment case, they will usually be a solicitor. However, if the case goes to court a solicitor may not always be able to represent you and may instruct a barrister to speak on your behalf.

Statutory redundancy payment   A payment made by the employer to an employee when the employee is made redundant and calculated with reference to the employee's number of completed years' service. To qualify for a statutory redundancy payment, an employee must have been continuously employed for at least two years.

TUPE   Transfer of Undertakings (Protection of Employment) regulations. This is relevant to any redundancy decisions or changes in terms and conditions where a business or part of it is transferred from one owner to another.

Whistleblowing   Whistleblowing is 'making a protected disclosure' under PIDA (the Public Interest Disclosure Act). In essence, the disclosure needs to be in the public interest, and something dishonest or unreliable done by your employer which people should know about. It is not just restricted to criminal activity, such as fraud, but it can also be a breach of regulations or civil law, like discrimination in the workplace.

Without Prejudice   This means that whatever is said or done on a without prejudice basis cannot later be used in tribunal or at work in any other context than negotiations. If the parties in a dispute have discussions on a 'without prejudice basis', those discussions are confidential between the parties.

Appendix Two

About Monaco Solicitors

Our mission is helping employees to get fair deals when leaving their jobs. We do this by negotiating settlement exit packages for our clients, and also by publishing our knowledge of employment law on the internet so that people can access the information for free and represent themselves.

To date we have had almost a million visitors to our website, thanks to the quality, range and depth of the employment law advice that we provide.

The team at Monaco Solicitors is one of the most accomplished and senior teams of specialist employee-side lawyers in the UK. Each and every member of our legal team is an outstanding lawyer armed with the knowledge and credentials to overcome employers in settlement negotiations and court cases. We pool our knowledge and work together closely on difficult cases, so our clients get the benefit of the whole team's experience when they instruct us.

Locations

We represent clients right across the UK, as we're able to carry out all communications via phone and email. The only time when it is necessary to travel is to attend courts and tribunals, and we are happy to do this when needed, but the vast majority of our cases settle out of court before they get to that stage.

Results

We have negotiated countless millions of pounds for our clients and our results show that in around 95% of our settlement agreement negotiations we achieve a significant increase in the exit package amount. The reviews on our website are nearly all five star, simply because we pride ourselves in providing a personal yet efficient and professional service to all our clients.

Perspective

Because we only represent employees and never the employer, there is no conflict of interest. This is in contrast to most employment law firms, which represent businesses too. They are naturally inclined to stay on good terms with your employer because one day that company may become their client.

We have no such incentive. If your employer conducts itself ethically then we will get along just fine in a negotiation. If your employer acts unfairly or illegally, however, then we will not hold back from unleashing the full force of our legal firepower against them.

Clients

Our clients include employees, entrepreneurs, managers, directors and more. We work with everyone from junior employees who have been the subject of discrimination at work, to clients earning £300,000+ who have disputes about their bonuses.

Cases

We handle all the types of employment law case mentioned in this book, and more. You could be being made redundant, or you might have a dispute at work. Disputes can include statutory claims such as unfair and constructive dismissal, redundancy, whistleblowing and discrimination. They can also include contractual claims such as restrictive covenants, notice pay, bonuses, commissions and share options.

Advice

Each case is different and therefore the specific advice will be different too, but some of the common steps which we can help you take include:

- Advise you on the strengths and weaknesses of your case
- Advise you on the value of your case
- Negotiate with your employer or guide your hand in negotiations
- Review and sign your settlement agreement
- Attend courts and employment tribunals

Website

Our website contains more resources by far than any other employee solicitors' website in the country. The resources include written guides and videos on how to negotiate, letter templates and examples which you can adapt for your particular case and the settlement agreement calculator, which tells you how much you should get in your case. Visit the website at www.monacosolicitors.co.uk